POTIDAEA
Its History and Remains

POTIDAEA

Its History and Remains

By John A. Alexander
PROFESSOR OF HISTORY
GEORGIA STATE COLLEGE

UNIVERSITY OF GEORGIA PRESS

ATHENS

TO

MY PARENTS

IN

GRATEFUL MEMORY

©

COPYRIGHT 1963

UNIVERSITY OF GEORGIA PRESS

LIBRARY OF CONGRESS CATALOG CARD NUMBER: 63-15862

Publication of this book was aided by a grant from the Ford Foundation

PRINTED IN THE UNITED STATES OF AMERICA

BY FOOTE & DAVIES, ATLANTA

CONTENTS

◻

LIST OF ILLUSTRATIONS

◻

PREFACE

◻

THE HISTORY of ancient Greece during the three or four centuries preceding the final supremacy of Philip of Macedon in 338 B.C. is essentially the story of a score of independent city-states, united by a common language, religion, and general culture, but separated by localism and the love of political freedom and autonomy. These elements of unity and separation shaped the course of Greek civilization to such an extent that the history of some of the more important states represents a sort of cross section of the history of Greece itself.

The history of Potidaea offers such a cross section, in spite of the limitations of our literary and archaeological sources. From the founding of the city as a colony of Corinth (ca. 600 B.C.) to its capture by Philip II in 356 B.C., and even to the establishment of Cassandreia on the same site forty years later, nearly all the major events of the history of Greece are represented. In fact, it is mainly from isolated comments on Potidaea's participation in these events that the history of the city has been pieced together with some degree of continuity; as for the domestic developments, aside from general inferences, the coinage of the city, and the scanty archaeological remains from the site, our sources have completely failed us. The same holds true regarding the history and archaeology of Potidaea's neighbors in Chalcidice.

The cause for this scarcity of information about Potidaea and the Chalcidic region in general is not difficult to ascertain. Ancient historical works dealing with this area have perished, and with the exception of one site, Olynthus, no appreciable excavations have been undertaken on these ancient sites. The works of ancient authors who wrote on the history of Pallene, for example, which naturally must have contained much information about the local history of the towns in that peninsula, have not survived. Dionysius of Halicarnassus mentions Hegesippus of Mecyberna (whom, incidentally, he describes as an archaeologist) as having written a book entitled *Palleniaca*. Unfortunately, only a few fragments of this book remain, and those do not bear on Potidaean history. Another writer, Philonides, also from Mecyberna, probably wrote a history of Pallene; both he and Hegesippus are mentioned by Stephanus of Byzantium. Only the works of Herodotus, Thucydides, and Xenophon remain as our main sources, but even here the information on Potidaea and Chalcidice in general is far from satisfactory. The main interest of these writers was to relate the activities of the leading states of Central Greece and the Peloponnesus, particularly Athens and Sparta; therefore their references to the cities of Chalcidice are almost entirely limited to events related to the history of these two states. Other contemporary or later writers add but few details to our knowledge of the history of the Chalcidic region.

In spite of the limitations of both literary and archaeological sources, the evidence available reflects the important role Potidaea played in the major events of the classical period in Greek history. The same role, even greater in some respects, was played during subsequent periods by Cassandreia, at least until its destruction by the Huns during the reign of Justinian in the sixth century of our era.

As a member of the staff of the fourth archaeological expedition to Olynthus in 1938 under the direction of the late Professor David M. Robinson of The Johns Hopkins University, I had the opportunity to visit the site of Potidaea-Cassandreia and to study the topography and extant remains. The Potidaean period in the history of the site was submitted in 1939 under the title "Potidaea" as a dissertation for the doctorate. A debt of gratitude is due Dr. Robinson by those of us privileged to have had him as a teacher. His constant interest in our work, his ready assistance, and his fine example of industriousness can hardly be forgotten. In the mind of Dr. Robinson the story of Potidaea ranked second to that of Olynthus. In fact, both cities had so much in common and their respective histories were so interrelated that one might be tempted to speak of them as the "twin cities" of Chalcidice.

Since 1939 I have been able to review the entire evidence on Potidaea's history and to revise or supplement it accordingly, taking into consideration the more recent publications of importance on Potidaea's history. Of particular significance are the monumental work of Meritt, Wade-Gery, and McGregor, *The Athenian*

Tribute Lists, vols. II-IV (Princeton, 1949-53) and of Gomme, *A Historical Commentary on Thucydides,* vols. I-III (Oxford, 1945-1956).

It is hoped that studies of this type, dealing with important cities of antiquity, may serve as collateral reading for courses in ancient history and in the history of European civilization. It is with this in mind, at least partially, that the present work on Potidaea's history and remains has been finally prepared.

I am indebted to my sister-in-law, Miss Eva Tsiropoulou, for securing for me on a recent visit to Greece the photograph used in Fig. 1, Plate XVIII. The photographs used in Plates I-XXI were taken by me in 1938. Some of these have suffered somewhat through the passing of time, but their usefulness has by no means been impaired. In Plate XXII I am indebted to The Johns Hopkins Press for permission to use the Potidaean coins illustrated in Robinson's *Excavations at Olynthus.* The two maps that accompany the text were prepared for me by my former colleague of the Geography Department at Georgia State College, Professor W. R. Walker, to whom I am greatly indebted.

I also express sincere thanks to the Ephor of Antiquities of Macedonia, Ch. Macaronas, and to his predecessor, N. Kotzias, for placing at my disposal for study all the Potidaean and Cassandreian material, both at the Thessalonica Museum and on the site. To Mr. Macaronas I am also grateful for a copy of the "Nea Potidaea Canal Plan" from which Map 2 has been adapted.

A previous version of this manuscript was read in 1949 by my former professor of Greek Art and Archaeology at Washington University, Dr. George E. Mylonas, and by my former colleague (now Professor Emeritus) of the English Department at Georgia State College, Dr. H. O. Smith. Another colleague of the English Department, Dr. Jack Biles, has read the text of the manuscript in its present form. To all three of my readers I wish to express my gratitude for their helpful comments and encouragement. Finally, my sincere thanks are also due to the director and staff of the University of Georgia Press for their suggestions and cooperation in preparing the manuscript for publication.

JOHN A. ALEXANDER

Georgia State College
Atlanta, Georgia

I

LOCATION AND TOPOGRAPHY OF POTIDAEA
PRESENT REMAINS

□

POTIDAEA, a colony of Corinth, was situated on the isthmus of
the peninsula of Pallene, the westernmost of the trident-like
southward projections of Chalcidice. The name of the city is
derived from the Corinthian (Doric) term for Poseidon, a god
greatly honored on the isthmus of Corinth. The relative similarity
between the isthmus of Corinth and that of Pallene, where the
new town was to be founded, probably occasioned the adoption
of the name Potidaea.[1] The ancient writers are in full agreement
as to the location of the town on the isthmus of Pallene. Whenever the location of Potidaea is mentioned, it is spoken of as being
at the neck of the peninsula. Characteristic of this uniformity of
opinion are the statements of Thucydides (I, 56) speaking of the
Potidaeans as living "on the isthmus of Pallene"; of Xenophon (V,
ii, 15) mentioning Potidaea as being "on the isthmus" of Pallene;
of Strabo who writes (VII, 330), "it lies on it" (the isthmus).[2] Because the isthmus is a geographically well-defined spot and because
there is specific mention in ancient authors that the city was located here, no doubt can be raised as to the identification of the site.

The modern traveler to the peninsula finds a canal cut through
the isthmus (Map 2). The work on this canal was started in 1935
by the Monx-Ullen Company and completed in 1937, except for
minor finishing work. The canal has a length of about 1,200
metres, a width of 40 m., and a depth of 6-7 m. Small boats with
a displacement of 20′ are able to pass through, thus facilitating
traffic among the various seacoast towns of the Thermaic and
Toronaic Gulfs.

Before the present canal was cut through the isthmus, traces of
trenches were still distinguishable in several places along the line
now occupied by it. From the Greek word for trench the place
was named *Handaks*.[3] Apparently in ancient times also a canal
had been cut through the isthmus, as may be gathered from the

1

statement of Strabo.[4] How early this canal was cut is not known.
With the passing of time, however, it was filled up, leaving only
a few traces as a mark of its existence.

Crossing the canal on the ferry-boat (Pl. VII), one notices
remnants of the towers of a mediaeval wall (Pl. IX, 1, 2) which
has much ancient material employed in its construction. Many
towers of the wall are still standing, though much ruined, and
extend the entire length of the isthmus. At the east end about
60 m. from the shore the wall changes its course and extends
directly northeast for about 70 m.; then, ending in a tower, it
reaches the shore. With the exception of the tower the wall has
been included in the canal (Pl. X, 1). From this tower the wall
extends about 50 m. to the northeast where it also ends in a tower
at the shoreline. The western end of the wall is similarly constructed, terminating in a tower on the shore (Pl. VIII, 1, 2);
however, a cross-wall which forms almost a right angle intersects
the main wall about 150 m. inland from the western terminus.
The cross-wall extends southward for about 75 m. and ends in a
tower situated on elevated ground near the shore (Pl. III, 2, to
the left). Thus the area facing the sea between the main wall and
the southward extending cross-wall must have been used as a
harbor (Pls. III, 2 and VIII, 1).

We cannot say how closely this mediaeval wall followed its
ancient predecessors. Struck believes[5] that the substructure of the
later wall dates back to the classical period. Of this we cannot be
certain because no parts of the substructure exposed so far can
definitely be assigned to the walls mentioned by Thucydides or,
even later, to the walls of Hellenistic times. Remains of an earlier
wall (Pl. IX, 1) visible especially on the right as one enters Pallene
probably belong to the time of Justinian.[6] The mediaeval walls
were restored during the war of liberation (1821-29) when the
Greeks of the entire peninsula of Cassandra defended themselves
at the isthmus against the Pasha of Thessalonica.[7]

A few remains from another wall can be seen farther south at
about 900 m. from the north wall and parallel to it.[8] Much of the
material employed in the construction of these walls has been
taken from ancient remains. From a passage which was broken
through the north wall and which thus gives the appearance of
a gate, the name Portes,[9] occasionally still used, was given to
the place.

Not much is known about the walls of the ancient town. They
extended the entire length of the isthmus and thus cut off the

peninsula from the rest of Chalcidice. Perhaps the mediaeval walls followed, in general, the lines of the ancient walls. During the work on the canal, traces of ancient wall construction, apparently classical, were reported to have been found;[10] and Mr. Kotzias, then Ephor of Macedonia, who had followed the canal work, prepared a study on the walls of ancient Potidaea.

Evidence for the existence of ancient walls, both during the Potidaean and the Cassandreian periods, is abundant. Of special interest are the passages in Herodotus, VIII, 29, where the author relates the unsuccessful attempt of the Persian Artabazus to pass in front of the north wall, probably at the east extension, into Pallene at low tide. This statement sets the earliest date for the construction of the wall at 479 B.C. when this incident happened.

Later Aristeus, after the battle in front of the north wall in 432 B.C., was more successful in an attempt to enter the city. He advanced directly through the sea and passed along the breakwater in front of the sea wall, as Thucydides tells us.[11]

The strength of the walls is substantiated not only by the failure of the three-month attack of Artabazus, but even more so by the two-year siege in 432-429 B.C., during which the reputed skill of the Athenians in attacking walls was defied. The attempt of Hagnon and Cleopompus to overcome the walls may be noted in particular. They brought engines up to the walls and tried by every means to capture the town, but in vain.[12] The Potidaeans themselves had such great confidence in the strength of their walls that, according to Diodorus, they left few men to defend them and centered their attention on the Athenian attacks from the harbor instead.[13] That there was also a second wall to the south of the city is attested by Thucydides.[14] One of the demands in the Athenian ultimatum to Potidaea before the revolt of 432 was to raze the wall toward Pallene to the ground.

Passing the walls one enters the modern town Nea Potidaea, whose first houses are only about 200 m. from the north wall. The town received its present name in 1924 when a refugee settlement was organized here. It was formerly known as Pinaka or Portes. Its population is about 700. Ancient material has been abundantly used in the construction of the houses, and a typical site is illustrated on Pl. XVI, 3. The road from Thessalonica to the interior of Pallene crosses the town. From the canal the ground rises gently both to the east and to the west, with higher elevation toward the east.

From the highest point on the east knoll, to the left as one

enters the town (Pl. III, 1), the visitor has a panoramic view of
the surroundings. To the east the Sithonia peninsula is sighted,
separated from Pallene by the narrow Toronaic Gulf or Gulf of
Cassandra. Farther east appear the peaks of Mt. Athos in the
peninsula of Acte. To the north, the hills of Olynthus can be seen
and, in the background, the Polygyrus mountains. To the west,
the spacious Thermaic Gulf, now the Gulf of Thessalonica, is
limited by the land of Thessaly. The mountains of Olympus, Ossa,
and Pelion present a magnificent view from here. Toward the
south is Pallene with its small hills and beautiful forests. In immediate view is the marshy shore to the east beginning just below
the slope of this elevated point. This marshy area extends a considerable distance north of the canal, even as far as Hagios Mamas
(Pl. VI). The view of the area south of the canal can be clearly
seen in Pls. V, 1, 2 and VI.

Directly north of the canal the terrain is gently rolling. A
similar terrain but at a lower elevation can be seen to the
west, south of the canal. Along the east side of the peninsula,
there are continuous chains of knolls, more or less corresponding
to others on the west side. Between them, as one looks beyond the
modern town to the south, other knolls can be seen (Pl. II, 1, 2).

The western knolls are cut off by the sea, giving the appearance
of a series of arch-like formations (Pls. III, 1, 2 and IV, 1). These
formations continue for a considerable distance toward the south-
ern section of Pallene. From these blunted hillocks it is evident
that the western side of the peninsula has been most affected by
the sea, and that its configuration must have completely changed
since ancient times. No sandy shore, as on the east coast, is visible
now, but certainly ships once found a landing on this side also
(Pls. III, 1, 2; VIII, 1), for we note in particular the Athenian
expedition against Mende and Scione in 423 B.C., which stopped
at Potidaea first and then started toward Mende.[15]

The effect of the sea since ancient times in changing the formation of the west side of the isthmus, and of Pallene in general, is
clearly indicated by the temple of Poseidon, of Roman date, the
western part of which has been completely cut away. This temple,
although necessarily near the sea, originally must have been built
at least a short distance from it.

About a kilometer south of the modern town, on the road to
the interior of Pallene, the pumphouse of the water system is
located. Much ancient material was employed in the construction

of this building. The water is slightly salty, but not so much as that of the four wells in the town itself. The modern Potidaeans often wonder about the ancients' water supply. The walls of the pumphouse, with the exception of the west wall which is of brick, are made primarily of ancient, large, well-cut stones of poros. Two drums of poros columns are built into the west part of the south wall.

On an elevation which rises gently away from the pumphouse toward the east is the Mount Athos Metochion Dochiariou, also known as Kapou Metochi (Pl. IV, 2), in the construction of which ancient material has also been used. The Latin inscription given by Demitsas[16] and others is still to be seen slightly to the east of the northern entrance to the chapel. The stone is of reddish marble and is placed vertically on the wall. The famous stele (0.80 m. in height, 0.35 m. in width) containing a decree of Cassander and dating ca. 306-297 B.C. was also found here and is now at the Mt. Athos Monastery Dochiariou.[17] In addition, a funerary monument (0.78 m. in height, 0.77 m. in width) in the Gymnasium of Valta was found in the Metochi.[18] The monument depicts a banquet scene and bears on the top the inscription: To Hero Heropythos. The date of the monument cannot be determined with certainty. Probably it belongs to the first half of the third century, if not to an earlier period. P. Foucart, uninformed of its provenance, wrongly attributed it to Ephesus and developed the interesting theory that it is a dedication to a true *hero*, Heropythos, who may be the person mentioned in Arrian, *Anabasis*, I, 17, 11.[19]

Many of the walls of the other buildings of the Metochi are still partly preserved. The interior walls of these buildings are plastered, and so no observations could be made. Many pieces of marble were among the fallen ruins; a few seem to have belonged to works of sculpture, but were so weathered that it was impossible to conclude anything from them. Two drums of poros columns belonging to two columns of a portico-like building were seen north of the chapel. One had 20 flutings, but the other seems to have been unfluted. Other fragments of columns were seen, as well as a fragment belonging to a marble capital which was built into the east wall of the northwest building of the Metochi.

The knoll on which the Metochi is situated is a rather extensive one. It slopes gently both to the south and the west; to the north it is separated from the second knoll in line from the canal by a ravine, and limits the southward extension of the marshy shore by running out into the sea. (*See* Pls. II, 1; V, 2; VI).

A construction belonging to the Metochi and located farther to the southwest is the so-called Pyrgos, tower (Pl. II, 1), built in 1863. It served as a windmill, but is now abandoned; near it is the Metochi called Simopetra. Ancient material has also been employed in its construction, and it was here that an ancient funerary monument inscribed "Antigona Euphanou" was found. It is a stele measuring 1.30 m. by 0.40 m. and is archaic in style.[20]

An amazing thing about the entire area around the modern town, extending even to the north of it beyond the canal and south to the region beyond the Metochi and the Pyrgos, is the almost complete absence of trees. There are only a few fig and olive trees south of the Metochi. The famous forests of Pallene start slightly south of the Pyrgos and extend farther into the interior.[21] The work of reforestation had already begun in 1938 with the intensive encouragement of the Greek Government. However, the entire section is divided into numerous plots and is intensively cultivated.

Unfortunately, the site of Potidaea has not been favored as yet by any extensive excavations. Only in the case of Olynthus, of the Chalcidic group of cities, has the scanty information in the ancient sources been supplemented by archaeological work. The four campaigns at Olynthus (1928-1938), under the direction of D. M. Robinson, added to the limited number of Potidaean coins extant and to our understanding of the important role Potidaea, as a colony of Corinth, must have played in this region. The majority of the extant bronze coins of Potidaea have been found at Olynthus; in addition, the five silver coins which seem to date before 500 B.C. have supplemented our knowledge of the early issues of Potidaea. The Corinthian division of the coinage of the Chalcidic cities, the Polyxenas and Neumous inscriptions from Olynthus in the Corinthian alphabet, the Corinthian influence on the Olynthus mosaics and bronzes—all of these in some measure also reflect Potidaea's influence.[22]

It is true that Professor Pelekides of the University of Thessalonica carried on preliminary excavations on the site of Potidaea, but on a small scale.[23] In the course of these excavations, which lasted for about three weeks, Pelekides found two buildings of Roman times on the southwest side of the modern town. The building near the west shore (Pl. IV, 1), much destroyed by the sea, measures about 20 m. in length. It was thought by the excavator to be a temple *in antis,* sacred to Poseidon, judging from the torso of a statuette of the god and from many leaden weights found in the building. Trial trenches were also dug, both in the space between Nea Potidaea and the mediaeval walls and to the south of the town, which yielded only graves assigned by the excavator to the early Roman times. Other finds from these excavations were the head of a statuette, a small fifth-century sculptured base, and a fourth-century life-size female protome of clay.

From time to time valuable contributions to the entire history and archaeology of the site have been made by discoveries by the citizens of Nea Potidaea in their fields or yards. In 1945, for example, a marble female head, dated in the second or beginning of the third century A.D., was found; in 1947, two heads of statues as well as a bilingual inscription (Greek and Latin), dated toward the end of the first century A.D. and commemorating the construction of a gymnasium at the expense of a certain A. Cornificius Tarantinus,[24] were uncovered.

The cutting of the canal also unearthed several archaeological objects. Most of these objects belong to the period after 316 B.C., when the site received the name Cassandreia from King Cassander of Macedonia. With the exception of a few finds which are in the Thessalonica Museum,[25] these objects were placed in the schoolhouse and in the newly erected town hall of the modern town. Eventually all were to be transferred to the town hall.

During the German occupation of Greece in World War II many of these archaeological remains were plundered or misplaced. The exact number is difficult to ascertain. According to the report on *Works of Art in Greece, the Greek Islands and the Dodecanese, Losses and Survivals in the War,* issued by the British Committee on the Preservation and Restitution of Works of Art, Archives, and Other Material in Enemy Hands (London, 1946, p. 21), only "a small collection of vases and other objects of little intrinsic value which was in the Elementary School have been plundered." Mr. Macaronas, Ephor of Antiquities of Macedonia, reports[26] that the small collection at the schoolhouse was seized by the German soldiers who settled there in April, 1941. Among the losses, he specifically mentions an agonistic inscription and three marble statues. These objects and others were photographed by the author in 1938, and a sample of what they were may be seen on Plate XXI, 1, 2.

THE ARCHITECTURAL REMAINS

The finds that can be assigned to the Potidaean period are three capitals of columns, a triglyph, several blocks with dove-tail and H-type clamps, and a few fragments of terracotta statuettes. In addition, a fragment of a terracotta tile with a figure of Pegasus stamped on it, and a conical loomweight with the inscription ΠΡΑΜΕΝ[Η] probably belong to the fourth century.

The three capitals of columns are of poros material and are of the Doric order.

1. Pl. XV, 1. This is the largest capital of the group, but more worn. It was located near the N. wall and on the old Thessalonica-Cassandra road. Between the echinus and the beginning of the shaft there are three necking grooves. The capital measures at the abacus 1.35 m. in length; the height of the abacus is 0.20 m., of the echinus 0.25 m. to the necking grooves which measure 0.05 m.; the shaft is 0.10 m. and has 20 flutes each of which is 0.14 m. wide and 0.02 m. deep. The diameter of the shaft is 0.88 m. and the square hole in the center measures 0.125 m. x 0.14 m. x 0.11 m.

2. Pl. XV, 2. This capital, found near the one above, is slightly smaller having an abacus of 0.96 m. in length and 0.14 m. in width. The echinus measures 0.185 m., the necking grooves 0.04 m. and the shaft 0.06 m. The diameter of the shaft if 0.65 m. and the square hole in the center 0.12 m. x 0.12 m. x 0.06 m. There are 22 flutings in the shaft each measuring 0.11 m. in width and 0.015 m. in depth. Traces of plaster shown by the echinus indicate that it served as building material, probably in the mediaeval wall.

3. Pl. XVI, 1. This capital was found toward the S.E. part of the modern town. It is much smaller than the two above, but a little better preserved. The abacus measures 0.70 m. in length and 0.08 m. in thickness; the echinus 0.14 m.; the shaft 0.56 m. in diameter. There are 20 flutings, much worn away.

One hesitates to attach any definite date to these capitals. Probably they belong to the very early history of the town. The first two were originally found on the north side of the mediaeval wall, in a place now included in the canal. Considering their early style and their location one cannot escape the temptation of associating them with the temple of Poseidon which Herodotus mentions as being in front of the city. The temple of Poseidon is the only temple of which there is definite mention; but any association of these architectural remains with this temple is, though interesting, merely conjecture.

Near the first two capitals there is a poros block (Pl. XVII, 1), probably a metope or a part of a stylobate, with a T-shaped clamp. This block measures 0.98 m. x 0.51 m. x 0.34 m. It has a raised border measuring 0.02 m. in height and 0.08 m. in width. The horizontal bar of the clamp is 0.09 m., the vertical 0.12 m.; the depth of the groove is 0.05 m. A part of a parastas (Pl. XVII, 2) and a fragment of a column (0.71 m. x 0.60 m.) with 20 flutings are also found near the capitals. Other fragments of columns are to be seen built into the mediaeval wall, as well as in buildings in the modern town (Pl. XVI, 2: 0.95 m. h., 0.50 m. diameter at the top; 20 flutings).

The triglyph and the blocks with dove-tail or T-shaped clamps were discovered in the canal and were placed on the S. side near the E. opening (Pls. V, 2; XII, 2; XIII, 1, 2; XIV, 1, 2). The triglyph (Pl. XIII, 1) is of hard poros stone; the only parts preserved are the upper part of the grooves, the projecting smooth band above, and a section of the metope to the right. The dimensions of the block are 0.29 m. in height, 0.70 m. in length and 0.40 m. in depth; the preserved height of the grooves 0.15 m., their width 0.11 m., their depth 0.07 m. and the distance between them 0.10 m.; the height of the smooth band above 0.14 m.; the preserved part of the metope to the right measures 0.03 m., the height of the band above is 0.10 m. On the top of the triglyph block to the left there is a T-shaped clamp. The horizontal bar of the clamp measures 0.11 m., the vertical 0.12 m.; the width of the cutting is 0.04 m., the depth 0.06 m.

A poros rectangular block with a T-shaped clamp is represented on Plate XIII, 2.

Plate XIV, 1 shows a poros block with a dove-tail type of clamp. The block measures 0.70 m. x 0.43 m. x 0.20 m.; the clamp is 0.08 m. long, 0.03 m. deep, and has a great width of 0.09 m. and a short width of 0.05 m. Adjoining this block was another with a similar type of clamp but mostly worn away.

Another rectangular block was located nearby (Pl. XIV, 2). It measures 0.78 m. x 0.40 m. The dove-tail clamp at the top is 0.09 m. long, and has a great width of 0.08 m. and a short width of 0.04 m.

The Terracottas[27]

1. Head of a terracotta male figurine, probably of a Silenus. Found in the house of Th. Ghiles. Ht. 0.034 m, w. 0.023 m. (across

nose). Nose chipped off. Broken and hollow behind. Light buff clay. Traces of red paint, especially noticed on left cheek. Wears a cap. Hair is falling on the side from under cap and is modelled in wavy lines. Beard is not modelled.

2. Part of a vase in the form of a satyr head. Found in the house of S. Paschalides. Ht. of fragment 0.029 m., ht. of face 0.02 m., th. of clay 0.002 m. Flat in back except for a stamped depression around a hole. Black glaze on head and at the back. Large opening in the mouth. Eyes and eyebrows prominent. Nose flat.

3. Head of a female terracotta figurine with part of the left side of body preserved. Found in the fields. Ht. of head 0.02 m. Solid in back of head. Traces of rectangular vent in back. Wears hat. Hair falls from under hat onto the shoulders in ridges, but not well modelled. Face is nicely modelled. Left arm, covered by garment, is bent at elbow, and hand is under chin.

4. Female terracotta figurine. Broken below waist. Ht. 0.074 m., w. 0.038 m.; th. of clay 0.004 m. Buff clay. Back of head solid; trace of a rectangular vent below. Figure wears a veil. Features of face are worn. Head is slightly turned to left. Left arm is bent at elbow and hand reaches chin. Right arm extends downward, but is broken at wrist. Seems as if the right hand held the garment. Two folds of drapery fall straight down at right side of body.

The above terracottas were, in 1938, at the school office of Nea Potidaea; though much worn, they give the impression of belonging to the fourth century.

5. Female protome of clay. This protome was discovered during the excavations of Professor Pelekides in 1928 and is dated in the fourth century B.C. Cf. *J.H.S.*, XLI, 1929, p. 234.

6. Seated terracotta figurine, now in Dresden. Ht. 0.16 m. The figure represents Attis and is described and illustrated in the *Arch. Anz.*, XL, 1925, p. 153, no. 117, fig. 50. The type is closely related to those found at Amphipolis and falls stylistically in the fourth century B.C., probably in the first half of that century.[28]

7. Female terracotta figurine, now in Dresden. Ht. 0.147 m. The figure is represented standing on a rectangular base. It wears a chiton and a himation which are rendered in nice folds. For an illustration of the figure see *Arch. Anz.*, XL, 1925, pp. 155f., no. 121, fig. 51.

8. Standing female terracotta figurine, now in Landesmuseum, Granz, Germany, no. 4252. Ht. 0.105 m. It was found near Potidaea. The facial features are partly chipped off. The figure wears a himation which also covers the head. The drapery is seen, in beautiful folds, at the lower part of the legs. The arms, bent at the elbows,

are straight in front, but under the himation. Cf. F. Winter, *Die Typen der Figurlichen Terracotten*, II, p. 46, 8.

The loomweight of clay was found in the fields and was placed in the school office. It is of the conical type and has one perforation near the top. Its shape is the same as the Type 8 loomweights found at Olynthus.[29] The interesting fact about this loomweight is that it bears an inscription written with whitewash across the side. The inscription reads: Πραμέν[η]. The word seems to be a form of πρίαμαι (buy), participle πριάμενος, or πέρνημι (be sold), Attic perfect πέπραμαι. The latter derivation of the form πραμένη seems to be the more probable with the reduplication πε omitted or washed away. It is also probable that the word may have stood for a proper name, though there is no parallel for it.

The stamped fragment of a tile, also displayed in the school office, was found by A. Perales in 1932. The stamp is square and contains a representation of Pegasus.[30]

THE BRONZES

In addition to the above finds, we might mention several bronzes acquired by the Department of Greek and Roman Antiquities of the British Museum. These bronzes are said to have come from Potidaea and are published by Forsdyke in the *British Museum Quarterly*, VI, 1932, pp. 82f., pl. XXXIII; and VIII, 1934, p. 108, pl. XXXV, a-e. Forsdyke speaks of them as geometric bronzes and remarks that nearly all the types can be paralleled by Early Iron Age material in Macedonia.[31] The most important of the group are a spearhead, a spiral fibula, a fibula with buttoned catch-plate, several beads, a little jug (9 cm. h.) with incised decoration, and a series of pendants. In the group published in Vol. VIII, 1934, above, in addition to such bronze ornaments as spiral bracelets of single coils and ornamental rings, several beads of amber, bone, carnelian, and glass are mentioned, but because of the circumstances of the discovery of these beads,[32] their date is somewhat uncertain.

These objects from Potidaea find exceptionally good parallels in Olynthian material. These similarities as well as Corinthian or Potidaean influence are pointed out by Robinson in the *Excavations at Olynthus*, Part X, *Metal and Minor Miscellaneous Finds*. The Potidaean spiral fibula previously mentioned, for example, in the British Museum (*Br. M.Q.*, VI, 1932, p. 82, pl. XXXIII) is compared with Type I from Olynthus, dated as pre-Persian (Robinson, p. 98 and n. 125). Another fibula of bone (Type IV) found in an Olynthian *apotheke* with Corinthian scyphus fragments and an aryballus (dated ca. the first half of the sixth century B.C.) is described by Robinson (p. 101) as "one of the first signs of commercial importation to Olynthus" and "perhaps from Ionia or from Corinth through Potidaea."

Several bronze heads were also found at Olynthus. These are of the "barrel" or cylindrical type, as Robinson describes them. Similar heads from other sites, including Potidaea, are usually dated between the years 800-600 B.C. (Robinson, *op. cit.*, pp. 65, 67, and n. 23). The Potidaean type (*Br. M.Q.*, VI, 1932, p. 82, pl. XXXIII) is compared with these.

The single coil spiral bracelets from Potidaea (*Br. M.Q.*, VIII, 1934, p. 109, pl. XXXVb) are compared with a similar type from the Olynthus finds (pp. 68, 74, n. 32, and pl. XIV). Some bronzes from Olynthus, identified as buttons (Robinson, p. 76 and pl. XV, 251), are quite similar to the Potidaean bronze rosettes in the British Museum (*Br. M.Q.*, VI, 1932, p. 82, pl. XXXIII, a rosette with six petals and with flat loops at the back; a slight variety in VIII, 1934, p. 109, pl. XXXVa, described by Forsdyke as a fibula-plate, has a bronze hook and part of an iron pin at the back).

In the Olynthian specimens of bird pendants, classified as Type I (a common archaic type), Robinson sees a possible Corinthian influence "through the neighboring Potidaea" (p. 117). These pendants are dated in the seventh or, more likely, in the sixth century B.C. The bird-cage pendants of bronze from Potidaea (*Br. M.Q.*, VI, 1932, p. 82, pl. XXXIII) have counterparts in the Olynthus Type II (Robinson, *op. cit.*, pp. 118, 119, and n. 194).

Two other bronze pendants of Olynthus Type III, one globular in shape with a "prolonged tip at bottom, no knobs, slender neck with vase-like lip" (Robinson, *op. cit.*, p. 122, pl. XXIV, 408), the other, elongated in shape, "with knob at lower end and eye for suspension at upper end" (Robinson, *op. cit.*, p. 123, pl. XXIV, 414), have parallels (*loc. cit.*, and notes 206 and 207, respectively) with two in the British Museum from Potidaea (*Br. M.Q.*, VI, 1932, p. 82, pl. XXXIII). The Potidaean pendants may be dated as early as the eighth century B.C.[33]

In this discussion of the relationship of Potidaean and Olynthian bronzes, the bronze shield found at Olynthus during the 1938 campaign (Robinson, *op. cit.*, pp. 443-46, pls. CXXXV-CXXXVII) is of interest. Robinson, commenting on Furtwängler's idea (*Olympia*, IV, pp. 163ff.) that the shields discovered at Olympia were of Corinthian manufacture "in view of Corinth's fame in bronze," remarks that "the Olynthian shield may also have come from a Corinthian bronze foundry, but it is equally possible that it was made in a local bronze foundry at Olynthus itself by someone (possibly from Potidaea, the nearby Corinthian colony) who was familiar with Corinthian work" (Robinson, *op. cit.*, pp. 445f. and notes 222 and 223).

ARCHAEOLOGICAL IMPORTANCE OF THE SITE

From the preliminary excavations of Professor Pelekides, from other finds which have been discovered to date, and from our conclusions from literary sources about the greatness of the cities of Potidaea and her successor Cassandreia which flourished on this site, it becomes evident that the soil still hides valuable remains. Further excavations, if undertaken, would explain many points now obscure and would provide the most important information in the reconstruction of the life of these two cities throughout their entire history.

II

FROM THE FOUNDING OF POTIDAEA
TO THE PERSIAN WARS
ca. 600-490 B.C.

□

THE SITE of Potidaea was colonized by Corinth; the circumstances, however, and the date of its founding are hidden in obscurity. Yet from a general survey of the activities of the metropolis in the seventh and sixth centuries B.C., and from other considerations, one may arrive at an approximate period for its founding.

One thing is certain, the city was settled before the Persian wars. It is first mentioned by Herodotus[1] who says that Potidaea and the other cities of the Chalcidic peninsula formed a part of the Persian host. Later the city took part in the battle of Plataea by sending 300 of its citizens to fight on the side of the Greeks.[2] How much the settlement of the site by Corinth pre-dated these great events cannot be determined with absolute certainty. Struck,[3] following Kiepert, places the settlement of the town by Corinth in the eighth century B.C. The reason for such an early period is not given. From what we know, however, Corinth's early colonial activity during the latter part of the eighth century and the first half of the seventh century was toward the western Greek world, leaving the Euboean cities, her rivals in colonization, a free hand in the eastern and northern parts of Greece.[4]

It was toward the end of the eighth century (734 B.C. is given as the traditional date) that Corinth founded Corcyra by Chersicrates and Syracuse by Archias.[5] Whether Corinth founded any other colonies at this period is difficult to say. Müller assigns the founding of Ambracia to the time of the Bacchiads,[6] but O'Neill gives Gorgus, brother or son of Cypselus, as the *oecist* of this city.[7] Through the settlement of Corcyra, Corinth sought to control the trade route to Italy and Sicily, and also to have access to the trade of the people of Epirus.

The ruling family at Corinth at this time was the Bacchiads,

14

descendants of the Dorians. Their relations with Corcyra were not as cordial as might have been expected. Enmity arose between the two immediately, Herodotus tells us.[8] The colony became wealthy and prominent, and soon was the rival of the metropolis. This unfilial attitude is attributed by O'Neill[9] to two factors,— to the establishment of a Democratic party in Corcyra as a result of the oppressive attitude of the Bacchiads, and to trade jealousies. Relations between the two cities led to the great naval battle of 664 B.C., the first to be recorded in Greek history. The battle resulted in the humiliation of Corinth; thus the authority of Corinth was overthrown for a while, and Corcyra became autonomous and supreme on the west shore.[10]

The Bacchiads were also in conflict with the commercial classes of the city, who, owing to extensive trade, had become rich and powerful. They wanted a voice in the government, but were denied it.[11] Cypselus, a member of an ancient family who was related to the Bacchiads through his mother, Labda, became their leader. In 657/6 B.C., according to the traditional date, he overthrew the government of the Bacchiads and assumed leadership. Cypselus was an able general and kind to the people. He inaugurated for Corinth a colonial policy, later carried on by his son Periander. Besides Ambracia, two other colonies, Leucas and Anactorium, are said to have been founded by him.[12]

After the death of Cypselus, Periander, his eldest son, became ruler of Corinth (627 B.C.). He enjoyed a great reputation as a statesman and as a patron of art and literature. During his reign Corinth became a powerful city. Its wealth was increased by commerce and by the taxes paid by wealthy men. The lower classes were left untaxed and were for some time more or less contented. The building program provided opportunities for employment. But laws restricting individual liberties were introduced and the powerful and wealthy elements were repressed.[13] Periander took every precaution to protect himself from the discontent that followed.[14] In order to dispose of the surplus population and the discontented elements, he continued his father's colonial policy with even greater zeal,[15] thereby gaining both economic advantages for Corinth and the extension of his own political ambitions.

In the Lelantine War at the end of the seventh century B.C., Periander sided with Chalcis and Samos against Eretria, Megara, and Miletus.[16] Perhaps this incident might have suggested to him the possibility of a foothold on the fertile peninsula of Pallene, where Eretria was supreme. Possibly, too, the idea of a settlement in this region might have come during the reign of his father after the loss of Corcyra, which event lost Corinth the control of the western trade. It was after the loss of her power in these regions that Corinth turned her attention to the northern shore of the Aegean Sea.

The location of Potidaea was too inviting for Corinth. Happily situated on the threshold of Pallene, the city could prosper and, at the same time, open up the boundless supply of timber much needed for the building of Corinthian triremes.[17] Thus, Potidaea's location, both in regard to security and economics, admirably satisfied the principles generally observed by the Greek city-states in selecting colonization sites.[18]

But whatever may have been the immediate occasion for the settlement of the site, it is most probable that the city was founded during the period of the Cypselids' reign, for after their fall (583 B.C., according to the traditional date) Corinth seemed to be on the decline.[19] It is very likely that the site was colonized during Periander's reign, as indicated by the statement of Nicolas of Damascus[20] that Evagoras, the son of Periander, was the oecist of the colony.[21] It may be added that extant Potidaean coins and the treasury of the city at Delphi may be assigned to about the middle of the sixth century B.C. These considerations, plus the ability of Potidaea to withstand so successfully the vigorous attack of the Persian satrap Artabazus in 479 B.C., favor an early founding, for they imply a certain degree of organization and material prosperity which would normally require a great many years of existence.

PRE-CORINTHIAN OCCUPATION OF THE SITE

A question arises as to whether the site of Potidaea was inhabited to any extent prior to the coming of the Corinthians. Unfortunately, definite information is almost non-existent. What little there is leads only to a mere probability of a pre-Corinthian settlement on the isthmus of Pallene. It will be instructive, however, to take note of this probability, slight though it is.

The peninsula of Pallene apparently was named after a city, which in turn derived its name from Pallene, the daughter of Sithon, king of the Odomantes in the Thracian Chersonese, and of Archinoe, daughter of Neilos, or the Nymph Mendeis, for whom the city of Mende seems to have been named.[22] The original name of the peninsula, according to the ancient writers, was Phlegra.[23] The location of the city of Pallene is not known. However, if indeed the peninsula did derive its later name from the city, it is then natural to expect that the city was located within the peninsula or, at any rate, near it; for only thus would such a derivation be intelligible. One would expect, further, that the city of Pallene must have been of some importance or that it commanded an important location in that peninsula. Stephanus Byzantius speaks of the city as being a πόλις Θράκης.[24] But the term Θράκης as used by Stephanus is not a well-defined district, and, in fact, it is a term used loosely among ancient historians and geographers. Potidaea itself is spoken of by the same writer as πόλις Θράκης, while Cassandreia, built later (316 B.C.) on the same site, is called πόλις Μακεδονίας, πρὸς τῇ Θράκῃ. An anonymous geographer, generally identified as Scymnus of Chios, speaks of the city of Pallene as being located on the isthmus.[25] One does not know how much credence should be placed in a statement of this sort, but at any rate it suggests the possibility that the town was located near the isthmus.

Such a location would easily have led to the application of the name to the whole peninsula. A parallel is easy to find. Cassandreia was founded on the site of Potidaea, but later the whole peninsula was named Cassandra, a name which has survived to the present day. But while the latter case is a fact, the former, in view of the lack of concrete evidence, depends only on analogy and mere probability.

That the peninsula was inhabited to some extent before the arrival of the Greeks from Euboea and Corinth seems to be certain.[26] Greek mythology says that the original inhabitants of the peninsula, then called Phlegra, were the giants, and that here the conflict between them and the gods took place.[27] According to another version, when Heracles came to Phlegra after the fall of Troy, he found the place inhabited by a barbarous nation which he defeated in battle.[28] Dionysius of Halicarnassus identified the original inhabitants as the barbarian Krousaioi, whom, he says, Aeneas and the Trojans found when they stopped at Pallene.[29] Undoubtedly there is some fact behind these accounts. In the same passage Dionysius tells us that the Trojans spent the winter season at Pallene and that they built a temple to Aphrodite and founded the city Aeneia.

We find an echo of Achaean connection with Pallene in the stories about Scione, an important city in that peninsula and one that is variously represented as an Eretrian or a Chalcidian colony. The Scionaeans, having no legitimate parent city, traced their descent to the Achaeans' return from Troy, and thus connected themselves with the Pallenians of Peloponnesus. Their founders, they claimed, were Achaeans, who, driven to Scione by a storm, settled there.[30] The territory between the sites of Potidaea and Aeneia was called Krousis or Krossaia, and in the sixth century B.C., according to Herodotus, was occupied by Thracian tribes.[31]

Considering these stories and the importance of the location of the isthmus, one might be justified in assuming that the site of Potidaea was to some extent inhabited. The Corinthians came to terms with these original inhabitants, and the female head on the early Potidaean coins, with the curious arrangement of the hair to a point at the top of the crown, probably may be attributed to these earlier influences. Another consideration is the fact that, as a general rule, the Greek cities planted their settlements on inhabited spots; it seems to have been an exception to send colonists to an uninhabited site.[32] Potidaea very likely did not constitute an exception.

THE RESOURCES OF THE NEW CITY

Pallene is the least mountainous and most productive of the three peninsulas of Chalcidice.[33] It produces even today a considerable amount of grain. Vineyards are cultivated in the interior part of the peninsula, especially in the region of ancient Mende, famous in antiquity for its wine. In modern times the region around Potidaea has proved to be unsuitable for the cultivation of grapes. A few vineyards have been planted north of the canal, but the product is very poor. The heavy forests of the peninsula in ancient times were a great source of wealth to the cities. They afforded material for the building of ships.[34] Corinth depended on Potidaea for the supply of timber for her triremes.[35]

Potidaea, situated at the very entrance to the peninsula, must have controlled the commerce between the cities of the interior and the mainland of Chalcidice. Mendaean wine passed through Potidaea. According to Athenaeus,[36] Cassander, the founder of the city named after him on the site of Potidaea, wished to find a special kind of wine vessel since a great quantity of Mendaean wine was exported from Cassandreia, and Lysippus, the sculptor, in order to please the king, invented a special kind of earthenware vessel. Naturally, similar trade may be assumed for the pre-Cassandreian period.

Much of the trade of the mainland of Greece with the Chalcidic region may have passed through Potidaea. The city's location, with a place suitable for beaching ships both at the east and west sides of the isthmus, attracted foreign vessels. Only Potidaea among the cities of Pallene and the region toward the mainland, with the exception of Mecyberna, could claim at least a low shore suitable for beaching ships.[37] It is quite probable that Potidaea possessed an actual harbor, most likely on the east side of the isthmus since it appears more suitable. Diodorus,[38] in relating the Athenian siege of Potidaea in 432-429 B.C., notes that the besieged city successfully resisted the attacks from the harbor. This point could be affirmed with certainty if one could accurately date the remains of an ancient embankment discovered during the work at the east end of the canal. These remains were of large stones which crossed the canal in an oblique line, extending toward the northeast, and are indicated on the Nea Potidaea Canal Plan as the center line of an ancient jetty (see Map 2).

Some evidence, though not specific, for another harbor on the west side of the isthmus may be derived from two passages in Thucydïdes. In describing the successful attempt of the Corinthian Aristeus to enter Potidaea following the battle at the isthmus in 432 B.C., the historian relates[39] that Aristeus, after forcing his way through the Athenian lines, passed along the breakwater which was apparently located on the west side, and arrived safely within the town; later,[40] in reference to the Athenian expedition against Mende, fifty ships sailed from Potidaea and came to land first at Poseidonium. In view of the number of ships involved and of the location of Poseidonium, a safe harbor on the west side of the isthmus may be assumed with some degree of certainty.

Finally, because of Potidaea's friendly relations with Corinth, because of her favorable location for commerce and trade, and because of the fertility of the surrounding territory, the city soon achieved wealth and prominence and became one of the most important cities in Chalcidice.[41]

GOVERNMENT

Throughout the entire history of Potidaea there is no documentary evidence of political organization with the exception of a passing reference in Thucydides (I, 56) to magistrates under the title *epidemiourgi* which were sent annually from Corinth. No inscription has been found as yet with even the slightest hint as to the type of government in the city; no names of magistrates have been recorded, either in literary or epigraphical texts, or on any of the coins from the city. Our knowledge must remain incomplete until some evidence is uncovered in future excavations on the site itself.

A source of information, however incomplete, may be sought in the founding of colonies and in the relation of Potidaea to Corinth. The importance attached to the foundation of colonies was very great. It must have been a matter of great concern to the Greeks colonizing cities to select a suitable site for their colonists, since it became customary to ask the approbation of the Delphic oracle. If the answer of the god was favorable, a leader (the oecist) was appointed to accompany the colonists to their new home. In the case of Potidaea, according to a fragment of Nicolas of Damascus, the leader appointed was Evagoras, the son of Periander. What the exact functions of a leader were after he conducted the members of the colony to their destination is not known. Probably he took part in organizing their new city.

Religion afforded an excellent means for the colonists to express their filial devotion. It was the custom for them, upon leaving their original home, to take with them the sacred fire from the hearth in the prytaneum of their parent city. Upon their arrival, the sacred fire was placed in the public hearth of their new home. The chief deities were also transplanted and worshipped in the colony. Ample evidence for the custom, in the case of Potidaea, is to be found especially in the coins (*see* Chapter V).

The citizens of the parent city were granted special honors at the festivals of the colony, and representatives from the colony were sent to attend the principal festivals in the parent city.[42] Corinth was highly honored by all of her colonies except Corcyra. This fact is evident in the Corinthian's speech before the Athenian assembly in the Corcyraean affair of 433 B.C.[43] The Corinthian embassy to Athens at that time took great care to contrast the disloyalty of Corcyra with the loyalty and honor received from the other colonies. Potidaea's history throughout is marked by cordial relations with Corinth.

The colony also, as a general rule, adopted the political institutions of the metropolis. The constitution, at least in its origin, was more or less based on that of the parent state.[44] We may assume that a form of oligarchy, on the Corinthian model, was instituted at Potidaea, which seems to have lasted throughout the history of the town, though specific evidence is lacking. It was the general practice that, as soon as a new settlement was organized, it became politically independent of the parent city.[45] But the Corinthian policy did not follow the general practice. Corinth was trying to keep her colonies in some way dependent upon the sovereign state.[46] This fact may explain the hostile attitude of Corcyra to Corinth and her efforts to offset Corinthian interference.[47] The extent of actual interference in the other colonies cannot be determined. It seems that the colonies had acknowledged from the beginning Corinthian hegemony and carried on amicable relations with their metropolis.[48]

The colonial policy of Corinth has been interpreted as an attempt to found an empire, the government of which was to be entrusted to members of the ruling family.[49] The practice of sending out a leader with each new settlement helped, in this case, to keep the colony in some way dependent on the metropolis.[50] The extent of such a relationship cannot be fully realized, since our evidence on the point is obscure. However, a glimpse of what the Corinthians expected of their colonies is available from the speech of the Corinthian embassy before the Athenian assembly. The Corinthian ambassadors point out that they founded the colony of Corcyra in the hope of becoming its political leaders and of being treated with due respect.[51] Such a policy of Corinthian political leadership in the colonies necessarily must have had its beginnings early in the history of Corinthian colonization.

In the case of Potidaea, a certain amount of political influence must be conceded. Corinthian interference must have been exercised by a board of magistrates called *epidemiourgi*.[52] The Athenians, after the Corcyrean affair in 433 B.C., sent an ultimatum to Potidaea demanding, among other things, that it expel the Corinthian *epidemiourgi* and that it not receive any of them in the future.[53] The mission of these *epidemiourgi* is not certain. It seems, from the narrative of Thucydides, that their presence at Potidaea was considered very dangerous for Athens. Their presence, then, is an indication that Potidaea, though an ally of Athens, continued even in this period to pay some allegiance to the parent state.[54] It is a sign also of Corinth's policy to interfere in the internal administration of the city and to exercise some control.[55]

Thucydides' reference to the *epidemiourgi* does not furnish anything that might permit an idea either of their number or of the nature of their power and their functions. In fact, there are no parallels for the form except in inscriptions of the second and first centuries B.C. from Delphi, where *epidemiourgus,* or the plural, appears.[56] In some Delphic decrees they exercise the functions that in other cases are assigned to the *archontes* or *tamiai;* in others, they are charged to administer the *xenia* to the *proxenoi;* and in one case they are to take charge of the engraving of the decree.[57] The simpler form, *demiourgus* or *damiourgus* (the Doric), is very common. *Epidemiourgus,* then, must mean an upperdemiourgus, and Müller makes the analogy with *epistrategus* in Egypt in the time of the Ptolemies, meaning upper or superior strategus.[58]

While there are no early parallels for the term *epidemiourgus,* the existence of the office of demiourgus is attested by epigraphical as well as literary evidence, and an inquiry into the use of the latter term will naturally help us to form some notion of the former. Hesychius[59] regards the demiourgi as a Dorian magistracy and speaks of them as   οἱ ἄρχοντες τὰ δημόσια πράττοντες, ὥσπερ ᾿Αθήνῃσι οἱ δήμαρχοι. But that they existed also among non-Dorians is well attested.[60] Schömann remarks that the term implies a constitution not oligarchical, but one that granted certain rights to the Demos.[61]

The functions may have differed from city to city, but it is evident that some form of political significance was attached to the name in every case.[62] In Elis they appear to have been established for a long time, and were considered as magistrates of great importance.[63] During the Peloponnesian War they are mentioned in the treaty between Athens on the one part, and Argos, Elis, and Mantinea on the other.[64] In this treaty the Elean and Mantinean demiourgi acted together with the Boule of their respective cities. In many cities the office of the demiourgi carried with it the privilege of eponymy, as, for example, at Aegium in Achaea, Cnidus, and Camirus.[65] In the case of Camirus, Foucart makes the observation that the demiourgus of this city was the prytanes at Rhodes and the epistates at Lindos.[66] At Stymphalia, he was the magistrate charged to summon the assembly of the people.[67] In Arcadia the senate, composed of 50 members, was called *damiourgoi*.[68]

The significance of the Corinthian *epidemiourgi* in Potidaea, especially during the early history of the town, may be assumed therefore to have been similar to the *demiourgi* of the other cities. Gaillemer[69] compares the office of the *epidemiourgi* to that of the harmosts of Sparta and to the *Kytherodikes* whom the Spartans sent to Cythera. O'Neill compares the office with the *episcopi* sent by Athens to its subject cities and with the harmosts of Sparta, but speaks of the *epidemiourgi* as being "functionaries whose survival signified rather a union of affection and religious observance, than a political connection."[70] The use of *epi* in front of the original term adds higher importance to the title of this magistracy. Schömann translates *epidemiourgus* as "supreme magistrate."[71] Is it not possible that the simple term *demiourgus* designated a Potidaean magistrate and the compound *epidemiourgus* a Corinthian? While the influence of these Corinthian officials at Potidaea cannot be determined with any degree of certainty, it can be assumed that their yearly appointment strengthened the ties between the parent city and the colony, and was the basis of Corinth's claim before the Athenian assembly (Thuc., I, 38) of the close relationship with her colonies.

RELIGION

The colonists transplanted to their new home the chief deities of their parent city. Among the Corinthian deities established at Potidaea, Poseidon received the highest honors. Poseidon was the "Lord of the Isthmus," according to Pindar,[72] and a Doric temple was erected to him on the isthmus of Corinth. To the Potidaeans, whose city was named after Poseidon, the god was now the "Lord of the Isthmus" of Pallene and his worship was held in great honor. A temple and a statue of the god are mentioned by Herodotus as being located in front of Potidaea, just outside the north wall of the city; the tidal waves that caused the destruction of a great part of the army of the Persian Artabazus in 479 B.C. were attributed by the Potidaeans to Poseidon, because the Persians had profaned his temple and his statue.[73]

Because of this incident, one might infer that Poseidon might have been worshipped under the cult-titles of *Thalassios, Pontios,*

Pelagios. On the isthmus of Corinth, where Poseidon was greatly honored and many sacrifices were offered to him annually, the cult-title was *Hippios*.[74] This is the cult-title that seems to have been dominant also at Potidaea. The image of Poseidon as Hippios appears on the obverse of all the Potidaean tetradrachms and drachms. Either a rider on a protome of a horse or a full figure of horse and rider, both naturally referring to Poseidon Hippios, is represented on the hemidrachms; only a horse, the animal sacred to Poseidon, is on the obols. On the reverse of the bronze coins are found a winged Pegasus and the symbol of Poseidon, the trident. Probably the image on the coins is a reflection of the statue of Poseidon which Herodotus mentions along with the temple.

Poseidon was regarded as a trainer of horses, and his cult as Hippios was very significant.[75] Many places held this special cult in honor. Besides Corinth and Potidaea, Poseidon as Hippios was worshipped in Thessaly, Attica, Arcadia, Elis, Patras, and other places.[76] The horse was his favorite animal and in legends the god is represented in that form. It was the sacrificial victim in his cult.[77]

The star often represented beneath the horse on the silver coins of Potidaea was meant, according to Svoronos, to give a planetary character to the horse.[78] In two later Potidaean tetradrachms, a dolphin, one of the attributes of Poseidon, takes the place of the star.

The worship of Poseidon must have continued even after the founding of Cassandreia on the site of Potidaea (316 B.C.). Professor Pelekides, during the excavations conducted on the site, discovered a building southwest of the modern town (Nea Potidaea), partly destroyed by the sea, which he thinks probably belonged to a temple of Poseidon (Pl. IV, 1), because of the torso of a statuette of the god and a number of leaden weights from fishing nets found in it.[79]

Another god who must have been worshipped at Potidaea was Apollo. The Potidaeans dedicated a treasury in honor of Apollo in his sacred precinct at Delphi; and an archaic inscription on a marble base speaks of a dedication of a Potidaean to Apollo. In addition, a large marble stele (height 1.40 m., width 0.71 m., depth 0.115 m.) has been found with a relief of Apollo holding the lyre.[80] The date of this monument is late, probably from the third century B.C., but is suggestive of the earlier worship.

Evidence for the worship of Athena at Potidaea is found in the representation of the head of the goddess in a Corinthian helmet on the bronze coinage of the city. No monument has yet been found to any other gods or goddesses that might have been worshipped at Potidaea. The female figure on the reverse of the Potidaean silver drachms, hemidrachms, and obols has been identified by some as Aphrodite and would indicate the worship of that goddess at Potidaea. But the identification of this figure as the nymph Pallene seems to be more probable.

The worship of Hera could be documented if one could restore, with any degree of certainty, the word Ἡραῖα in an inscription from Nauplium, where the name of Potidaea appears (the first two syllables are restored).[81] The inscription was put up by the city of Hermione in honor of a certain Nauplian victor in several athletic contests. If the restoration of the name of Potidaea in the beginning of the last line is correct, as it appears to be, we then have in this document the only mention of athletic contests at Potidaea. These contests, naturally, were held in honor of some god or goddess. The word Ἡραῖα may be suggested to fill the un-restored part in line 5, but the certainty of the restoration cannot be established. The date of the inscription must be before 356 B.C., for after the capture by Philip, the city fell into an insignificant position, and no local autonomy, by any means, could have been maintained.

Of the heroes, Heracles must have been very popular, since tradition connects him with the isthmus of Corinth, where he slew the giant Alcyoneus,[82] as well as with Pallene, where, according to another version, he took part in the fight between the gods and the giants.[83] The stories about Alcyoneus and the giants and their struggle with Heracles were transplanted, according to the author in *R.E.*, Suppl. III, p. 921, to Chalcidice through the Corinthian colony Potidaea.

THE POTIDAEAN TREASURY AT DELPHI

Potidaea at some period of her existence dedicated, like her parent city, Corinth, a treasury at Delphi (Pl. XVIII, 1). Neither the circumstances, however, nor the exact date of the dedication is known. Ever since the beginning of the excavations in the sacred precinct, scholars have attempted to identify the treasury with one of the many uncovered.

It is always customary, when the exact date of a construction is not given, to assign it to some important event in the history of the town. In regard to the treasury of Potidaea, it has been taken for granted that the building antedates the revolt of the city from Athens in 432 B.C., which resulted in the expulsion of the inhabitants and the resettlement of the town by Athenian colonists (429 B.C.).[84] Because of the absence of information about events in Potidaea from both her founding to the invasion of Xerxes and from the battle of Plataea to the revolt against Athens, scholars have assigned the period immediately after the famous repulsion of the Persian army under Artabazus (479 B.C.)[85] as the period in which the city erected the treasury at Delphi. There appears to be no objection to such a date for the Potidaean treasury. In fact, this important event in the history of the town is almost too inviting as a reason for the dedication of the building. But we know almost nothing of the history of Potidaea before the Persian wars. Naturally there were other events which must have been recorded in the local histories, but because of their scant connection with the affairs of any of the great powers, Athens or Sparta, these local events were not included in the works of Athenian writers. Thus, we are not justified in any way in assigning the building of the treasury to the period immediately following the Persian defeat, the only important event known, unless other evidence comes to the support of such an assignment.

The only literary evidence we have that Potidaea ever erected a treasury at Delphi is found in a brief statement of Pausanias.[86] The author, in speaking of the Syracusan treasury, definitely states that it was built from the spoils taken from the Athenian defeat; whereas, in referring to the Potidaean treasury, he merely says that it was an indication of piety to the Pythian god.

It is clear that if the Potidaean treasury had been built as a result of the victory against the Persians, Pausanias would have so stated, especially since the victory was of such great importance. In mentioning the treasuries of the Thebans and the Athenians in the same paragraph, he states the event that led to their erection.[87] In fact, it is true that in all the treasuries mentioned by him, the event commemorated is given and it is only in the case of the Potidaean treasury[88] that Pausanias states that it was built "for the sake of piety." Would not one be justified in expecting Pausanias to mention the event of 479 B.C. if the treasury had really been built because of that event?

Another consideration might support the view that the treasury does not necessarily belong to the Persian period. The happy outcome of the resistance of the Potidaeans against the Persians was attributed by them, according to Herodotus, to Poseidon and not to Apollo,[89] and consequently we may assume that a thank-offering or an image of the god of their deliverance was dedicated in his temple at Potidaea. It seems difficult indeed to explain the building of a treasury in a precinct of Apollo when the Potidaeans themselves attributed the defeat of the Persians to Poseidon, their patron god. It is more probable that Potidaea, following the example of her parent city which under Cypselus had built a treasury at Delphi,[90] dedicated her own treasury at some time before the Persian wars.

The exact location has been a matter of no small controversy. The treasury has been sought in different places in the sacred precinct, and different structures from time to time have become candidates for the title "Potidaean." From Pausanias[91] one doubtless gets the impression that both the Syracusan and the Potidaean treasuries were near the Athenian. This should be kept in mind together with the more or less certain dates of these two treasuries. For the Potidaean treasury, a structure built not later than the first quarter of the fifth century (accepted by all as the last possible date, on historical grounds, for the treasury) must be located. To be identified as Potidaean, this treasury must be near another one (that of Syracuse) which answers Pausanias' statement that it was built "from the spoils of the great Athenian defeat"; and, since an inscribed poros block was found near the Athenian treasury,[92] there must be evidence of an earlier Syracusan building on the same site.[93]

Of the various structures that have been identified from time to time as "Potidaean" and "Syracusan," the following groups are worthy of consideration: V, VII; XIII, XIV; VIII, IX.[94] Group V, VII has been accepted by Dinsmoor[95] as representing the Syracusan and Potidaean foundations, respectively. These foundations are located to the south of the Athenian treasury and on either side of the first turn of the sacred way toward the north. Their proximity to the Athenian treasury would satisfy the statement of Pausanias. Dinsmoor observes[96] that Pausanias passed their foundations while writing about the three war treasuries, and that after he finished reading their inscriptions, he mentioned the treasuries of Syracuse and Potidaea (V and VII).

There does not seem to be any serious objection to Dinsmoor's argument about treasury no. V, although other scholars have variously identified it.[97] No. VII, however, seems to be more suitable for a Boeotian treasury rather than for a Potidaean, and has been generally accepted as such.[98] It is a poros building with H clamps and is dated in the first half of the fifth century. The objection raised to its identity as Potidaean is that many blocks, both *in situ* and scattered nearby, bear inscriptions in the archaic Phocian alphabet which represent masons' names common in Boeotia.[99] Besides, another foundation, no. VIII, is better suited to the narrative of Pausanias and fits into his discussion in a more logical order of the treasuries.

The group of foundations XIII and XIV can be easily rejected, not only because their distance from the Athenian treasury does not fulfill the requirement of the narrative of Pausanias, but also because their late foundations do not fit either the early Syracusan treasury or the date of the Potidaean.[100]

The group of foundations VIII and IX, behind the Athenian treasury, remain to be considered. Both have been variously dated, but in no case later than 475 B.C.[101] The northern one, which is also the smaller of the two, seems to have been rebuilt toward the end of the fifth century; thus it fits the two dates required for the treasury of Syracuse[102] and has this advantage over V. Many of its stones, identical with those *in situ*, have been found built into two nearby constructions.[103] The other treasury, VIII, must be the Potidaean,[104] as all other possibilities have been eliminated. Both VIII and IX have been assigned to Potidaea, but with question marks, by Pompow in an article on *Delphi* (*R-E.*, Suppl. IV, cols. 1274-1278 and nos. 38, 39). De La Coste-Messelière (Au Musée de Delphes, p. 412) thinks that VIII can in no way be assigned to Syracuse, but that there is sufficient evidence for its being assigned to Potidaea. The same author (p. 471 and n. 6) maintains that the original structure of IX was pillaged at the beginning of the fifth century B.C. and considers the possibility that the foundation might belong to the old treasury of Athens. To Syracuse he assigns a small foundation (no. 13 in his plan) located between treasuries IV and VI.[105]

Treasury no. VIII (Pls. XVIII, 2; XIX, 1, 2; XX, 1) is a rectangular building constructed of good poros stone and measures at the euthynteria 8.40 m. by 6.30 m., and at the orthostate, 6.05 m. by 8 m. The building was divided by a cross wall into a vestibule and a cella. Remnants of the cross wall can still be seen near the south wall (*see* Pl. XVIII, 2). The wall is best preserved on the west side, and the greatest height is 1.87 m. from the euthynteria. In the south wall double orthostate was used, part of which is visible near the southwest corner (Pl. XIX, 1). This double orthostate measures 0.53 m. in h., 0.80 m. in l. and 2 x 0.35 m. in d. The east wall is the least preserved; only a few blocks can be seen *in situ*. The north wall, which is preserved almost to its entire length, is especially interesting, for here material from older structures can be seen. Near the east end of this wall on the interior side there is a block, under the second course from the top, bearing dove-tail clamps on both ends (*see* Pl. XIX, 1, 2) and a horizontal groove between. The third block to the south bears traces of a similar clamp. The date of these dove-tail clamps is placed by De La Coste-Messelière in the first third of the sixth century B.C. The re-used material must have come from structures that were built after the first sacred war and razed to the ground at the time the temple was reconstructed (548 B.C.).[106]

Both the double T and the dove-tail clamp can be found in other parts of the building. Specifically, a T clamp is seen on a block above the re-used material with the dove-tail clamps; there is a similar clamp on the outer side of the double orthostate; a dove-tail clamp is found at the northwest corner of the building.

Curiously enough, the Potidaean treasury, in dimensions as well as in proportions and general plan, is very similar to the building identified as the treasury of the Sicyonians (Pl. XX, 2) and dated by De La Coste-Messelière at about 500 B.C.[107]

Dedicatory Inscription of a Potidaean at Delphi

There is only one inscription which can be definitely dated within the first century of Potidaea's existence.[108] It is inscribed on a marble base and represents a dedication of a Potidaean to Apollo at Delphi. The inscription is now in two fragments which were found by Lolling in 1888 and 1896, respectively,[109] near the theatre and reads as follows:[110]

Θευγένες Πυθοκλέο[ς ἀνέ]

θεκε τὀπέλονι Ποτεδα[ιάτας]

Δόμις ἐποί[ε or -εσε]

The dedication is in the Corinthian alphabet, while the signature of the artist is not in that alphabet and has larger letters.[111]

There is no doubt that the dedicator is a Potidaean; both his
name (Theygenes) and the patronymic (Pythocles) are very common Greek names.[112] The ethnic Ποτεδα[ιάτας] placed at the end
causes no difficulty, since there are numerous parallels.[113] The
artist's name in the last line cannot be identified.[114] He does not
seem to have any relations with the Corinthians. His name has
been read as Δόμις and M does not stand for the Corinthian Ξ, as
in the first two lines, iota is not represented by a three-bar sigma
but by I, and E not by a form of B although the form E appears
in the ethnic Ποτεδα[ιάτας] in the second line. The name Δόμις
itself is very unusual and this is the only inscription in which it
appears.[115] The suggestion of Δῶμις or Δοῦμις does not help. The
alphabet in which he signs his name may as well stand as Boeotian,
Phocian, Locrian, Chalcidian, Eretrian.[116] The reading of iota
after omicron in the verb of the third line belies the Boeotian
origin of the sculptor, according to Perdrizet, as the iota is omitted
from ποιῶ in archaic inscriptions from Boeotia.[117] Phocian or
Delphic origin is not considered impossible by Perdrizet, for, as
he observes, forms of ποιῶ with the iota appear in inscriptions
from these places. A Chalcidic origin for the sculptor, also, is not
impossible, for both the iota and the four-bar sigma are to be
found on the inscription on the base of the Eretrian Bull at
Olympia.[118] The monument has been dated in the second half of
the sixth century B.C., but not later.[119] Its importance cannot be
overestimated. Besides showing the devotion of the Potidaeans to
Apollo Pythios, it is the only documentary evidence extant from
the period before 480 B.C. With the treasury at Delphi, the
architectural remains on the site of the ancient town, and the
silver coins, the inscription helps to fill the gap which exists in
the history of Potidaea from its founding to the Persian wars.

III

POTIDAEA DURING THE PERSIAN WARS
490-479 B.C.

□

THE FIRST literary reference to Potidaea is to be found in Herodotus' account of the invasion of Greece by Xerxes, in 480 B.C.
Herodotus carefully relates the detailed itinerary which the Persian fleet followed after leaving Doriscus.[1] The fleet came to
Acanthus and sailed through the canal. Following this, the historian of the Persian wars ascribes to the fleet a "periplus" of the
entire coast of the peninsulas of Sithonia and Pallene. Every seacoast town is included in this cruise. Whether the whole fleet or
just a detachment undertook the operation the author does not
mention. It is absurd, however, to think that the entire fleet is
meant here. Doubtless a base for these operations was established
at first on the south shores of Sithonia, and then at Pallene, and
both bases used as starting points for the exploration of the two
peninsulas.

That this was the procedure which must have been followed is
suggested by Herodotus in paragraph 123.[2] He states first that
the fleet held a straight course from Ampelus, the headland of
Sithonia, to Canastraeum, the headland of Pallene, and requisi-
tioned ships and men from the towns of the latter peninsula.
Previously he had stated that the fleet, after rounding Ampelus,
passed the Greek towns on the west coast of Sithonia as far as
Olynthus[3] and received ships and men from all of them. To reconcile these two statements is not difficult. What probably happened is this: after rounding Ampelus a detachment of the fleet
resumed the operations around the Toronaic Gulf, while the
main part must have waited on the south coast of Pallene. Potidaea
then, along with the rest of the seacoast towns, furnished ships
and men. There is no mention of the exact number of ships and
men furnished by Potidaea alone. An estimate of the ships and

men supplied by the Greeks of Thrace and the islands off Thrace is placed by Herodotus at 120 ships and 24,000 men.[4]

THE REVOLT AND THE SIEGE OF POTIDAEA

The next mention of Potidaea by Herodotus is found in VIII, 126-29, when the city was besieged by Artabazus, Xerxes' general, in 479 B.C. As soon as the people of Potidaea saw the King's army marching toward the Hellespont and heard that the Persian fleet had fled from Salamis, they openly revolted. Their example was followed by the rest of the people of Pallene and they apparently formed an alliance with Potidaea.[5]

Among the troops that accompanied Xerxes to the Hellespont was a body of 60,000 men under Artabazus. These men, according to Herodotus, were selected by Mardonius to escort the King as far as the passage and then to return. Herodotus does not say if there were any other motives behind the escorting idea. Perhaps Mardonius was anticipating adverse reaction on the part of the northern Greek cities, as Xerxes had indirectly been advised by Themistocles, the Athenian commander at Salamis, that the Greeks would attempt to destroy the bridge on the Hellespont. Perhaps, also, the Persian general, doubtful of future dealings with the Greeks, sent Artabazus with a substantial force in order to make sure that any future retreat might not be blocked. Both motives might have influenced Mardonius. Grundy[6] suggests that the main motive was in regard to the supply service and to organize the "new line of communication."

Xerxes was now in Asia. When Artabazus returned to Greece, passing near Pallene, he found the Potidaeans in revolt. The other cities of Pallene had followed the example, and Olynthus, a town occupied by the Bottiaeans at that time, was suspected of similar action.[7]

Artabazus immediately laid siege to Potidaea and Olynthus. Olynthus apparently succumbed fairly soon; the inhabitants were killed and the city was handed over to Critobulus of Torone and the Chalcidian Greeks.[8] Perhaps this cruelty against the Olynthians was meant to terrify the Potidaeans and the rest of Pallene. It certainly achieved the opposite end. Having captured Olynthus, Artabazus threw all his forces against strongly-fortified Potidaea.[9] The north wall of the city, running from sea to sea and cutting off the peninsula from the mainland, rendered all access to the town and the rest of the peninsula difficult to land forces. The besieged Potidaeans and their allies offered strong resistance and successfully withstood all the attacks of the enemy.

Their bravery, however, would not have been fully rewarded had not the plot of the Scionaean general, Timoxenus, been discovered in time. Timoxenus was in command of the contingent from Scione within Potidaea and had agreed with Artabazus to betray the town.[10] Herodotus does not mention how the agreement was first made and what the motives governing it were. Possibly Persian gold played its part.[11] Timoxenus communicated with the Persian commander by means of letters wrapped around an arrow and concealed with feathers. The arrow was shot to places previously agreed upon.[12] Fortunately for the Potidaeans and their allies, the plot was accidentally disclosed. An arrow shot by Artabazus missed the mark and hit the shoulder of a Potidaean. The letter in its shaft was discovered and taken to the generals who must have represented the different cities of Pallene. They decided, however, not to punish Timoxenus on the charge of treason, lest the title of traitors should be attached to the Scionaeans hereafter.[13]

Another event occurred during the siege that could have decided the fate of Potidaea.[14] Since the walls of Potidaea were from sea to sea and the Persians had no ships with which to cross over to the south side of the city or to make sea attack, they were unable to hold a complete blockade of the town. But after three months of vigorous struggle, there happened to be an unusual ebb tide which lasted for some time.[15] Evidently the besiegers failed to take advantage of this opportunity in time; otherwise, they could have circumvented the wall and entered the town.

Artabazus finally tired of the long drawn out siege and ordered his troops to march along the marshy shore; when they had traveled only two-fifths of the way a great flood-tide came, greater, as Herodotus reports it on the testimony of the natives, than any other that had ever occurred.[16] Many of the Persians, unable to swim, were drowned; those who could swim were killed by the Potidaeans who had quickly sent boats.[17] The number of men lost is not given, but the Persian commander in despair raised the siege and led the remnants of his troops to Thessaly, where Mardonius was wintering. Thus, Potidaea and the other cities of the peninsula were saved.

The cause of the tidal waves was attributed by the Potidaeans

to the wrath of Poseidon against those who had profaned the
temple and statue of the god which stood in the suburb of the
city.[18] It is possible that the tide was the result of volcanic dis-
turbances, quite common in Greece and the Aegean region. Such
phenomena as the high sea and the low sea were ascribed to
Poseidon; and the Potidaeans, who regarded him as their protec-
tor and placed his image on their coins, quite naturally attributed
their safety to the god's intervention.

PARTICIPATION AT PLATAEA

The battle of Plataea followed, and Potidaea sent, according to
Herodotus, 300 of her citizens to fight on the side of the Greek
allies. This contingent from Potidaea, at the suggestion of the
Corinthians, was stationed by Pausanias near the 5,000 Corinthians.[20] The Corinthians, the Potidaeans, the Orchomeneans, and
the Sicyonians were facing the Medes on the Persian side.[21] No
other city of the Chalcidic peninsula is mentioned by Herodotus
as having taken part in this battle.

After the battle of Plataea, the spoils were gathered together;
first a tithe was dedicated at Delphi; another, apparently from
what remained, at Olympia; and a third at the isthmus of Corinth.[22] The remaining booty was divided, according to Herodotus,
among the various states that had taken part in the battle. Exact
details as to the basis for each city's apportionment are not indicated. Doubtless both the relative worth of the service rendered,
as implied in Herodotus,[23] and the relative size of the troops sent
by each city, as Diodorus believes,[24] played their parts.

The participation of the Potidaeans entitled them to have their
name engraved on the monuments that were erected in commemoration of the battle. On the monument at Delphi, the well-
known serpent-column, the word Ποτειδαιᾶται appears; Pausanias
also read the name of the Potidaeans on the pedestal of the votive
statue of Zeus at Olympia.[25]

In spite of this evidence and Herodotus' testimony, the participation of the Potidaeans in the battle of Plataea has been doubted
by some scholars.[26] The trustworthiness of Herodotus' list has
been suspect since this list has fewer names than that of the
Olympia monument, as given by Pausanias.[27] In spite of the differences between the list of Herodotus and the inscriptions on the
two monuments, it is difficult to discredit the evidence of Herod-

otus in the case of Potidaea. His account of Potidaea's participation seems too vivid to be questioned. After all, it is not impossible that the city did take part in that battle. Macan,[28] referring
to the passage of Herodotus, comments that it is far from clear
how the Potidaeans came to Plataea. But this should not be a
disturbing factor. Lack of specific information as to the ways and
means that brought them to Plataea cannot be taken as justification to keep them out of Plataea. The Potidaeans, if anxious to
fight against the Persians, could have found a way to get to Plataea.
If there were barriers on land in the presence of the Persian army
in Thessaly, there was the open sea.

The whole question would be easier to decide if more definite
facts were known concerning the eligibility of states to have their
names inscribed on the monuments of Delphi and Olympia.
Bauer,[29] attempting to explain the differences between the two
monuments, suggested the possibility that the privilege of having
a name inscribed on either monument was granted to any city
for contributing to the cost of that monument as well as for having fought at Plataea or Salamis. This explanation, however, is
not supported by any evidence. The statements of Herodotus and
Thucydides, as well as the heading of the Delphic inscription, are
clear on this point.[30]

It has generally been accepted on good evidence that the names
on both the Delphic and Olympian monuments represent not only
those states that fought at Plataea, but also those which took part
at Salamis. The original intention, then, of the erection of these
two monuments as a commemoration of the victory at Plataea
was soon modified in order to include also the victory at Salamis;
and the cities that took part in either of the two battles were entitled to have their names inscribed on both monuments.[31]

The inclusion on the serpent-column at Delphi of names of
cities that fought at Salamis explains the difference that exists between this list and the one given by Herodotus for Plataea. The
cities named in the list of Herodotus as having taken part at
Plataea are included in the Delphic list, with the exception of
the Paleans and Mantineans.[32] Meyer's view[33] that Herodotus included the Potidaeans in his list of the states which fought at
Plataea because he found their name on the inscribed serpent-
column is refuted by How and Wells in their commentary on
Herodotus.[34] Since the monuments commemorated the victories
of both Plataea and Salamis and contained the names of those

cities that rendered service in either, why was the name of Potidaea in the inscriptions of Delphi and Olympia if she had not
taken part at Plataea? Certainly she rendered no service to the
Greek cause at Salamis; in fact, she contributed ships and men
to the fleet of Xerxes.

Rawlinson,[35] commenting on the order in which the names
appeared on the Delphic inscription, believes that the principle
of importance rules as far as the 7th or 8th coil; then the geographic principle prevails. He explains the irregularities which appear in the geographic sequence by saying that they were perhaps
due to later additions made at the beginning or the end of the
original lines of the document.[36] According to the same author,
the name Ποτειδαιᾶται is included among the possible later additions.[37] There is no reason to believe that the name was in-
serted later. Granted that it was, upon what basis was this later
addition made on the document? Rawlinson, aside from including Marathon as being commemorated by the monument, which
is probable, makes a statement that the inscription was a commemoration of those cities "which came into hostile collision
with the Persians throughout the war," and not those which
fought at Plataea alone.[38] From this it may be inferred that the
Potidaean resistance to the siege of Artabazus in 479 B.C. must
have been considered responsible for the city's appearance on
the inscription. There is absolutely no evidence supporting this
supposition. If the Potidaeans were mentioned on the monument
simply because of their resistance to Artabazus, we would have
expected Herodotus to refer to this fact. He does so in the case
of the Tenians,[39] who, because of their service at Salamis, were
included in the Delphic inscription. Furthermore, other cities of
Pallene had revolted against Persia and had sent troops to help
Potidaea against the siege of Artabazus; Olynthus also was besieged and destroyed by that general. Yet none of these cities is
included in any of the Plataea monuments.[40]

With the exception of coils four and seven which have four
names each, and with coil three containing only two names, the
coils have three names each. The inscription then gives the appearance that the original arrangement was in groups of three,
and Potidaea appears at the end of the fifth coil, after the Styrians
and the Eleans. It does not seem likely that this coil contained
only two names. Moreover, there is not the slightest indication
that the letters in the word were incised later than the majority

of the names, although such a case of later incisions is pointed out by Frazer[41] and Hicks-Hill[42] in the names of the Tenians and Siphnians. In reference to these two names, it may be added that they are found at the end of the seventh and fourth coils respectively, the coils containing four names each.

Perhaps the point of later additions would be made clearer if we knew something about the time when both the Olympia and Delphi monuments were inscribed and the procedure followed in arranging the names of cities on the former monument. Pausanias possibly copied down as many names as he could make out on the Olympia monument, but certainly in the order in which he found them on the pedestal. He mentions the Potidaeans between the Eleans and Anactorians.[43] On the Delphic monument the Potidaeans appear after the Eleans also. If Pausanias copied down the names in the order in which they appeared and had any regard for their arrangement, the position of the Potidaeans does not give the impression of a later addition.

It is interesting to note at this point that Ambracia and Anactorium are mentioned by Herodotus as having taken part in the battle of Plataea, and the names of both cities appear on the inscriptions of the two monuments. Leucas also is mentioned but appears only on the serpent-column. These three cities, like Potidaea, were colonies of Corinth.

Finally, we may introduce the testimony of Aristotle in support of Potidaea's participation in the battle. In the *Rhetoric,* commenting on the necessity of acquaintance with the elements of a topic under discussion before drawing a conclusion, he cites, as an example, the Athenian conduct toward the Greeks as an element of censure and states that the Athenians subjugated and reduced to slavery the Aeginetans and the Potidaeans who, as allies, had fought with distinction against the barbarian.[44] While this passage has not been noted by authorities on the question, the information that can be derived from it is significant. It shows that it was an established fact among the ancients that Potidaea was allied with Athens and the other Greek cities against Persia and played an important part in that struggle.

In summary, the evidence indicates that the Potidaeans did take part in the battle of Plataea. In fact, they had every reason to participate, for their position, in view of their previous revolt, would have been perilous had the battle ended in favor of the Persians.

IV

FROM THE END OF THE PERSIAN WARS
TO THE REVOLT FROM ATHENS
479-432 B.C.

◰

AFTER THE defeat of the Persians at Plataea and Mycale in 479 B.C. the desire among Greek cities for a political union as a defense against any recurrent Persian invasion was more powerful than ever. The Greeks followed up their victories and proceeded to liberate the Greek cities which were under the Persian rule. Thus a fleet, composed of Peloponnesian, Athenian, Island, and Ionian ships under the command of the Spartan Pausanias, sailed for Cyprus and liberated many of the cities of that island from the Persians; it then seized Byzantium, which was strongly defended by Persians.[1]

It seemed for a while that Sparta would continue the principal role she played at Plataea and become the leader in the tendency toward Panhellenic cooperation against Persia. The Greek cities of Asia Minor were the prime movers for such a unified action, for they were in immediate need of protection against the constant attacks of Persia. The medizing attitude of Pausanias, however, and his mistreatment of the Ionian allies resulted in his recall to Sparta to answer charges; and the allies persuaded Athens to assume the leadership against Persia.[2] Therefore, when the Spartans sent Dorcis to take the place of Pausanias, the allies were not satisfied with him as a commander,[3] and he was recalled soon afterwards.

Sparta from the very beginning showed that she was unfit to undertake the leadership in a war which required maritime strength; moreover, she could not trust her generals to remain incorruptible when fighting on distant fields. The recent behavior of Leotychidas,[4] who was sent to Thessaly to punish those who had sided with Xerxes and Mardonius, and of Pausanias at Byzantium, played the major role in inducing the Spartans to surrender their supreme command of the Greek forces against Persia.

After the recall of Dorcis, no Spartan general was sent to supersede him. The leadership then fell upon Athens—a task which she was ready and willing to undertake. After all, being superior in fleet strength, Athens was the most natural leader.

The Athenians, having agreed to lead this group of allied maritime states, began in the winter of 478/7 B.C. to organize the Confederacy.[5] Delos was selected as the seat of the Confederacy, where an annual synod was to be held. Each of the allied cities had a vote. The main purposes of the Delian Confederacy were to prevent any future attempt by Persia to subjugate Greek cities, to liberate all Greek cities still under Persian domination, and to retaliate for the losses that Persia had brought on Greek soil by devastating the territory of the Great King.[6]

No further details about the policy and the organization of the Confederacy are known, except that the allies were obligated to share the cost for this unified action against Persia by supplying a quota of ships and men or a quota of yearly tribute. According to Herodotus and Plutarch, the contribution was based on the ability and the resources of each allied city.[7] It was left up to Athens, however, to determine the form of contribution.[8] The Athenian representative, Aristides, a fair man who was familiar with the comparative strength and resources of Greek cities, was assigned the task of drawing up the first assessment. Aristides' discharge of that duty met the approval of the parties concerned; the fixed contributions that he assigned to each city were regarded as equitable and moderate even to the period when the Delian Confederacy evolved into the Athenian Empire. The sum of the first assessment was 460 talents.[9] This sum must have included the contributions in ships; the existence of a monetary equivalent for ships could be accepted as definite from the beginning of the Confederacy and is confirmed by Thucydides for the later period when the allies began to convert their assessment from ships to money.[10]

Unfortunately, we have no satisfactory account of the history and development of the Delian Confederacy or League. There is no definite information, for example, about the League's original extent, or the form and amount of contribution of each member before 454 B.C., when the seat, apparently for reasons of security and on the motion of the Samians, was transferred from Delos to Athens.[11] Information concerning the time Potidaea entered the League, the form of her original contribution, and her relations

with Athens between 479 and 432 B.C., aside from the quota lists
following the year 445/4 B.C. (when the name of the city first
appears) and from the coinage of the city during this period, is
based on probabilities. These suppositions depend upon Potidaea's
participation in the Persian wars, the Athenian activities in the
Thraceward region, and the general policy of Athens toward the
allied states.

The revolt of the cities of Pallene and Olynthus against Persia
following the departure of Xerxes from Greece and the successful
defense of Potidaea against the attack of Artabazus seemingly left
Potidaea and the cities of Pallene the only independent states in
the Chalcidic peninsula for the time being. Subsequently, Potidaea alone is reported to have sent a contingent to Plataea to
fight against the Persians. One would naturally expect this anti-
Persian attitude of Potidaea to have found expression when the first
news of the formation of a league against Persia was announced.
In the absence of any evidence to the contrary, one might reasonably assume that the city was among the first to join the Delian
Confederacy and to provide its assigned share in the common
effort. Probably the other cities of Pallene followed the move too.

The news of an alliance must have been heard with great relief
not only in Pallene, but in all the Greek cities of Chalcidice which
had temporarily become subject to the King. In spite of the Persian defeat at Plataea, fear of Persia was still present. According
to Herodotus,[12] the Persians remained for a while in control of
every important stronghold, such as Doriscus and Eion, on the
coastline of Chalcidice and Thrace.[13] It is not at all impossible
that, in view of the circumstances and the feeling of common
danger, the Chalcidic cities were among the first to participate
in this equal alliance.

According to Walker,[14] the most the alliance could claim in
the Thraceward district at the time of the first assessment of Aristides (first half of 477 B.C.) were Chalcidice and the islands of
Thasos and Samothrace. West in his article "The Tribute Lists
and the non-Tributary Members of the Delian League" gives a
partial roll of the charter members of the League, in which he
includes the names of the islands Ceos, Cythnos, Siphnos, Naxos,
the two Euboean cities Chalcis and Eretria, and Potidaea. All
these states had fought against Persia and their names were inscribed on the serpent-column of Delphi. Meritt, Wade-Gery, and
McGregor[16] discuss extensively the original membership of the

Delian Confederacy and include, as part of the Thracian panel of the quota lists, the names of a number of cities of the Chalcidic peninsula together with Potidaea. An annual assessment as large as 460 talents suggests widespread alliance from the very beginning.[17]

Assuming that Potidaea had not entered the League by the time of the first assessment, the next opportunity must have been presented during the Thraceward campaign of Cimon in 476/5 B.C. It was Cimon who expelled the Persian garrisons from all the Greek cities on the Thracian coast and the Hellespont.[18] Potidaea and the other cities of Chalcidice would have found it convenient to enter the League at this time, if they had not already done so. The most definite statement that can be made, however, is that Potidaea and the other Chalcidic cities had definitely accepted membership at the time Aristides was acting as assessor, if the literal translation of a statement in Thucydides is correct.[19] Thucydides' statement refers to the terms of the Peace of Nicias (421 B.C.), which provided for the autonomy of certain towns in Chalcidice and of others near it, with the obligation to pay to Athens "the tribute of Aristides' time." The terms of the peace thus suggest that Potidaea, being so near the Chalcidic cities and also having fought against Persia, must have entered the League at the same time, provided she was not already a member.

THE TRIBUTE OF POTIDAEA

There is no specific evidence as to the form of Potidaea's contribution to the Confederacy. The early records of the tribute, unfortunately, have not been preserved; the extant records begin with the year 454/3 B.C., when the treasury was removed from Delos to Athens.[20] It was up to Athens, the hegemonic power, to decide whether a member state should furnish a quota of ships and men or a quota of tribute. We know that Potidaea actually possessed ships, as she contributed to the fleet of Xerxes and also used ships during Artabazus' siege.[21] With her nautical background, Potidaea probably preferred, or was assigned, to contribute her quota in ships instead of money.

The absence of the name of Potidaea from the first two periods of the Athenian assessment, if not accidental because of the fragmentary condition of the inscriptions, suggests that she originally contributed ships instead of money. Potidaea appears as having paid monetary tribute in the second year (445/4) of the third assessment period, and the name of the city as well as the tribute is restored for the preceding year. It cannot be shown that the city paid a monetary tribute earlier than the beginning of the third assessment. Meritt in his *Documents on Athenian Tribute* suggests that Potidaea has a serious claim for the assessment of 450 B.C., but, he remarks, "West has made a strong case for inception of tribute payment only at the beginning of the third assessment period (446/5)."[22]

More recently, Meritt, Wade-Gery and McGregor, re-examining the evidence in *The Athenian Tribute Lists*,[23] arrive at more definite conclusions. It appears that fourteen other cities, in addition to Samos, Chios, and Lesbos, continued to contribute ships instead of money as late as 454 B.C.; the final move by Athens to have her allies convert ships to money contributions was not undertaken until about 450 B.C. and was completed by the end of the second assessment period (447/6) with Potidaea being the last to convert her obligation to money.

It is very likely that Potidaea finally decided, or was prevailed upon, to commute her quota of ships to payment of money about 446/5 B.C., if not a little earlier, but definitely by 445/4 B.C., when the name of the city and the monetary tribute appear on the quota lists for the first time. This apparent persistence of Potidaea in supplying ships instead of cash may be explained on the grounds of autonomy and prestige that this form of assessment offered and, possibly, on Corinthian influence as evidenced by the presence at Potidaea of the epidemiourgi sent annually by Corinth.[24] In any event, the gradual evolution of ship quota to money payments in the assessments of the Confederacy must have finally affected Potidaea's contribution and, in either 450/49 or 446/5, the normal assessment periods, the city changed her status to that of a tributary ally.

Many factors could have brought about the change. Thucydides attributes it to the attitude of the Confederate allies themselves;[25] they found it convenient, he reports, to pay money and be free from any personal service in the fleet; so they prevailed upon the Athenians to adopt such a measure. But it seems also that the change was appealing to Athens and was especially favored by Cimon. By such a change, a more homogeneous and more efficient fleet could be provided, and the practice gradually became an established Athenian policy following the Peace of Callias in 450/49, which terminated the war between Athens and Persia.[26]

It is from the extant quota lists that we get a glimpse of the history of Potidaea and her relations with Athens during the third quarter of the fifth century.[27] A glance at these lists will show that relations were cordial at least down to 440/39. It has been assumed that the city had changed her status to that of tributary ally in 446/5 and her name and amount of tribute paid were restored on the quota lists for that year; but this cannot be regarded as definite. Potidaea's name first appeared in the year 445/4, with the amount of tribute recorded as six talents; the same amount is recorded for the entire period, with the exception of the fragmentary entry for the year 442/1. However, this also can be restored with certainty as six talents.

The name of Potidaea has not been preserved on the tribute lists of 439/8, 438/7, and 437/6, while the amount is missing from two other lists, 436/5 and 434/3. In reference to the years 439/8 and 438/7, the inscriptions of the Thracian district are fragmentary and the names of only four cities for 439/8 and of six for 438/7 are preserved or can be restored.[28] The quota list for the year 437/6 is not preserved.[29] In the absence of any definite evidence as to events in the Thracian district during these years and because of the fragmentary condition of the inscriptions, it is difficult to make any statement in regard to the relations of this region to Athens. The name of Potidaea appears again in the year 436/5. The amount of the tribute is not recorded, but in the following year, 435/4, the usual six talents appears. Such a record might lead to the belief that nothing had happened thus far to mar the relations between Potidaea and Athens.

In the year 434/3, the name of Potidaea appears on the quota lists, but the amount paid is not preserved on the stone. The following year shows an increase to fifteen talents, and this amount could, with some justification, be assumed also for 434/3, an assessment year. The explanation for the unusual increase, whether it came in 434/3 or in 433/2, is not an easy one. The increase was not the result of any previous failure on the part of Potidaea to pay her tribute, since the name of the city appears with six talents for 435/4 and for the year before with the amount missing.

The authors of *The Athenian Tribute Lists* consider the increase in Potidaea's tribute "in no way disturbing" and are inclined to associate it with "disciplinary measures" on the part of Athens preceding the revolt of Potidaea in 432 B.C.[30] It is difficult to accept this view. It would have been an unwise policy for Athens to exert this type of discipline in 433/2 because of any Potidaean sympathy toward Corinth during the latter's conflict with Corcyra and Athens, immediately preceding or following the battle of Sybota (usually dated in the fall of 433 B.C.). A policy of this type would have invited trouble in a locality where a more conciliatory attitude might have been expected. Moreover, had so striking an increase been assessed for such reasons at a time so near to the revolt, some mention of it could have been expected in the account of Thucydides.[31] On the other hand, if the increase to fifteen talents can be attributed to the preceding year, as appears quite probable, there is no need to assume any pressure on Potidaea, since the relations of Corinth and Athens were in no way critical at that time. The reasons for the increase would then have to be sought elsewhere.

Furthermore, if by raising the tribute the exertion of pressure for any implied or expressed Corinthian sympathies is to be assumed in the case of Potidaea, then the increase in the tribute of Scione to fifteen talents in 435/4, unless erroneously recorded, is more difficult to explain in view of the fact that the amount is reduced to four in 432/1. Scione had regularly paid six talents a year, especially during the third assessment period 446/5-443/2. For the next two years, only the name of the city appears and the tribute entry of six talents is restored; in the period to 431/0, both the name of the city and the amount of tribute are preserved only for 435/4 (fifteen talents) and for 432/1 (four talents). The rise to fifteen talents, therefore, for 435/4—the only entry for this assessment period—is puzzling.

The authors of *The Athenian Tribute Lists* suggest the possibility of a stone-cutter's mistake in recording the amounts paid by Scione and Potidaea for that year.[32] This is not at all improbable, especially since the names of these two cities follow each other on the inscription, Potidaea (col. VI, 5), then Scione (col. VI, 6). If the stone-cutter or the clerk who provided the copy had mistakenly inverted the figures, it follows that Scione continued to pay her usual amount of six talents until 432/1, when her tribute, for some special reason (probably loyalty to Athens or assistance to her during Potidaea's revolt), was reduced to four talents, while Potidaea paid fifteen talents in

435/4. The increase could probably have begun in the preceding year, or even at the beginning of this assessment period (438/7).[33]

Had the tribute lists for the Chalcidic region been sufficiently preserved, they might have given a clue to the trend in the amount of tribute paid during the assessment period of 438/7 to 435/4. The portion preserved, however, does indicate some increases in tribute, though not so striking as in the increases of Scione (or Potidaea) for 435/4 or of Potidaea for 433/2. Aphytis and Mende in Pallene are included in the cities whose tribute was increased. During 446/5-443/2, Aphytis paid one talent a year, while Mende appears with five talents. In the present assessment period (438/7-435/4), the tribute of Aphytis is increased to three talents, and that of Mende to eight. In the case of Mende the tribute of eight talents is indicated at the beginning of the assessment period. This evidence, though slight, is suggestive of the possibility that, if Potidaea's tribute was increased during this assessment period (as the Scione-Potidaea inverted record for 435/4 seems to indicate), that increase might more likely have taken place at the time of the reassessment in 438.[34]

In such a case, there is more reason to assume that the increase in Potidaea's tribute came not as a punishment, but as a result of other considerations. It may be that the six talents paid by the city since 445/4 was not indicative of her wealth or ability, so that a readjustment was finally in order; or it may be that the reassessment came at a time when the city enjoyed a period of prosperity, perhaps partially caused by the friendly relations between Corinth and Athens. This Potidaean prosperity combined with the strengthening of Athenian power in the Thraceward region—through the founding of Amphipolis on the Strymon or Brea on the west coast of Chalcidice between Therma and Aeneia[35]—may offer the best explanation for Potidaea's increase in tribute. Witness also the tribute from the cities of Bottice (neighbors of Potidaea), which was almost doubled during the same period,[36] as well as the increase in the tribute of Aphytis and of Mende.

That Potidaea's increase, however, must have played a substantial role in stimulating discontent toward Athens cannot be denied; it must have been regarded as unfair by the Potidaeans when they were already paying without interruption more than many others in the region. This, combined with other factors such as limitations to their autonomy (as evidenced by the coins) and their relations with Corinth, hastened their revolt in 432 B.C.

By comparing the tribute of Potidaea with that of the other important cities of the peninsula of Pallene and Chalcidice, such as Aphytis, Mende, Scione, Acanthus, Torone, Neapolis, and Olynthus, some idea of the relative wealth and importance of the town may be obtained.[37] If the tribute, as is generally believed, was assessed mainly on the basis of the resources of the cities of the Athenian Empire, the following facts become evident from a study of the amounts paid by these cities: Pallene seems to surpass the other two peninsulas (Sithonia and Acte) in wealth, for the Pallene cities paid about twice as much tribute as did the cities of Sithonia and Acte combined; the cities of Pallene paid nearly as much as the rest of Chalcidice; the amount Potidaea paid—six talents annually down to 435/4—is greater than that paid by the majority of the cities in Chalcidice and is equaled only by the amount paid by Scione and Torone and is surpassed only by that of Mende which generally paid eight talents (as in 452/1, 438/7, 436/5. etc.), but five talents in 444/3 and 440/39.[38] From this brief comparison, it seems that Potidaea held an important position among the Athenian allies in the entire Chalcidic peninsula and surpassed many of them in resources and wealth. These resources and wealth may be explained partly on the basis of strategic location and on the city's relations with Athens and Corinth, the greatest maritime powers of the mainland.

Relations with Athens and Corinth

Potidaea's position appears unique in that while maintaining the status of an ally or tribute-paying member of Athens, she managed also to remain a loyal colony of Corinth. As to what part Potidaea played within the Delian Confederacy or the Athenian Empire, we are completely without information; we are equally uninformed as to any Athenian or even Corinthian influences on the city, except for the presence of the Corinthian *epidemiourgi* whom the Athenians finally ordered expelled in view of the imminence of hostilities with Corinth in 433/2 B.C. The fact that Athens allowed this Corinthian element to be sent annually to Potidaea may be taken as an indication not only of the city's good behavior, but also of a certain degree of autonomy—more extensive when its obligation to the Delian Confederacy or

Athenian Empire was a quota of ships and men, but somewhat limited when the conversion to cash was adopted.

It is quite reasonable to assume that Potidaea's form of government, which apparently was modelled after that of Corinth and therefore oligarchic in character, must have remained intact until the city was finally captured and its inhabitants expelled by Athens (430/29 B.C.).[39]

We hear of no Athenian personnel at Potidaea, such as the *episcopoi* or overseers, or of a "Board of Magistrates," commonly described as "the archons in the cities," or of a military garrison. The narrative of Thucydides[40] describing the circumstances leading up to the revolt of Potidaea from Athens in 432 B.C. gives no such indication. The presence of *episcopoi,* however, whose duty it was to look after the interests of Athens in the allied cities and, more specifically, the collection of tribute, could be expected. Their presence must have involved no limitation to local autonomy, however, provided acceptable behavior was maintained on the part of the allied city.[41]

A certain amount of limitation to Potidaea's autonomy may be found in the judicial sphere, with the extension of the jurisdiction of the Athenian courts, as the evidence available regarding the tributary states seems to imply.[42] Limitation on Potidaean coins of large denominations is also evident. Judging from the extant issues, the minting of tetradrachms appears to have come to an end about the middle of the fifth century as a result of the Athenian coinage decree.

Though we have no information about any strained relations between Potidaea and Athens before the revolt in 432 B.C., there may have been periods of tension. One such occasion might have become serious between 460 and 451 B.C. when Corinth, the metropolis of Potidaea, was fighting against Athens for her economic, even political, survival.[43] Corinth's position was made to appear hopeless for a time by the Athenian occupation of Naupactus (ca. 460) at the west entrance to the Corinthian Gulf, the alliance of Megara with Athens (459),[44] which gave rise to the First Peloponnesian War, and, finally, the capture of Aegina by Athens (457/6).[45] O'Neill,[46] in his excellent account, sums up the plight of Corinth as one of helplessness and despair, with the Corinthian and Saronic Gulfs having become Athenian lakes, so that the city was completely excluded from the avenues of trade.

Corinth survived this critical period and soon recovered, not so much through her own efforts as through Athenian retreats elsewhere, such as the disaster in Egypt, which eventually produced a favorable climate for the signing of the Five Years' Truce between Athens and the Peloponnesians (451 B.C.).[47]

One wonders about the attitude of Potidaea toward the critical situation of Corinth, and whether or not Corinth tried to create some diversion for Athens in the North, particularly in Pallene. The "extreme hatred" of Corinth toward Athens, as Thucydides describes it,[48] may have found some expression in the reputed loyalty of Potidaea to Corinth. The Corinthian epidemiourgi at Potidaea may have encouraged and incited the pro-Corinthian sentiment in the city. Unfortunately, evidence is lacking; a possible echo, however, of Athenian difficulties in Pallene may be found in the *Eumenides* of Aeschylus (lines 295-296), produced in 458 B.C., soon after the outbreak of the First Peloponnesian War. Reference is made in the play to the Phlegraean plain as one of the places from which Athena might come to aid Orestes.[49]

The authors of *The Athenian Tribute Lists*[50] point to lines 762-774 in the *Eumenides* as alluding "clearly to the war" (the First Peloponnesian War); "an allusion to the campaign in Egypt," they remark, "is often detected in lines 292-295," and, further, if these lines "do refer to the fighting in Egypt, then very possibly lines 295-296, . . . will refer to some sort of trouble in Pallene, and this would surely mean Poteidaia." This interpretation leads them to suggest that "it is not impossible that Poteidaia remained recalcitrant till Kimon made his Five Years' Truce in 451" B. C.

In any case, it would have been strange if Corinth, in the midst of her struggle for survival, had not seized the opportunity for Athenian diversion in Pallene, even though the circumstances then may not have been as ripe as during the period immediately preceding the revolt of Potidaea from Athens in 432 B.C.

Subsequently, however, with the Five Years' Truce and later the Thirty Years' Peace (447/6), a "new look" in Periclean policy (with reference to the Empire) came into existence. This change in policy aimed at raising the prestige and influence of the Empire by consolidating it internally and by promoting friendly relations with its neighbors.[51] Corinth was satisfied with the terms of both the Truce and the Peace; her position in the Corinthian Gulf was restored and with it, her trade with the west. The conciliatory policy of Pericles, exemplified especially by the founding of a

Pan-Hellenic colony at Thurii (443 B.C.),[52] was reciprocated later by the Corinthian attitude toward the revolt of Samos from Athens in 440/39 B.C. It was mainly Corinthian diplomacy that prevented the Peloponnesian League from intervening in support of Samos.[53] Whether there was any special agreement, contemporaneous with these developments between Corinth and Athens, which brought about such friendly relations, we do not know. Irrespective of any agreement, Corinthian self-interest must have played its part.[54] As long as Athens respected Corinth's sphere of influence, the western sea-route in particular, the latter could acquiesce to Athenian activity within the empire or elsewhere.

Potidaea's ties with Corinth could have invited preferential treatment when Athenian-Corinthian relations were friendly, or could have easily aroused the suspicion of Athens when these relations were reaching a critical point. It is within such a dual allegiance that Potidaea tried to shape her course. At times this could not have been an easy task; but there was no other choice. Ultimately, a choice had to be made and Potidaea sided with Corinth against Athens. The circumstances that led to this decision are given in detail by Thucydides.[55] Suffice it to say here that the defensive alliance between Corcyra and Athens in 433 B.C., following the crisis of Corcyra and Corinth over Epidamnus, finally embroiled Potidaea and thus provided one of the "grievances" for the Peloponnesian War.

V

THE COINAGE OF POTIDAEA TO 432 B.C.

□

POTIDAEAN first issues can be dated stylistically as far back as the middle of the sixth century B.C. Seltman remarks that Potidaea started to coin money not long after 550 B.C.[1] A *terminus ante quem* of the first coins has been established by the discovery of the Hoard of Tarentum, in which three Potidaean tetradrachms were included.[2] This Hoard was abandoned about 510 B.C.[3]

Tetradrachms were the first coins to be issued by Potidaea. They bear on the obverse the image of Poseidon Hippios on horseback, holding his trident, and on the reverse an incuse square. The standard followed is the Euboic-Attic, with a minimum weight of 16.04 grms. and a maximum of 17.70 grms. Fractions of tetradrachms were also struck before 500 B.C.[4] Here the Potidaeans did not follow the Euboic-Attic system, but the Corinthian; that is, the tetradrachm was divided into drachms and their fractions, as at Corinth, instead of into didrachms, as at Athens.[5] The other cities of Chalcidice adopted the divisions followed by Potidaea. In this a manifestation of the Corinthian influence through Potidaea is evident. At the same time, we might assume that Potidaean issues preceded those of other cities in this region.

DENOMINATIONS AND TYPES OF POTIDAEAN SILVER COINAGE

GRAMMES

	Minimum	Maximum	
Tetradrachms:	16.04	17.70	Poseidon Hippios. Rev. Incuse square.
Drachms:	2.16	2.86	Poseidon Hippios. Rev. Female head.

GRAMMES

	Minimum	*Maximum*	
Hemidrachms:	1.09	1.36	Horseman on a protome of a horse, or on entire horse. *Rev.* Female head.
Obols:	0.36	0.39	Free horse. *Rev.* Female head.

CLASSIFICATION OF COIN ISSUES

On the basis of style and historical considerations, the coinage of Potidaea down to 432 B.C. may fall into two periods:

    I. From the middle of the sixth century to ca. 479 B.C.
    II. From ca. 479 to ca. 432 B.C.

These periods are represented by silver coinage. A third period, which falls mainly in the fourth century and is represented wholly by bronze coins, will be treated in connection with the historical events following the repatriation of the Potidaeans by Sparta ca. 404 B.C. The main guide for a chronological classification is the style of the coins themselves.[6] There are dangers involved in a chronology on the basis of style. Stylistic variations are often misleading; the difference may be the result of two engravers who, though working during the same period, may differ in ability. Again, coins may be found which actually belong to a later period but which, because of intentional copying of a particularly revered design, resemble coins of a preceding period.

In the matter of chronology the coinage of Potidaea has one advantage which at the same time has its inherent dangers. The Potidaeans, most likely, were reproducing on their coins the image of the statue of Poseidon, which was, according to Herodotus,[7] in front of the city. In the case of the tetradrachms, there are differences in style among individual coins. The danger lies in the possibility that the archaic image of Poseidon might have been reproduced in later periods in which the coin would not normally belong. This becomes evident when we consider the smaller denominations, which on the obverse have the figure of Poseidon, but on the reverse, instead of the incuse square, show a female head. On these smaller coins, some very early,[8] the treatment of the female head shows a distinct advance, while the figure of Poseidon on the obverse remains practically the same. Of course this may be explained as artistic conservatism in the figure of Poseidon or on the inability of the engraver to attain in such a small space an advanced artistic treatment of the god on horseback.

A more accurate chronology would have been possible if more Potidaean silver coins were extant and if those found revealed the relations of the dies used. Die-sequence combined with stylistic comparisons and historical considerations would make it possible to arrive at a safer chronological sequence. With material presently available, however, the only chronological arrangement of the coins that may be formulated is one which is subject to future investigation.

The division of the silver coinage into two periods is demanded only by the artistic advance exhibited in certain specimens of both the large and small denominations. But it is very difficult to say where period I ended and period II began. A natural impetus, however, for the advance in style of the coins classified in period II might be expected to have taken place immediately following the retreat of the Persians from Plataea. It is fitting to place the beginning of period II in this year (479 B.C.). At the same time the possibility that the archaic type, as represented in period I, may have continued to be issued in some cases in period II must not be disregarded. But certainly the more mature artistry seen in these later coins places them in a class of their own.

CHRONOLOGICAL SEQUENCE OF PERIOD I
(ca. 550-ca. 479 B.C.)

Period I may be divided into two groups, A and B. The division is not meant, by any means, to put up fixed boundaries for the minting of representative coinage in each group, but rather to emphasize the stylistic advance attained in the entire period. The only suggestion for such a division is the fact that the discovery of the Hoard of Tarentum, which was abandoned about 510 B.C.,[9] offers a chronological point before which certain types of tetradrachms were issued; but this point cannot be established as a terminus of these issues since no complete stylistic break between them and what followed can be detected. It seems logical, however, to group together the coins from the period ca. 550-510 B.C., exemplified by the Potidaean tetradrachms of the Tarentum Hoard and issues similar to them, and to classify separately those coins which show a stylistic advance. In general, group A falls within the period from ca. 550-ca. 510 B.C., and group B from ca. 510-ca. 479 B.C.

The following coins are representative of Period I:

A. ca. 550-ca. 510 B.C.

a. *Tetradrachms*

1. Poseidon Hippios, nude, on horse walking right; he holds, almost horizontally, the trident in his right hand and the reins in his left.[10]

Rev. Small incuse square diagonally divided into four triangles. Weight, 17.20 grms. Brussels, in the *Hirsch Collection*. Babelon, *Traité,* I, no. 1636.

Other examples: Pl. XXII, a-c = Robinson, *Excavations at Olynthus,* VI, pl. VIII, 131, 132, 133 (weights, 16.01, 16.23, 16.56 grms.);[11] Babelon, "Trouvaille de Tarente," *Rev. Num.,* XVI, 1912, pl. II, 5, 6 (weights, 16.56, 16.80 grms.); Naville I, pl. XXVI, 796, with symbol (wt. 17.09).

2. Poseidon Hippios, nude, on horse walking left, wears long hair and holds the trident in his right hand and the reins in his left. Beneath the horse Π, and to the right above 0 ($= .0\,\Pi$).

Rev. Incuse triangle divided by two lines in the form of a T into three parts.

Weight 17.70 grms. Babelon, "Trouvaille de Tarente," pl. II, 4 = *Jameson Collection,* pl. XCVI, 960A (dated ca. 520 B.C.).

3. Similar to left, holding trident in his right hand and the reins in his left.[12] Beneath the horse a star with eight rays.[13]

Rev. Incuse square as in no. 1.

Weight 16.86 grms. Luynes. Babelon, *Traité,* I, p. 1149, no. 1638, pl. LII, 6 = Gaebler, pl. XX, 18. Another example in London (wt. 17.39), Wroth, *Num. Chron.,* XXXI, 1892, p. 7.

b. *Drachms* (Tetrobols)[14]

1. Poseidon Hippios nude, on horse walking right; in the right hand he holds the trident and in the left the reins; beneath horse a star with seven rays; in the field at the left above, the symbol for the letter koppa. Border of dots.

Rev. Female head in archaic style to right; wears necklace; the hair represented by dots is arranged in a long point at the top, and falls in long tresses on the neck; the entire in linear square in incuse square.

Weight 2.73 grms. Pl. XXII, d = Robinson, *Excavations at Olynthus,* VI no. 134, and pls. IX and XXIX. A similar one may be found in *ibid.,* III, no. 65 and pl. IV (wt. 2.59 grms.). Another example, but slightly advanced, in Gaebler, *Die Antiken Münzen,* III², p. 104, pl. XX, 21, with seven-pointed star, but with traces of Π in right below, and distinct 0 behind right arm of Poseidon.

2.   Similar to left, with a five-pointed star beneath horse and an exergue line. Oval shape of flan.

Rev. Similar head, but horizontally engraved. In linear square in incuse square.

Weight 2.57 grms. Paris. Babelon, *Traité,* I, no. 1640, pl. LII, 8. Another in London, Head, *British Museum Cat., Mac.,* p. 100, no. 6 (wt. 2.52 grms.). For similarity in the treatment of the obverse cf. the tetradrachm in Babelon, pl. LII, 6.

No. 1953 in *Weber Collection,* pl. 75 (wt. 2.72 grms.) = Gaebler, pl. XX, 22, is a similar type with five-pointed star, but the flan is round instead of oval and the female head is not horizontally engraved. The style on the obverse of this coin may be compared to that on the tetradrachm 3 above. With *Weber Collection* no. 1953 may be compared for the obverse the drachm illustrated in Naville I, pl. XXVI, 801 (wt. 2.76 grms.). The style of the figure of Poseidon and of horse is very similar, and has also the five-pointed star and the exergue line. The female head, however, on the reverse of this coin resembles that on the reverse of a drachm in Gaebler, pl. XX, 21, mentioned in no. 1 above.

c. *Obols* (Tritemoria)

1.   Horse galloping to right. Exergue line.

Rev. Female head with very pointed facial features, protruding eyeball with no indication of eyelids. Hair treated in archaic style and comes to a point at the top in similar fashion to preceding. Incuse circle.

Weight 0.36 grms. Babelon, I, p. 1153, no. 1649 = *Weber Collection,* pl. 75, no. 1955, and *Num. Chron.,* XXXVII, 1898, p. 254 and pl. XVI, 14.

Another similar example is illustrated in Naville I, pl. XXVI, 803 (wt. 0.44). Traces of a symbol seen beneath horse.

The examples given above are distinguished by their very

archaic, schematic representation of the figures, both of Poseidon and of horse; the figures are not well-proportioned, and the modelling is very crude. The muscles of the body are not indicated. The trident does not show in front of the horse's body. A slight advance in the general treatment of the type can be noticed in the varieties of tetradrachms given under no. 3 above. The female head on the reverse is very archaically treated. It shows pointed facial features; no modelling; the eye is of almond shape and is engraved in incised lines with eyeball in full view. The point to which the hair is arranged at the top of the crown is very pronounced.

B.   ca. 510-ca. 479 B.C.

a.   *Tetradrachms*

1.   Similar type to preceding, but a distinct advance in the modelling in the figure of Poseidon and especially in that of the horse. The type is to the right and beneath horse a star with four rays.

Rev. Again, the incuse square is diagonally divided into four triangles.

Weight 17.25 grms. Berlin. Gaebler, pl. XX, 19.

A slightly better modelling in the horse can be seen in the coin illustrated in Naville I, pl. XXVI, 797 (wt. 17.10). Beneath horse a six-pointed star. Another example, though worn, with six-pointed star, is illustrated in *McClean Collection,* pl. 116, no. 11 (wt. 17.15).

2.   Similar to the right with border of dots. Beneath horse an eight-pointed star. In the field to right traces of a letter (Π ?). More life is added to the attitude of the horse.

Rev. Incuse square is irregular and gives appearance of three small incuse triangles.

Weight 16.59 grms. *Weber Collection,* pl. 75, 1952. The same one (wt. 16.59) is in Naville IV, pl. XVII, no. 444.

3.   Similar to no. 1, with seven-pointed star beneath horse, Π just below head of trident, and with traces of an O above trident. Vigorous attitude of horse, beautiful, rounded modelling.

Rev. The usual incuse square.

Weight 16.75 grms. Berlin. Gaebler, p. 104, pl. XX, 20.

Another one (wt. 17.57 grms.) in Babelon, I, pl. LII, 5 (= Head, *H.N.²,* p. 212, fig. 128; *Cat., Mac.,* p. 99, no. 1) with a border of dots, seven-pointed star beneath horse, and trace of the

letter Π below head of trident; hair mass distinguishable. Still another example in Berlin (wt. 17.47); cf. A. de Sallet, *Besch. der
Ant. Münzen,* II, p. 123, no. 1, pl. V, 49. Cf. also with example
of Hirsch *Cat.,* XIV, pl. 8, no. 187 (wt. 16.04 grms.), trace of star,
border of dots. Body of Poseidon crudely represented, but horse
nicely modelled.

4.   Type similar to no. 3. Symbol beneath horse not distinguishable. No legend.

Rev. Same incuse square diagonally divided.

Weight 16.97 grms. *Weber Collection,* pl. 75, 1951.

The obverse shows a distinct advance over what has preceded.
Figure of Poseidon appears powerful. Beard of the god clearly
distinguished, muscles of the body indicated, and the chest em-
phasized. The trident for the first time shows the part on the side
of the horse and of Poseidon.

b.   *Drachms* (tetrobols)

1.   Similar type to right. Beneath horse Π and between front
legs O. Trident shows clearly on side of body of horse and
Poseidon.

Rev. Incuse square divided into four small squares by crossing
relief lines. *Fleur-de-lis* in lower left and upper right squares.

Weight 2.42 grms. London. Head, *H.N.*[2], p. 212 = Wroth,
Num. Chron., I, 1900, p. 276, pl. XIII, 4 = Babelon, *Traité,* I,
pl. LII, 7.

This coin is unique; it differs from the rest of the drachms in
not having the representation of the female head on the reverse.
Such departure from the usual reverse type cannot be explained.
For the artistic qualities of the obverse it may be compared with
tetradrachm no. 4 above.

2.   Similar type. Beneath horse Π and exergue line.

Rev. Female head to right diagonally placed within linear
square in incuse square. Shows advance in the modelling of face.

Weight 2.87 grms. Gaebler, pl. XX, 23.

A similar female head is represented on another drachm illustrated in Naville VI, 664 (wt. 2.59 grms.). The obverse of this
coin may be compared with tetradrachm no. 1 (Gaebler, pl. XX,
19). A drachm in Naville X, pl. 14, 419 (wt. 2.43 grms.) shows
a better modelled female head. The obverse of this coin is slightly
worn, but has Π beneath horse and an exergue line. A similar

specimen but more advanced is in Robinson's collection. Cf. *Excavations at Olynthus*, III, p. 26, n. 39.

CHRONOLOGICAL SEQUENCE OF PERIOD II

(ca. 479-432 B.C.)

In the year 479 B.C. Artabazus, unable to capture Potidaea after a three-months siege, retreated into Thessaly to join the forces of Mardonius. A little later the Persian army was defeated at Plataea, in which battle 300 Potidaeans had participated on the side of the Greek allied forces. The Persian danger was over. The period immediately following these events must have been very favorable for increased activity in the Potidaean mint. Judging from these events, we must assume that, politically and economically, the city was well founded. Not only was the city able to withstand successfully the long siege of Artabazus, but she also sent troops to Plataea. Potidaea was the only city of the entire Chalcidic peninsula to be represented in that battle. Following that memorable event, after the tithes to the gods were set aside, the booty was divided. The Potidaeans must have received their share. Potidaea soon joined the Attico-Delian alliance, but this relationship with Athens did not affect the monetary policies of Potidaea during the early part of this period.

It has often been suggested that Athenian monetary policy, to have a monopoly of silver and to restrict whenever possible the issues in the metal in allied cities to smaller denominations, had its origin after the organization of the Attico-Delian alliance.[15] Numismatic evidence for such a policy at this period is available in the case of some cities.[16] But the policy had a more general application and became fixed when the *symmachia* changed into an *arche* following the transfer of the treasury from Delos to Athens (454 B.C.).[17] Epigraphical evidence proves conclusively that such a policy prevailed at least from about 450 B.C. This date has been established by M. Segre and is based on the discovery in 1933 of a large fragment of a monetary decree on the island of Cos. In his article, "La Legge Ateniese Sull' Unificazione della Moneta," published in *Clara Rhodos*, IX, 1938, pp. 151-78, Segre, with the help of the already-known fragments of the monetary decree found in various cities,[18] has been able to reconstruct the Coan fragment. These fragments represent copies of the original decree set up in the cities of the Athenian Empire. Meritt,

Wade-Gery, and McGregor in their restoration of the decree identify it with that of Clearchus.[19] On the basis of epigraphical, intrinsic, and extrinsic considerations of the Coan fragment, the decree has been dated about 449 B.C.[20]

In accordance with this decree the cities of the Athenian Empire must have ceased to issue coins after 449 B.C.; any that were issued were of small denominations on Attic weight and intended for local use.[21] It is significant to notice that from the middle of the fifth century, foreign money at Athens, with the exception of coins in gold or electrum, was accounted for in terms of weight and not monetary value.[22] Certain cities, however, continued coining money of large denominations even after 449 B.C. There is good reason to assume that a separate agreement was reached between these cities and Athens, and that special concessions were granted to them. This is the case, as far as the Thraceward district is concerned, of Abdera, Acanthus, Maroneia, and perhaps a few others.[23] There is no indication that Potidaea was one of them. Judging from the extant issues, the city was not excluded from the provisions of the monetary decree. Potidaean tetradrachm issues came to an end about the middle of the century while smaller denominations may have continued down to 432 B.C., when the city was besieged by Athens and the silver coinage came to an end. Thus two chronological divisions for the silver coinage of period II are distinguishable: A. from ca. 479 to ca. 450 B.C., and B. from ca. 450 to ca. 432 B.C.

A.   ca. 479-ca. 450 B.C.

a.   Tetradrachms

1.   Poseidon Hippios, nude, on horse walking left. The trident is held in the right hand, but obliquely in stabbing position. Trace of trident is seen extending behind head. The reins are held in the left hand. Beneath horse a dolphin to left and an exergue line. In the field above both to the left and to the right there are indistinguishable letters, probably ΠOT.

Rev. The usual incuse square divided into four triangles by diagonal lines.

Weight 16.92 grms. Naville I, pl. XXVI, 798 = Naville X, pl. 14, 418.

This is one of the most interesting tetradrachms of Potidaea. It surpasses all the others in artistic quality. The figure of Poseidon is better engraved; the muscles are indicated. The figure of

the horse is powerfully represented; it exhibits masterful modelling of the muscles, especially in the head and legs of the animal.

This tetradrachm may be compared with another which is very
similar and exhibits the same qualities but is not as well preserved. Cf. Hirsch *Cat.*, XIII, pl. 14, 446 (wt. 16.27).

b. *Drachms* (tetrobols)

1. Poseidon Hippios on horseback to right, with the trident
in the right and the reins in the left hand. Bearded (?). Hair
gathered at the back *en masse*. Beneath horse a star with seven
rays.

Rev. Similar female head, but advanced treatment, especially
in the face. In incuse square.

Weight 2.61 grms. Naville V, pl. XL, 1331.

Similar to Babelon, I, no. 1641, pl. LII, 9 (wt. 2.43).

2. Similar. Hair can be distinguished falling on shoulder.
Beard indicated. Better modelling in the body of Poseidon. Beneath horse Π.

Rev. Similar female head. Traces of linear square; the entire
in incuse square.

Weight 2.70 grms. Gaebler, pl. XX, 24. For this coin *see* also
Imhoof-Blumer, "Nymphen und Chariten auf Griechischen Münzen," in *Jour. Int. Arch. Num.*, XI, 1908, p. 57 and for the reverse
pl. IV, 29.

A very similar coin is illustrated in Cahn's *Catalogue* 68, pl. 27,
1197 (wt. 2.70 grms.). Head of Poseidon is partly off flan, also
the head of horse and the prongs of the trident. Incuse square
on the reverse, with the linear square not distinguishable. Another coin resembling no. 2 is found in Naville I, pl. XXVI, 800
(wt. 2.79). Poseidon's long hair falling on the shoulder can be
distinguished. Beneath horse legend Π.

3. A variety of no. 2, but with traces of a star beneath horse
and better modelling in the female head on the reverse. Linear
square distinct in incuse square.

Weight 2.86 grms. London. Head, *Cat., Mac.*, p. 100, no. 4 =
Babelon, I, p. 1151, no. 1644 = Gaebler, p. 105, pl. XX, 25.

Approximately similar to the preceding is illustrated in *Weber
Collection*, pl. 75, 1954 (wt. 2.52 grms.). The obverse is slightly
worn, and traces of a symbol can be seen beneath horse. The
female head on the reverse constitutes the best example of the
entire group.

B. ca. 450-ca. 432 B.C.

The following coins definitely present an artistic advance over those discussed previously. There is no evidence to deny their classification in this period, which, stylistically, they fit. The monetary law of Athens, while preventing issues of larger denominations, seems to have had no effect on issues of smaller coins meant to be used locally. It is interesting to notice that the coins so far extant which can safely be classified in this period consist of hemidrachms and obols. There are no drachms which can be assigned with any degree of certainty to this period, although their issue may have continued after 450 B.C.

a. *Hemidrachms* (diobols)

1. Naked horseman on protome of a prancing horse to right. In the field below horse's head the letter Π.

Rev. Female head to right, with long hair falling on the neck. Naville VI, pl. 23, 665.

Weight seems to be incorrectly given as 2.16 grms, too high both for the size and the type of the coin.

A great resemblance is seen between this coin and that illustrated in Naville I, pl. XXVI, 802 (wt. 1.25 grms.). In the latter coin the horse is more powerfully represented.

A similar type is given also in Gaebler, pl. XX, 26 (wt. 1.13 grms.).

2. Horseman to right. Exergue line.

Rev. Female head to right. Incuse square.

Weight 1.09 grms. Hirsch *Cat.*, XIII, pl. 14, 447. Nice modelling of body of Poseidon and of horse.

Face of female figure is not clear but shows same style as that on the preceding coins.

With this coin we may compare the one mentioned in Babelon, I, p. 1151, no. 1646 (wt. 1.25 grms.) = Head, *Cat., Mac.,* p. 100, no. 8; also, Head, *loc. cit.,* no. 7.

The most interesting thing about these hemidrachms is the female head on the reverse. The hair is not represented with dots, except for a few above the forehead, and does not come to a point at the top as on the drachms, but is drawn to the back and apparently falls free on the neck. The ear is covered except for the lower part; the face is not like that on the drachms. This might, perhaps, be the representation of a different personality. This is difficult to decide because of the small size of the coin. It is possible, however, that with the change in the representations on the obverse (instead of the Poseidon Hippios of the tetradrachms and the drachms we find the horseman on a protome or on an entire horse on the hemidrachms), there also occurred a change on the reverse. Such a change in the figure on the reverse of the hemidrachms would pose another difficult question: What does the new figure represent?

b.   Obols (tritemoria)

1.   Free horse to right.

Rev. Female head to right, with hair arranged to a point at the back. In incuse square.

Weight 0.49 grms. *Weber Collection,* pl. 75, no. 1956. Cf. Weber, *Num. Chron.,* XXXVII, 1898, p. 255, pl. XVI, 15 = Babelon, I, p. 1153, no. 1648 = Gaebler, p. 105, pl. XX, 27. In all references this coin is cited as tritemorion. The coin is not clear, and although the type is similar to the obol in period I, illustrated in *Weber Collection,* pl. 75, 1955, the style of this coin is more advanced. The horse on the obverse is more spirited, and the female head on the reverse does not have the pointed features that are seen on the former coin.

The female head which is seen on the reverse of the drachms, hemidrachms, and obols has been variously identified. The rendering of the coiffure adds to the uncertainty of the identification. The formation of a point at the back of the head and a fillet passing from above the forehead to the temple has suggested to some observers that this is actually a cap and not the hair. Head speaks of the figure as wearing a spiked leather cap covered with dots.[24] Casson refers to the figure as wearing a spotted *alopekis*.[25] Svoronos, on the other hand, in his translation of Head's *Historia Numorum* (1898), p. 279, speaks of the "conical arrangement" of the hair. The same interpretation is held by Babelon, who describes the figure as follows: "Les cheveux gravés au pointillé sont retenus par un bandeau: ils sont arrangés en une longue pointe au vertex et de longues mèches retombent sur le cou."[26]

The view of Svoronos and Babelon seems to be the more nearly correct. The dotted part above the forehead certainly represents the treatment of the hair. There is no difference in the treatment of this part and the part above the fillet. If the engraver wanted to represent a cap he would have made some distinction between it and the hair. The dotted lines falling on the neck, which are a continuation of the dotted surface, cannot be leather straps; they are tresses of hair. The point at which the dotted surface (hair) ends at the back of the head is admittedly peculiar, but may be regarded as an influence of local custom. It is more pronounced in the early specimens by the addition of one dot at the end.

Compare the hairdress on the latest examples of drachms with that on the female head (Arethusa) represented on the reverse of the Syracusan tetradrachm.[27] Here also we have a dotted surface representing the hair which is brought to a point at the rear of the crown, although slightly less pronounced than on the Potidaean representations. The strands of hair falling on the shoulder are also represented by dots. It is interesting to note that a fillet is worn higher on the head, in about the same position as in the Potidaean figure.

There is no absolute agreement as to the personality of the figure on the reverse either. According to Casson, the female head is that of an Amazon.[28] It is compared with the Amazon head on the coins of Soli in Cilicia,[29] wearing the spotted *alopekis* which Casson sees in the dotted hair on the Potidaean head.

For the reasons presented above, this view cannot be accepted; moreover, there is no absolute similarity between the figure on the Potidaean coin and that on the Soli.[30] Head, in *Historia Numorum* (p. 212), following Millingen (*Syll.*, p. 48), suggests that the female head may be a representation of the Nymph Pallene after whom the peninsula was named. Babelon also believes that the aspect of this figure makes it possible to interpret it as an ancient idol to be regarded as the companion to Poseidon Hippios in the local tradition. It is not at all improbable that the type may be a personification of the peninsula Pallene. Indeed, the situation of the city at the very entrance to that peninsula might have suggested to the Potidaeans the adoption of such a type for the reverse of their small denominations.[31]

Another plausible suggestion is made by Seltman, namely, that the figure is a representation of Aphrodite. He refers to the resemblance of the Potidaean type to the Aphrodite on the Corinthian drachms.[32] There also is a facial resemblance between the Potidaean head and the female head on the Syracusan drachms as well as similarities in the treatment of the hair. The idea that this figure may represent a Corinthian deity cannot be disregarded. In fact, such an idea is to be expected. Potidaea, being a colony of Corinth, naturally received from the parent city her religious cults. The fact that the head of Aphrodite appears on the drachms of Corinth suggests that the same goddess was selected for the Potidaean drachms. In addition, Aphrodite was associated with the god of the sea.[33] Even if the type is a representation of that goddess, local influence is apparent in the manner in which the hair comes to an absolute point at the top of the crown.

About 432 B.C. the silver coinage of Potidaea seems to have come to an end. At this time Potidaea allied herself with the Chalcidians and Perdiccas II of Macedon, and revolted from Athens. Corinth and the Lacedaemonians promised assistance to the revolting city. With Potidaea declaring her autonomy against Athens, and with fresh Corinthian influence upon the city, one might expect new issues of large denominations and of more Corinthian influenced types, but the extant coins provide no such evidence. It is quite probable, however, that the city began to issue bronze coins about this time. These bronze issues will be discussed in Chapter VII in connection with the Potidaean developments in the fourth century.

VI

DURING THE PELOPONNESIAN WAR
432-404 B.C.

◳

AFTER THE battle off the Sybota islands in the autumn of 433 B.C. which resulted in the partial defeat of Corcyra and in the humiliation of Corinth because of Athenian interference,[1] Athens had many reasons to fear a Corinthian retaliation. Retaliation is suggested in the speech of the Corinthian embassy to Athens before the battle took place. The Corinthian envoys, speaking before the Athenian assembly, advised the Athenians not to establish a precedent by receiving into their alliance Corcyra, Corinth's rebellious colony. They also reminded the Athenians that accepting Corcyra would bring war against Athens, and that many Athenian allies would be on the side of Corinth.[2] The implications of the Corinthians' words are clear. Corinth herself would strike against Athens with the same measure.

There does not seem to be any doubt in the minds of the Corinthians that in the Chalcidic region they would find ready means of retaliation. Corinth was conscious of the ill feeling existing among the tributary Chalcidic allies of Athens. Through her colony Potidaea, now a member of the Athenian alliance, Corinth enjoyed a great influence in this region. Potidaea, though a tributary ally of Athens, had kept up amicable relations with Corinth and continued to receive the annual magistrates, the epidemiourgi, from that city.[3] Friendly relations with Potidaea may have been one of the reasons why the Corinthians took great care to emphasize to the Athenians the allegiance paid by the other colonies to Corinth. No other city, they said, is liked so much by her colonies as Corinth.[4]

Doubtless the Athenians recognized the danger to which a conflict with Corinth would lead; hence the hesitation in the first assembly to accept Corcyra's offer of alliance may be explained.[5] At the same time they were afraid of Corinthian domination of

Corcyra, a thing which would upset the balance of power existing at the time. Therefore, in their second assembly, careful not to be considered the violators of the treaty with the Peloponnesians, the Athenians concluded only a defensive alliance with Corcyra[6] aimed at checking Corinthian subjection of that city. In the battle off the Sybota islands which followed, the Corinthian fleet was victorious over the Corcyraean, but was prevented from following up its victory by the intervention of the Athenian ships.[7]

There is no real evidence to indicate the attitude of Potidaea toward the Corinthian-Corcyraean conflict and toward the Athenian policy in relation to that conflict. Apparently the Potidaeans took no active part, but it seems reasonable that they were not apathetic spectators; their sympathies must have been with Corinth though they did not join the parent state as the other Corinthian colonies (Leucas, Ambracia, and Anactorium) did.[8] Perhaps Potidaea felt that any action on her part would be premature at this time, and therefore awaited developments at Corinth. The Potidaeans must have looked upon Athenian intervention with a certain indignation, however; this seems to be indicated by the demands they received from Athens soon after the conflict.

After the Sybota incident, relations between Corinth and Athens finally reached a critical pitch. The Corinthians, on their part, considered methods of reprisal against Athens,[9] and the Chalcidic region offered the best opportunity. During this period, there seems to have been a growing discontent with Athens among her allies in Chalcidice. The evidence is not clear, but the subsequent willingness of these allies to revolt is revealing. Pericles' attempts in the preceding years to consolidate the Empire must have caused some resentment. The founding of Brea (probably, ca. 438 B.C.), especially if the colony was located in the northwest part of Chalcidice, and of Amphipolis (437/6 B.C.) exemplifies this policy and certainly played a part. In addition, the new assessments and the increase in the tribute, particularly in the case of Potidaea (raised from six to fifteen talents), contributed their share in stimulating a feeling of discontent and the ultimate rebellion.

The Athenians suspected Corinthian designs and began to take measures to counteract any activity which might tend to involve their tributary allies in this area. As a precautionary measure they sent an ultimatum to Potidaea, probably soon after the payment of the tribute in the Dionysia of 432 B.C. (if not a little before), demanding that the city pull down its wall on the Pallene side, give hostages, expel the epidemiourgi sent annually from Corinth, and refuse to receive any in the future.[10]

The ultimatum was a firm step. The Athenian suspicion that Potidaea might be induced to revolt was heightened by the conduct of the King of Macedon, Perdiccas II. The king, estranged from the Athenians because of their alliance with his brother Philip and Derdas, the prince of Elimia, tried every means to stir up a conflict between the Peloponnesians and Athens. In Potidaea's position and her relationship with Corinth, Perdiccas saw a fine opportunity to involve Corinth and the rest of Peloponnesus in the affairs of the Athenian allies in the North.[11]

The Athenians were also busy. They immediately dispatched 30 triremes and 1000 hoplites under the command of Archestratus, son of Lycomedes, and two others[12] against Perdiccas. At the same time they instructed their generals to enforce the execution of the ultimatum given to Potidaea and to prevent any uprisings in neighboring cities.[13]

Upon receiving the ultimatum from Athens, the Potidaeans immediately dispatched two embassies, one to Athens and the other to Corinth. The purpose of the first was to persuade the Athenians to modify the terms of the ultimatum, and probably was used to gain time for preparations against an Athenian attack. The mission of the second was to find out what assistance Potidaea might expect from Corinth and the Peloponnesians in case of attack.[14]

The embassy sent to Corinth was successful; the Spartan magistrates promised that Attica would be invaded if there was an Athenian attack on Potidaea. The mission to Athens failed completely. The Athenians were totally unwilling to change any measures already taken against Potidaea. In fact, they informed the members of the embassy that the expedition of Archestratus against Macedonia was directed against Potidaea as well.[15]

When the Potidaeans learned of the failure of the embassy to Athens and of the success of the one to Corinth and Lacedaemon, they openly revolted in August/September of 432 B.C.[16] At the same time the Chalcidians and the Bottiaeans allied themselves with Potidaea against Athens.[17] Perdiccas also joined the alliance. He advised the inhabitants of the seacoast towns of Chalcidice to settle at Olynthus and told them they might have land in Mygdonia to cultivate while the war lasted.[18]

The circumstances that led to the revolt of Potidaea came to be regarded as one of the major causes of the Peloponnesian War.[19]

THE BATTLE OF THE ISTHMUS

When the Athenian expedition under Archestratus arrived in the Thraceward region, it found Potidaea and certain other allies already in revolt. The Athenian generals considered their forces insufficient to wage a two-front war (against both Macedonia and the rebel allies). They decided to turn their attention to Macedonia, their original destination. There they fought in cooperation with their allies, Philip and the brothers of Derdas, who had invaded Macedonia from the upper regions.[20]

Diversion of the Athenian forces from Chalcidice to Macedonia provided sufficient time for Peloponnesian troops to be sent to Potidaea, thus completing the town's defenses. The force sent was collected by the Corinthians who naturally were alarmed for the safety of their colony when they saw the Athenian fleet lying off the Macedonian coast. An army of 1600 hoplites and 400 light armed troops was quickly mustered and dispatched to Potidaea. This expeditionary force, composed of Corinthian volunteers and mercenaries from various Peloponnesian cities, was under the command of the Corinthian Aristeus, son of Adeimantus, who is described by Thucydides as being very popular at Corinth and a great friend of Potidaea. Aristeus and his troops reached Chalcidice forty days after the revolt and completed the defense of Potidaea before the arrival of the Athenian forces.[21]

Unfortunately, there is no indication in our sources as to whether Aristeus arrived in Chalcidice by sea or by land. It seems more likely that the troop movement was carried out by sea. The Athenian naval forces, the thirty ships of Archestratus, were not enough to intervene; besides, with Thessaly friendly to Athens and with the operations of Philip and the brothers of Derdas, a land movement would have presented more difficulties than a journey by sea. In addition, the element of speed and Corinthian anxiety for the safety of the colony are sufficiently indicated in the narrative of Thucydides; thus, transportation by sea would have brought Aristeus' forces to Potidaea in the shortest possible time.[22] Naval power was Corinth's stronghold, and there is no question that, following the battle of Sybota, she had ships available and ready;[23] those assigned to transport the forces of Aristeus might also contribute to Potidaea's defense against Athenian attacks from the sea.

Though there is no reference to Corinthian ships at Potidaea, their presence cannot altogether be discounted. Aristeus' suggestion of evacuating by sea all but 500 men of the entire Potidaean garrison (so that provisions within the besieged town might last longer) may be taken as an indication that more ships than what the Potidaeans themselves might have been able to provide were available for such an enterprise.[24] The presence of Corinthian ships, of course, is not certain, but the ability of Potidaea to successfully sustain the attacks from the sea[25] may not be entirely attributed to the garrison and her own naval resources.

When the news of the revolt in Chalcidice and of Aristeus' departure from Corinth with Peloponnesian reinforcements for Potidaea reached Athens, 40 ships and 2000 Athenian hoplites under the command of Callias were immediately dispatched. This force went first to Macedonia and found that the forces of Archestratus had just captured Therma and were besieging Pydna.[26] For a time, the forces of both Archestratus and Callias joined in the siege, but in view of the urgency of the Potidaean situation, the Athenian generals reached an agreement with Perdiccas and concluded a forced alliance. They then withdrew from Macedonia in order to proceed to Chalcidice.[27]

Here again the account of Thucydides does not indicate whether the Athenian forces moved from Pydna to the opposite side of the Thermaic Gulf by sea or by land. The statement that follows the information about the withdrawal from Macedonia is both concise and puzzling, and various emendations have been offered in order to clarify it.[28] The most probable interpretation of the text is as follows.[29] In the withdrawal from Macedonia, the Athenians might have been expected to have sailed from Pydna to the Chalcidic coast and to have landed somewhere between Therma and Aeneia, probably where Woodhead[30] places the Athenian colony Brea (a more logical corruption of the Beroea of the text). From here, they moved to Strepsa (the generally accepted emendation for the *khorion* of the text), which could be located south of Therma and not far from Brea.[31] Finally, after an unsuccessful attempt to capture Strepsa, they proceeded by land toward Potidaea. The total Athenian force now consisted of 3000 hoplites from their own citizenry, an undetermined number of allied troops, and 600 Macedonian cavalry commanded by

Philip and Pausanias; at the same time 70 Athenian ships were sailing along the coast.[32] Advancing by short marches, they arrived at Gigonus on the third day and made camp.[33]

In the meantime, Aristeus and the Chalcidians were making all necessary preparations. As soon as the Athenians left Macedonia, Perdiccas broke his alliance with them and joined the Potidaeans with 200 cavalry.[34] Aristeus was chosen by the allies as general of the infantry, while Perdiccas was placed in command of the cavalry. Aristeus placed his force, composed of Potidaeans and Peloponnesians, at the isthmus on the side toward Olynthus (about seven miles from Potidaea)[35] and held a market outside the wall of Potidaea. The other allies—the Chalcidians, the Bottiaeans, and Perdiccas—were stationed at Olynthus, and were to strike the Athenians as soon as the latter attacked Aristeus. They were to be informed by signals. Callias and the Athenian generals foresaw this arrangement, and sent the Macedonian cavalry under Philip and Pausanias and the other allies to take a station opposite the troops at Olynthus. This would check an enemy movement from that quarter. Then the Athenians proceeded toward the isthmus, where they found the Potidaeans and their allies preparing for battle.

In the ensuing engagement (September/October, 432), the wing commanded by Aristeus succeeded in routing and driving away the corresponding Athenian wing. But this partial victory was not followed up by the rest of the army. The Athenians had managed to defeat the Potidaeans and the rest of the Peloponnesians and forced them to retire within the walls.[36] Aristeus and his followers found themselves in a delicate situation; they were cut off from Potidaea. Aristeus decided to force his way to the town through the Athenian line instead of proceeding to Olynthus. Consolidating his forces, he marched full speed through Athenian missiles, passed along the breakwater, through the sea, and arrived safely inside the city, but not without some losses.[37] He proved to be more successful than Artabazus had been in 479 B.C.

The battle ended so quickly that neither the allies at Olynthus nor the Athenian troops stationed opposite them were able to take part. When the battle began, the agreed signals had been raised at Potidaea. The allies at Olynthus had advanced to render assistance, and the Macedonian cavalry had prepared to check their move. However, the battle was so quickly decided for the

Athenians that the signals were hauled down and the Potidaean allied troops retired within the walls of Olynthus. The Macedonian cavalry and the allied troops joined the Athenian camp outside Potidaea.[38]

In this engagement 150 Athenian hoplites and their general, Callias, were killed; on the side of the Peloponnesians and Potidaeans, nearly 300 lost their lives. After the battle, the Athenians set up a trophy and permitted the Potidaeans to bury their dead.[39] The event is commemorated by a sepulchral monument put up at Athens in honor of those who were killed in the battle.[40]

THE SIEGE AND CAPITULATION

Following their victory outside the walls of Potidaea the Athenians immediately began a blockade of the town. They erected a wall across the isthmus on the north side of Potidaea, thus cutting off communications between the besieged town and her allies at Olynthus.[41] This was far from a complete blockade, for the south side of Potidaea was not guarded. A complete blockade would have required a division of the Athenian forces, an unwise move at this time without any additional troops from Athens. As reinforcements, Phormio, son of Asopius, was sent from Athens with 1600 hoplites (October/November, 432 B.C.). Phormio established his headquarters at Aphytis, a town about seven miles southeast of Potidaea, and proceeded slowly toward Potidaea, ravaging the country along the way. He met no opposition and was able to complete the land blockade by building a wall on the south side of Potidaea, which cut off the town from the rest of the peninsula. The Athenian ships blockaded the town by sea.[42]

The complete containment of the town by both land and sea must have aroused great anxiety in Potidaea especially since no relief seemed to be forthcoming from Peloponnesus. The Olynthian allies, with Aristeus and his Corinthian and Peloponnesian troops among the besieged, apparently did not have the initiative to bring any assistance to the town. The fall of Potidaea seemed to be a question of time. Since there were not enough provisions for everyone in the town, Aristeus proposed that the troops be removed by sea, leaving only 500 men to defend the town. He offered himself as one of the defenders. [43] The proposal met with a refusal from the troops. But Aristeus himself with a number of followers eluded the Athenian ships and joined the Chalcidian allies in their battle with Phormio, who, when the blockading operations south of Potidaea were finished, had attacked the Chalcidians and Bottiaeans, ravaging their country.[44]

Aristeus, after he escaped from Potidaea, requested aid from Peloponnesus to relieve the blockaded town. He also cut off a large force of the Sermylians, as they showed no willingness to offer any assistance to the Potidaean cause.[45]

The Potidaean hope of relief from Sparta and Peloponnesus was not realized. The promised Spartan invasion of Attica to draw Athenian attention away from Potidaea did not materialize. The Corinthians and the rest of the Peloponnesians who came to Potidaea's aid directly after the revolt, were now themselves, with only a few, including Aristeus, excepted, among the besieged; and instead of being the expected relief, they were a drain on the supplies in the town. We do not know whether the Potidaeans were able to receive any material assistance from the outside during the siege; perhaps, if it were not for Archestratus' delay in proceeding against Potidaea which gave ample time to the town for securing provisions, the Potidaeans probably would not have been able to withstand the two-year siege. But having been well-provisioned from the start and with the protection of strong walls, they did manage to withstand a siege of that length.

Sparta was slow in taking the initial step against Athens. The Corinthians, however, were not at all idle; they tried every means to induce the Spartans to act, especially with Potidaea undergoing a vigorous siege and a number of Corinthian troops within the walls of the besieged city. Fearing the fate of their colony and of their own citizens,[46] Corinth employed everything in its power to also arouse the Peloponnesian allies against Athens. Allied representatives were summoned to Lacedaemon, and those with grievances against Athens stated them before the Spartan Assembly.[47] The Corinthians loudly accused the Athenians of having broken the truce and of injuring Peloponnesus. They strongly advised the Lacedaemonians to abandon their policy of inaction and urged them to send an army at once to Attica and thus relieve the pressure on their allies, particularly on the Potidaeans to whom the Spartans had pledged assistance. Finally, they reminded the Spartans that they would be breaking their treaty by forsaking allies they had sworn to defend.[48]

Following the speech of the Corinthians, some Athenian envoys who happened to be in Sparta on other business came forward and were allowed to address the Assembly. The intention of these envoys was not to answer the charges made against Athens, but to emphasize the great power of their city and to urge the Spartans not to act hastily on a question of such magnitude but to consider the dispute calmly and to submit it to arbitration.[49] Then both the allied and the Athenian envoys withdrew. After deliberation the Spartan Assembly put the question to a vote, and by a large majority decided that Athens had violated the treaty and was guilty of aggression. This meant that the Assembly was in favor of war.[50] The decision was announced to the allied representatives present, along with the plan to summon all the allies and to put to them the question of whether they should go to war against Athens.[51] Finally, in October or November of 432 B.C., an Allied Assembly met; most of the representatives, especially the Corinthians, favored war. The actual declaration of war on Athens was made, but hostilities really began in March of 431, when the Thebans attacked Plataea.[52]

Though war on Athens had been declared by the Spartan allies, no immediate relief came to the besieged Potidaea. For a while the Peloponnesian Confederacy, apparently in order to gain time to prepare for the war, busied itself with the sending of embassies to Athens. They insisted, among other things, that the Athenians raise the siege of Potidaea. These demands were vigorously refused by Athens.[53] The original besieging army of 3000 was still at Potidaea, and Phormio with his troops (1600 hoplites) was busy keeping the Chalcidians from bringing any assistance to the town. But the Athenian forces at Potidaea had proved insufficient to capture the town, nor was Athens able to send any fresh troops: her fleet was occupied in ravaging Peloponnesus,[54] and the Peloponnesians had finally invaded Attica.

It was about this time (summer of 431) that the Athenians, through Nymphodorus, a native of Abdera, won the alliance of Sitalces, King of Thrace. Nymphodorus, whose sister was the wife of Sitalces, was in great favor with the Thracian King. Nymphodorus had been invited to Athens and was made Athenian proxenus at Abdera.[55] Through his influence, Sadocus, the son of Sitalces, acquired Athenian citizenship. Nymphodorus also brought about an alliance between Athens and Perdiccas, restoring Therma to the Macedonian.[56]

Perdiccas and Phormio[57] now fought the Chalcidians. In the alliance with Sitalces the Athenians had sought a powerful assistant to crush the revolt of the Chalcidians and the Potidaeans.[58] No fresh troops were sent by Athens to the besieging forces at Potidaea until the spring of 430 B.C., when a fleet under Hagnon and Cleopompus (colleagues of Pericles) sailed against the Potidaeans and the Chalcidians.[59]

Whether Phormio was still in Chalcidice at this time is not known. He was probably recalled to Athens and Hagnon elected as general in his place. In fact, we learn from Thucydides[60] that about the end of the summer of 431 B.C. the entire armed force of Athens, except those employed in the siege of Potidaea, was in Megara. In another passage the historian definitely states that the troops of Phormio were not in Chalcidice.[61] These troops, therefore, escaped infection from the plague which was brought by the troops under Hagnon.

The armament under the command of Hagnon and Cleopompus, as far as we can gather from the text of Thucydides, included 4000 hoplites and an unspecified number of ships.[62] This force had just returned from Peloponnesus and was sent to Chalcidice equipped with engines for the siege of Potidaea. But the walls of Potidaea defied all the Athenian devices for storming fortifications, and nothing was accomplished.[63]

The operations of Hagnon and Cleopompus did not last long; their troops had been infected with the plague which spread so quickly that, out of the 4000 hoplites, 1050 died in about forty days. The infection also was communicated to the original 3000 hoplites. Hagnon was forced to leave the continuation of the siege to the original troops, and to conduct his men back to Athens.[64]

Aristeus, on the other hand, in spite of a valiant effort had not been able to bring substantial relief from any source to Potidaea. Even his final effort failed, and cost six lives, including his own. In the summer of 430 B.C. he had accompanied the Lacedaemonian ambassadors, Aneristus, Nicolaus, and Pratodamus, on a mission to Persia to persuade the Great King to help the Peloponnesians financially and to join the war against Athens.[65] Two others, Timagoras of Tegea and Pollis of Argos, were with them, but had no formal mission.[66] Now would have been a good time for Persia to interfere in the affairs of Greece. The envoys had to pass through Thrace; apparently at the instigation of Aristeus, they decided to go to Sitalces, the King, in the hope of persuading him to break his alliance with Athens and to send troops to help raise the blockade of Potidaea.[67]

Two Athenian envoys, Learchus and Ameiniades, happened to be at the court of Sitalces. They persuaded the King's son, Sadocus, who had already been granted Athenian citizenship, not to allow the Peloponnesian ambassadors to proceed on their mission to Persia. Sadocus seized the Peloponnesians on their way to the Hellespont and handed them over to the Athenian envoys, who conducted them to Athens. The Athenians were afraid that Aristeus might escape and cause still more mischief. Therefore the whole party was put to death without a trial as retaliation for the treatment of the Athenians and their allies at the hands of Lacedaemonians.[68]

Such was the fate of the valiant and forceful Aristeus. The death of this dangerous man eliminated for Athens the cause of many of her troubles in the Thraceward region. His death also eliminated all hope of assistance, Corinthian or otherwise, for the besieged people of Potidaea. The town was slowly reduced to complete starvation; the day of capitulation could not be far off.

The hunger and misery were so severe that, according to Thucydides,[69] there were cases of people eating one another. With the situation so desperate and no hope of outside assistance, the Potidaeans decided, in the winter of 429 B.C., to come to terms with the Athenian generals Xenophon, son of Euripides, Hestiodorus, son of Aristocleides, and Phanomachus, son of Callimachus, all of whom were conducting the siege operation at this time. The Potidaeans were very fortunate to receive from the Athenian generals unusually favorable terms of capitulation. The Athenian generals themselves were glad to come to terms with Potidaea, considering the fact that Athens had already spent 2000 talents on the siege and that her troops had also experienced many hardships. The Potidaeans with their families, the Corinthians, and the Peloponnesian mercenaries were allowed to leave the city freely; the men were allowed to take one garment, the women two, and a fixed sum of money for their journey.[70] Thus the Potidaeans left their homes and went to Chalcidice and other places to find shelter.[71]

The terms of surrender were not satisfactory to the Athenians at home, and the generals were blamed for the leniency shown the Potidaeans and for acting without authority from Athens. Probably, they were accused of taking bribes in return for such favorable terms. The Athenians must have expected Potidaea to surrender at discretion,[72] and expected to make up for the expense of the siege by selling the inhabitants as slaves. Whether any action was taken against the generals is not known, but Xenophon is found in command of operations in Chalcidice in the following year.[73]

THE ATHENIAN EPOIKOI

Soon after the capitulation of Potidaea the Athenians sent a number of their own citizens, as *epoikoi,* to colonize it.[74] Diodorus states that the number of settlers was 1000 and that both the city and the land were divided into lots.[75] The colonization is recorded on a marble base found near the Propylaea at Athens and inscribed: Ἐποίχον ἐς Ποτείδαιαν.[76] The original monument seems to have been a dedication made to Athena by the colonists before they left Athens. The date of the inscription can safely be placed in the year 429 B.C., since the settlement of Potidaea must have taken place immediately after the expulsion of the former inhabitants.

The relationship between the *epoikoi* and Athens is not clear. Their status in the new place of residence has been identified with that of *apoikoi* (normal colonists)[77] or *klerouchoi* (cleruchs);[78] the application of the term epoikoi to them has been understood to refer not to a new type of settlement, but simply to indicate "additional settlers," or those "slated to go" to Potidaea but not yet there, thus implying that upon arrival they were either apoikoi or klerouchoi.[79] There is reason, however, to believe that the use of the term epoikoi in Thucydides and on Attic inscriptions of the period implies a type of settlement which technically could not have been described either as a pure colony (with apoikoi) or a pure cleruchy (with klerouchoi), although it embodied some characteristics of both. To describe the epoikoi as "additional settlers" is to overlook the fact that the original inhabitants were expelled and the city occupied by Athenian troops until the official settlers (the epoikoi) arrived from Athens. Moreover, to limit the meaning of the term epoikoi to only those "slated to go" does not account for the fact that it continued to be applied to the settlers even after their arrival, as *I.G.,* II², 55 (11. 20-21, referring to epoikoi "who are in possession of Potidaea")[80] and Thucydides, VIII, 69 (describing the Athenians at Aegina, twenty years after their settlement there, as epoikoi) indicate. Apparently, this was a new type of Athenian settlement, with some special characteristics of its own resulting from unusual political or military circumstances relative to its establishment, yet not entirely different from the other two types.

It must be recognized that in Athenian colonization policies, especially during the period of the Empire, certain political, economic, and social factors entered into each type of settlement. Even further variations were allowed within each type depending on the circumstances of the founding and the status of the colony within the Empire. It is well to keep in mind the general features of Athenian settlements with apoikoi and klerouchoi while considering what evidence is offered for the settlement of Potidaea with epoikoi.[81] For the sake of clarity and brevity, the abstract terms apoecy, cleruchy, and epoecy are used to describe these settlements.[82]

An apoecy was founded in an unoccupied or thinly populated territory and formed a separate city-state with its own citizenship, administration, and laws. A cleruchy represents, as a rule, a settlement of Athenian citizens among whom part of the land of an allied state was divided; it formed no independent political unit and its members retained their rights and duties as Athenians within the existing city-state, the lands of which they occupied.[83] The epoecy, as far as it can be reconstructed from the two clear examples we have (that of Aegina in 431 B.C. and of Potidaea in 429 B.C.), represents an Athenian settlement on a site from which the original inhabitants had been expelled;[84] municipal organization is expected, but this implied no major change in the status of its members as Athenians;[85] the territory of an epoecy was more of an extension of Attica and served as a primary base for military operations.

The epoecy seems to exemplify something of an intermediate form between an apoecy and a cleruchy. With its well-defined territory and its municipal organization, it enjoyed a certain amount of independence; with its Athenian citizenship retained, it was subject to some form of taxation and supervision. Recognition of the special status of the epoecy may clarify some of the disputed points regarding settlements which do not fall into the category of either independent colonies or pure cleruchies, but contain features of both.

The evidence available from the epoikoi settlement at Potidaea seems to be clear on the point of municipal organization as well as on Athenian citizenship and taxation. A passage in Aristotle's *Oeconomica*[86] says that the Athenians at Potidaea, in order to meet the needs of the war, imposed an *eisphora*, or property tax, upon themselves. Accordingly, all citizens were obliged to register

their property—not collectively each in his own deme, but separately—where the property of each was located; those who had
no property were to assess their own person at two minae
(*epikephalaion,* head tax). When the assessment was made, each
person was to bring his due share to the city. The eisphora
was an extraordinary tax and was imposed upon all citizens—at
Athens upon metics as well—to meet financial emergencies.[87] The
reference to the epoikoi in the passage as "the Athenians who
reside at Potidaea" and the mention of demes indicate that Athenian citizenship was preserved within the framework of a municipal organization modelled after that of the metropolis.

Some evidence for the existence of demes, and even tribes, at
Potidaea may be derived also from an inscription found in 1938
at Hagios Mamas (a village between the sites of Potidaea and
Olynthus). The inscription refers to an Athenian Polyxenos, son
of Meixias, of the deme of Sounium, and of the tribe Leontis. The
inscription was probably brought from Potidaea and is dated
within the period of the Athenian occupation.[88]

With Potidaea under their control, the Athenians had established a strong base of operations against the Chalcidic cities. It
is difficult to say, however, whether or not the capture of the town
was worth the money and effort expended by the Athenians on
the siege. Certainly the expectation that the subjugation of Potidaea would check the revolt in Chalcidice was not fully realized.
Indeed it appears that a more unified action on the part of the
Chalcidic cities resulted, although at the same time the cities of
Pallene, for a time at least, were kept under Athenian control.
In any case, Potidaea, even in subsequent periods, proved to be
a strong base indispensable for any operations in this region.

According to Thucydides, the Athenians in the summer of 429
B.C. renewed operations in Chalcidice by sending 2000 hoplites
and 200 cavalry under the command of Xenophon and two other
generals.[89] Their attempt to capture Spartolus was unsuccessful,
for reinforcements from the Chalcidians aided the people of that
city to defeat the Athenians in a battle outside the town. The
Athenian troops were forced to take refuge in Potidaea, having
lost their three generals and 430 men. Later the remnant returned
to Athens.[90]

After this defeat the Athenians temporarily ceased operations
in the North. Their whole attention was drawn elsewhere, especially to Peloponnesus.[91] For the time being they contented them-

selves with their command of the isthmus of Pallene, waiting for a more opportune moment later to deal with the revolted allies in Chalcidice.

A reference to the Athenian soldiers at Potidaea is found in the first of a series of Athenian decrees about Methone.[92] This decree could be dated in the spring of 429 B.C.,[93] soon after the capitulation of the city and, possibly, before the arrival of the Athenian epoikoi. It provides, among other things, that Methone be granted certain privileges regarding the payment of her annual tribute to Athens (lines 3-16; 29-32);[94] that Perdiccas' interference in Methone be restricted (lines 16-23); and, further, that Athenian envoys inform Perdiccas that if the soldiers at Potidaea report favorably, the Athenian people will think well of him (lines 27-29).

Aphytis, among the cities of Chalcidice which had not revolted, received similar privileges about this time, as we learn from *I.G.*, I², 58 (dated about 428 B.C.) and *I.G.*, II², 55 (= II, 59) supplemented with two new fragments discovered during the 1938 Agora excavations. That the new fragments and *I.G.*, II², 55 belong to the same inscription there can be no doubt. Meritt has restored the inscription and has included it in *The Athenian Tribute Lists,* II, p. 75 and photographs on plates XII and XIII.[95] The mention of the Methone decree naturally places the present inscription after the spring of 429 B.C. This date is supported by the reference (lines 8-10) to the Athenian settlers (the epoikoi) who were sent to Potidaea following her capitulation. This reference is of particular interest to this study. The decree provided (lines 9-12) that the oath which the Aphytaeans gave to the epoikoi and to the Athenians (if the restoration of the latter is correct) and the decree itself should be engraved on a marble stele and placed in the city at Aphytaean expense, and finally records (lines 19ff.) the oath itself. The oath states that if anyone commits an aggressive act against the city of Athens or the epoikoi in Potidaea, the Aphytaeans in either case should offer all possible aid.[96]

On a sepulchral stele which contains a list of Athenian soldiers killed in various battles in one year, probably during 425/4 B.C., three men of the tribe Antiochis are recorded as having died at Potidaea.[97] There is no record of any battle taking place near Potidaea, though Athenian forces had resumed operations in the North about this time, the summer of 425.[98] From the insignificance of the number lost, we would imagine that these were victims of an ambush or some other minor military operation.

Spartan and Athenian Activity in the Region

With the appointment of Brasidas to command the Peloponnesian operations in Chalcidice,[99] events swiftly changed from a stand-still to more action. Consequently, the Athenian settlers at Potidaea must have experienced a great deal of activity as well as anxiety. Brasidas arrived in the region sometime after August of 424 B.C. with 1700 hoplites and soon managed to inflict severe blows upon Athens.[100] He induced Acanthus and Stageira to revolt and join the Chalcidic alliance; he captured Amphipolis and won over to his side all the towns in the peninsula of Acte except Sane and Dium.[101] He then went to Sithonia and in a surprise attack captured Torone, the most important city in that peninsula. Later he also took the fort Lecythus nearby.[102] The Athenians who survived escaped in boats to Pallene[103] and naturally came to Potidaea.

Sparta and Athens were in favor of peace at this time, and a one year armistice was concluded by both parties in April, 423 B.C.[104] The armistice, however, was disregarded by Brasidas, who, elated by his recent successes, had planned to land in Pallene and win the allies of Athens in that peninsula to his side. It was a daring plan, for with Athens in possession of Potidaea at the isthmus, the peninsula could be approached only by sea, while any Athenian force by both land and sea could endanger any of his successes here. Probably he was determined to bring about quick action in that peninsula and attempt to capture Potidaea before any Athenian force could arrive to prevent him.

The opportunity to go to Pallene was offered to him when Scione revolted.[105] It happened that the revolt took place two days after the truce was concluded between the Athenians and the Peloponnesians.[106] When Brasidas heard about the revolt, he crossed over to Pallene. Scione welcomed Brasidas, and he called an assembly and addressed the people of the town. He praised them for their boldness in defying Athenian power in spite of their nearly insular position (since Athens occupied Potidaea, it could cut off all Scione's land communications with the rest of Chalcidice). The speech was received with great enthusiasm and the Scionaeans publicly crowned Brasidas with a crown of gold as the liberator of Hellas.[107]

According to Thucydides, Brasidas soon departed from Pallene, leaving behind at Scione a small temporary garrison. Later, with

a larger force and with the help of the Scionaeans, he intended
to attempt the capture of Mende and Potidaea before any Athenian forces arrived.[108] It appears that he had already entered into
negotiations with parties within the two towns and that there
were conspirators in both Mende and Potidaea willing to deliver
these towns to him. We are informed about the Mendaean conspirators from another passage of Thucydides,[109] where the subsequent revolt is ascribed to their activity. There is no information about the activities of any conspiracy within Potidaea. It
does not seem likely that the conspirators were Athenian settlers;
others presumably were allowed to reside at Potidaea as metics
and might have been tempted to betray the town to Brasidas.

Brasidas, meanwhile, had refused to accept the terms of the
recent truce as far as they concerned Scione;[110] so the Athenians
at home, upon the motion of Cleon, decided to capture the town
and put all the inhabitants to death.

While the Athenians were preparing for the expedition against
Scione, another important town in the peninsula, Mende, an
Eretrian colony, revolted.[111] Doubtless the conspirators within the
town were encouraged to revolt at this time, even against the will
of the citizens of Mende, by the stern attitude of Brasidas in the
case of Scione and his willingness to help.[112] News of the Mendaean revolt infuriated the Athenians and they now speedily prepared to fight against both towns. An expedition was sent under
the joint command of Nicias and Nicostratus.[113] The Athenians
landed first at Potidaea, then continued down the coast to the
Poseidonium promontory.[114] From there they attacked Mende and
were successful in capturing the town. The lives of the citizens
were spared, but the instigators of the revolt were to be singled
out by the Mendaeans and punished. The old constitution was
restored.[115] After crushing the Mendaean revolt the Athenians left
for Scione, and by the end of the summer of 423 B.C. they completed a blockade of the town.[116]

During this time Brasidas, returning to Torone from a campaign with Perdiccas against Arrhabaeus,[117] found Mende in the
hands of the Athenians. Neither his attempt to retake Mende nor
to bring assistance to blockaded Scione was successful as long as
the Athenians were in control of the isthmus of Pallene and the
sea. In the spring of 422 B.C. he attempted a surprise attack on
Potidaea.[118] His troops approached the town by night, doubtless
on the north side. Grote[119] believes that Brasidas again had come

to an understanding with certain people in the town. Thucydides gives no indication here of any such understanding; therefore, it seems that Brasidas must have relied more on the element of surprise on this occasion.

Thucydides describes how the wall of Potidaea was guarded. Sentries were posted at definite intervals along the entire length of the wall. To ensure vigilance at night, a bell was passed to each sentry in turn; the first man passed the bell to the second and returned to his station, the second one passed it to the third, and so on. Therefore, when a sentry left his station to pass the bell, a space on the wall[120] was momentarily left unguarded. Brasidas selected such an opportunity to carry out his scheme. In the brief time the sentry was absent from his post, the Spartan succeeded in planting a ladder against the wall undetected. But his timing must not have been calculated correctly, for before his men could set foot upon the ladder they were observed, apparently by the returning sentry, and the entire scheme failed. Thus Brasidas was forced to hastily withdraw his troops from the town, not even waiting for daybreak.[121]

The End of Athenian Occupation of Potidaea

For the remaining period of the Peloponnesian War there is no reference to the Athenian epoikoi at Potidaea. That they continued to contribute their share, both militarily and economically, to the war effort of Athens cannot be doubted. As guardians of Athenian interests in the North, they were not expected to take any part in the Sicilian Expedition and thus were spared the disaster that followed.[122] Finally, as the war approached its end after the Spartan victory at Aegospotami (405 B.C.), the days of their residence at Potidaea were numbered. Soon the old inhabitants or their survivors would be repatriated, while they as Athenians were to leave for Athens to witness the humiliating defeat of their metropolis.

VII

FROM THE END OF THE PELOPONNESIAN WAR TO THE FOUNDING OF CASSANDREIA
404-316 B.C.

□

FOLLOWING the battle of Aegospotami, Lysander did not immediately attack Athens; instead, he conceived a plan whereby the city would be forced to surrender by starvation. He bade all Athenians abroad, whether on military duty, sent as colonists, or traveling on some mission, to return to Athens, threatening to kill any Athenian he found outside of Athens.[1]

Lysander sailed with 200 ships from the Hellespont to the island of Mytilene. He sent his vice-admiral, Eteonicus, with 10 triremes to arrange affairs in the Thraceward region.[2] The Athenian allies, in the meantime, revolted and went over to the Spartans. Athens herself was soon to capitulate.[3] The people who had been expelled by the Athenians from their cities during the war were repatriated.[4] It was about this time that the Potidaeans, who had been exiles since 429 B.C., must have had their homes restored to them. Evidently this took place before the siege and final capitulation of Athens in 404 B.C.

RELATIONS WITH SPARTA, CORINTH, OLYNTHUS, AND ATHENS

Lysander lost no time in organizing the new possessions in the interests of Sparta and of himself personally. Democratic constitutions, as a rule, were overthrown and native councils of ten, the *decarchies,* composed of members of oligarchical clubs and partisans of Lysander, were instituted in the various cities. These decarchies were to be sustained in power by a Spartan officer or *harmost* and a garrison.[5]

In the absence of any information to the contrary, it may be assumed that the form of government instituted by the repatriated Potidaeans was in line with the prevailing Spartan policy. West,[6] in discussing the general policy of Sparta, remarks that those cities which had been her allies since the beginning of the Peloponnesian War were left to manage their own affairs without the presence of harmosts and garrisons, and that the same was probably true in the case of the Chalcidic state and others in a similar category. Although Potidaea may not be regarded as a member of the Chalcidic state at this time, it is nevertheless quite likely that the same policy was applied to her also because of her status as an ally of the Peloponnesians at the time of her revolt from Athens in 432 B.C.

In any case, the arrogance and ambition of Lysander, the bitter complaints of the cities, and the remonstrances of the Persian satrap Pharnabazus forced the ephors to abolish the decarchies soon after Lysander's recall in 402 B.C. and to restore to the cities their traditional form of government.[7] The harmosts and the garrisons, however, were maintained for some time.[8] Even the moderate revival of the essential elements of Lysander's oligarchic system by King Agesilaus must have come to an end with Conon's victory over the Spartan fleet off Cnidus in 394 B.C., and the subsequent maritime expansion of Athens.[9]

The Potidaeans, following their repatriation, began to organize their political and economic life. They probably resumed friendly relations with Corinth; but whether they joined the Corinthian alliance at this time or took part in the "Corinthian War" (394-387 B.C.) on the side of Corinth, Argos, Thebes, and Athens, as their Chalcidic neighbors did,[10] is not indicated. It is most likely that they did. The "Peace of Antalcidas" that followed (more commonly known as the "King's Peace," arranged by the Spartan plenipotentiary and the Persian satrap Tiribazus in the name of the King Artaxerxes) provided for the independence of the Greek city-states of the mainland.

About this time (the date cannot be ascertained), Potidaea was invited by the Chalcidians to join their league. It appears as if the city was allied with the Chalcidians by the time of their treaty with Amyntas III of Macedon, which is variously dated within the years 393-383 B.C.[11] According to a stipulation in that treaty neither party could ally itself with the Amphipolitans, the Bottiaeans, the Acanthians, or the Mendaeans without the consent of the other.[12] Mende, then, among the cities of Pallene, was still holding out against the Chalcidians. It is, therefore, most probable that the other cities of the peninsula, including Potidaea, had already become allies of the Chalcidic League.[13]

From Xenophon we derive the information that Potidaea was already an ally by the time an embassy of Acanthians and Apollonians came to Sparta.[14] The mission of this embassy was to persuade the Spartans and their allies to interfere in the North, and check the growing power of Olynthus and her Chalcidic League. Cleigenes, speaking for the embassy before the Spartan assembly and the Lacedaemonian allies, stated that the most important cities had already joined the league.[15] Of these cities only Potidaea is mentioned by name.[16] From the word *hypekoous* used by Xenophon, one might conclude that Potidaea was a subject and not an independent ally of the Olynthians. But another passage in which the word *symmachos* is used in reference to the Potidaeans seems to clarify the situation and establish the true relationship of Potidaea as an autonomous ally of the Chalcidic League.[17]

The Acanthians and Apollonians at Sparta succeeded in persuading the Lacedaemonians and their allies to take some action, and preparations were begun for an expedition of 10,000 hoplites against the Chalcidians. The embassy also suggested that a Lacedaemonian be sent to Chalcidice as soon as possible with as large a force as could be mustered quickly to support those cities that had not yet joined the league. Such a force would also lend moral support to those that were coerced into the alliance and thus limit their usefulness.[18] The suggestion was accepted and in the early summer of 382 B.C. Eudamidas was sent with 2000 hoplites composed of Neodamodeis, Perioeci, and Sciritans.[19] As soon as Eudamidas reached Pallene, Potidaca, already an ally of the Chalcidians, voluntarily came over to his side. The Spartan placed garrisons in the towns that needed them, using Potidaea as a base of operations.[20] The Spartans at home, encouraged by their recent success in capturing the Cadmeia, the citadel of Thebes, were now more willing to send out forces against the Olynthians. Thus, toward the end of the summer of 382 B.C., Teleutias was sent with a command of 10,000 men. He increased his army on the way with hoplites and cavalry from Thebes as well as from Amyntas of Macedon and from Derdas, the archon of Elimia.[21] With this increased force he arrived at Potidaea, now a Spartan ally. After organizing his forces and apparently consolidating them with the troops of Eudamidas,[22] Teleutias left for Olynthus. The Chalcidian troops came out to meet him, and in the battle that followed Teleutias won an indecisive victory.

The following summer (381 B.C.), the Olynthians came out of their city, crossed the nearby river, approached the enemy position and forced Teleutias to battle. After a fierce fight Teleutias was killed, and his army was put to flight with the Olynthians in pursuit. The defeated army fled to various cities, wherever they could find refuge; many men went to Spartolus, Acanthus, and Apollonia, but the majority came to Potidaea.[23]

After the Spartan defeat Agesipolis was dispatched with a greater force.[24] Probably he, too, came to Potidaea and, regrouping the soldiers scattered in that region,[25] encamped near Olynthus. He succeeded in capturing Torone, but contracted a fever and was brought to Aphytis, where he died outside the temple of Dionysus.[26] He was succeeded by Polybiades, who after a close siege, forced the Olynthians to send ambassadors to Sparta suing for peace. The result of this peace was an alliance between the Chalcidians and Sparta in 379 B.C.[27] This treaty would not have affected Potidaea's relations with Sparta, for, as we have already seen, she had been bound by an alliance to Sparta since the first Lacedaemonian campaign against the Chalcidians. With the power of the Chalcidic League broken at least for a while, Potidaea and the other cities of Pallene were free of Chalcidic interference for some time. Potidaea's status as ally of Sparta was retained as long as Spartan supremacy in Chalcidice was recognized.

A few years later, with the revival of Athenian sea-power, the Spartans lost control of the Chalcidic peninsula, and the Olynthians began to act independently of Sparta. Olynthus began again her work of annexation and must have regained many of her former members and allies. The information we have about the activities of Olynthus and her league is very incomplete, and provides no satisfactory evidence regarding the relations of Potidaea and the league.

It has been generally accepted, on the basis of statements of Demosthenes, Isocrates, Deinarchus, and others referring to the campaigns of Timotheus in Chalcidice, that Potidaea was already an ally of the league at the time of these campaigns (364-2 B.C.).[28] It is thought that the campaigns were directed against the Olynthians,[29] and therefore any city captured in this region must have belonged to them. But this does not necessarily follow, nor must the statements quoted from literary sources be interpreted in this way. Doubtless Timotheus had as his main objective a check of the ever-growing power of the Chalcidic League, but this need not have detained him from taking cities other than allies or members of that league.[30]

The inscription (*I.G.*, II[2], 110) in which Menelaus, a mercenary general under Timotheus, is honored, and which knows only, as Kahrstedt puts it,[31] of Chalcidians and Amphipolitans, does not necessarily prove that Potidaea was an ally of the league. In fact, the evidence that has been generally quoted in favor of this point might be used to prove the reverse. Isocrates,[32] for example, may be interpreted to mean that Potidaea is independent of the Chalcidians. After mentioning the capture of Potidaea by Timotheus, Isocrates adds (XV, 113) that the general "in addition had fought against all the Chalcidians." The use of προσέτι in the text, which means "moreover," "in addition," is significant here, and probably suggests that Potidaea was not considered by Isocrates as a part of the Chalcidic League. Deinarchus speaks of the cities Timotheus conquered, but here again there is no implication as to which were Chalcidian; undoubtedly some were, but not all.[33] Nor can we definitely interpret Demosthenes' statement to mean that Potidaea was an ally or a member of the Chalcidic League at this time.[34] Moreover, there is no indication in our sources of any assistance from the league when Timotheus was besieging the town.

There is no definite evidence, literary or epigraphical, which can be cited to prove in any satisfactory degree that Potidaea was a member or an ally of the league during the interval between 479 B.C. and the Thraceward campaign of Timotheus in 364-2 B.C. New evidence, especially from the side of epigraphy, is needed. In the absence of such evidence we may assume that no alliance between Potidaea and the Chalcidic League was in effect, although friendly relations may have existed.

It would have been interesting, of course, if the coinage of Potidaea after her restoration in 405/4 B.C. could have thrown some light on her relations with the Chalcidic League. If the issues of the fourth century could be dated within fixed chronological limits, one might be able to determine whether Potidaea was ever a part or merely an ally of the league. But such chronological limits for the coins cannot be established. The only means of dating them is on the basis of their style, and such means does not admit exact chronology.

ATHENIAN CLERUCHS AT POTIDAEA

In 364 B.C. Timotheus undertook his Thraceward campaign and among the cities captured was Potidaea, which he took with the assistance of Perdiccas III of Macedon (364/3 B.C.).[35] Diodorus makes the statement that the general in the siege of Potidaea and Torone helped the besieged with Cyzicenes.[36]

Later, in the spring of 362 B.C., when Timotheus was succeeded by Callisthenes,[37] the Potidaeans expressed the desire to have Athens send cleruchs to their city; the Athenians obliged in 362/1 B.C.[38] The inscription containing the decree for the cleruchs is preserved.[39] According to the inscription, official representatives of Potidaea went to Athens and communicated the request of the inhabitants of their city to the Athenians. Upon the motion of Philippus, the assembly passed a decree granting the request of the Potidaeans. It is noteworthy that of the cities in this region which came under the influence of Athens at this time only Potidaea received cleruchs, and received them not as a result of force on the part of the Athenians, but because of an expressed desire of the Potidaeans.[40]

The attitude of the Potidaeans invites suspicion. Why were they so anxious at this time to receive Athenian cleruchs, when cleruchs had caused antipathy toward Athens in the preceding century? Possibly the explanation may be found in the desire on the part of the Potidaeans to establish better relations with Athens and so receive certain concessions; besides, the presence of Athenian cleruchs would strengthen their position against any encroachments of the Chalcidic League on their territory.

At any rate, the Potidaeans did not submit to Athenian domination,[41] and their status in the Athenian Confederacy must have been, according to Demosthenes,[42] that of allies rather than members. Their cordial relations with the Athenian cleruchs prompted the Athenians at home, upon the motion of Aristophon, to pass a decree (361/0 ? B.C.) honoring the Potidaeans for their friendly attitude.[43] It is interesting to notice that Demosthenes, in speaking of the Athenians settled at Potidaea, refers to them as "the Athenian apoikoi" (VI, 20) and "the Athenians who reside at Potidaea" (VII, 10), while the inscription indicates cleruchs.[44]

An interesting sidelight is the bronze dicast's ticket discovered in an Olynthian house during the 1938 campaign. The ticket is a palimpsest, and the later inscription in the Attic alphabet refers

to an Aristophon, son of Timandros, from the Athenian deme of
Phlya. According to Robinson, "it probably was brought there
in ancient times by a visitor or possibly by an Athenian from
Potidaea," and is dated in the first half of the fourth century.[45]
If the ticket can be connected with an Athenian from Potidaea,
it is inviting to suggest that it belonged to a cleruch and, therefore, could be dated between 362/1 and 356 B.C. when Athenian
cleruchs resided at Potidaea.

PHILIP AND THE FATE OF POTIDAEA

In 356 B.C. Potidaea became the victim of Macedonian expansion. Philip was quick to act, but the Athenians were slow to
realize his deceitful intentions. First, he conquered Amphipolis in
357 B.C., but failed to give it to the Athenians as he had promised.
Following the capture of this town Pydna fell into his possession,
since the Athenian fleet came too late to save it.[46] An alliance
between Philip and the Olynthians was then concluded,[47] and
Anthemus was given to the latter in return. The Olynthians
seemed to have a claim upon Anthemus,[48] and according to Diodorus[49] they also were very anxious to conquer Potidaea; Philip
promised that he would deliver that city to them too.

Demosthenes speaks of an alliance of Philip with the Athenians
of Potidaea,[50] saying that Philip had exchanged oaths with the
inhabitants of that city. Demosthenes does not describe the type
of alliance or the kind of oaths. In fact, there is no other information on this point. We have no grounds to refute the words
of the orator; besides, it is not impossible that the Potidaeans at
some time previous to their conquest by Philip, probably after
his alliance with the Olynthians, were suspicious of his intentions
and decided to ally themselves with him. Philip was ready to
give assurances to them, thus concealing his ultimate designs for
the time being.

Early in 356 B.C. Philip was ready to march against Potidaea;
with the help of the Chalcidians, he captured the city after a
siege.[51] Athenian aid arrived too late to save the town.[52] The
Athenian cleruchs were deprived of their possessions and sent
to Athens. There is no clear statement in our sources as to the
exact fate of the rest of the inhabitants. Demosthenes speaks of
the injustice that was done to the Potidaeans, and mentions that

the Athenian *apoikoi* were dispossessed and expelled, but fails to give any conclusive information as to the manner of injustice done to the Potidaeans proper, aside from the definite mention that their land was given to the Olynthians.

Thus far Philip had kept his promise to the Olynthians and at the same time succeeded in depriving Athens of her last stronghold in Chalcidice. A year after the capture of Potidaea, Demosthenes delivered a speech against Leptines (355 B.C.), in which he refers to Potidaea as being under the dominion of Philip.[53] Dominion of Philip over Potidaea may be understood to mean a domination by his allies, the Olynthians, to whom he had given the Potidaean possessions. We would expect the Olynthians, who were so anxious to have control over Potidaea and who helped Philip in the capture of the town, to prevail upon him not to destroy the town. They would not be satisfied to receive a town in complete ruins as a reward for their cooperation.

We do not know how much credence can be attributed to the statements of Demosthenes that Philip destroyed Olynthus, Methone, Apollonia, and thirty-two other cities in Thrace, destruction so complete that one could not tell whether those sites had ever been inhabited at all.[54] It is hard to believe that Philip would have aimed at such wholesale destruction. It is certain that he destroyed some cities, such as Olynthus, completely; it is more credible to assume that there was only a partial destruction of others. Partial destruction following subjugation might explain Demosthenes' apparent exaggeration.

It is interesting to note, and important for our contention, that Demosthenes, in all the cases in which he mentions Potidaea and her capture by Philip, never makes any remark which might be interpreted that the city was completely, or even partially, destroyed. In fact, if a complete destruction had taken place, Demosthenes surely would not have passed over it in complete silence, especially since the city was very important to Athens because of its location and was at the same time an ally and a residence for Athenian citizens, the cleruchs. Demosthenes, instead, limits himself to statements like the following:[55]

VI, 20: . . . that he [Philip] gave Potidaea to the Olynthians, after casting out the Athenian colonists, and he took upon himself your enmity, but to them he gave the land to enjoy.

VII, 9 . . . for he wishes to put this over you and to include it in the treaty as an acknowledgement on your part that you, as the injured party, do not hold him responsible for his aggressions on Potidaea, but that you confirm the lawfulness of his capture and possession of that city. 10: . . . Yet the Athenians who resided at Potidaea were deprived of their property by Philip, though they were not at war but in alliance with him, and in spite of the oath he swore to the inhabitants of that city. 13: . . . Do not forget, therefore, that the real object of the articles of this treaty is to exact an admission that you no longer have any reasonable claim to Potidaea.

VIII, 62: . . . no one could describe sufficiently how he [Philip] deceived the wretched Olynthians after he first gave them Potidaea and many other places. 65: . . . It was not safe at Olynthus to be an advocate of Philip's plans, unless the Olynthian commonwealth had shared in the enjoyment of Potidaea's possession.

In these quotations the orator fails to mention the exact nature of the fate of the inhabitants of the place except for the Athenian residents, who he definitely states were sent to Athens. The failure of Demosthenes to mention Potidaea by name, as he does in the case of Olynthus, Methone, and Apollonia,[56] may be interpreted as another indication that the town was not destroyed. Furthermore, the circumstances that led up to the capture of Potidaea do not justify the supposition that the city was completely ruined. In addition, how could Demosthenes speak of Potidaea as being given to the Olynthians when the whole town was in ruins? Again, how could he speak of Pydna and Potidaea and other towns not named, but which apparently were captured before 355 B.C. (date of the delivery of Demosthenes' speech against Leptines), as being subject to Philip if they were nothing but ruins?[57]

Other evidence concerning the fate of Potidaea and surrounding cities under Philip is noteworthy. The reference in Callisthenes, for example, is to plunder rather than destruction.[58] From Diodorus' account of the siege of Potidaea we learn that after capturing the city, Philip sent the Athenian garrison (the *apoikoi* of Demosthenes) to Athens and delivered the enslaved city and its outlying possessions to the Olynthians as a gift.[59] Diodorus also mentions that when Cassander founded Cassandreia, he "united with it as one city the cities of the peninsula, Potidaea, and many of the neighboring towns" and that he settled here "those of the Olynthians who survived, not few in number."[60] If Potidaea had been completely destroyed in 356 B.C., it would be difficult to interpret Diodorus' testimony. In such a case, one would ex-

pect Diodorus to have made some remark in reference to Potidaean survivors similar to his remark about the Olynthians, whose
city Philip did destroy in 348 B.C. The Olynthians are described
as "those who survived" the destruction of their city, while
Potidaea is merely mentioned as being incorporated into the new
town. Therefore, Potidaea must have been inhabited, to some extent at least, down to 316 B.C. (when Cassandreia was founded).

A similiar record is found in Libanius.[61] After mentioning Anthemus as being given to the Olynthians, Libanius states that
Potidaea, a possession of the Athenians, was handed over to the
Olynthians. Suidas speaks in the same terms and adds that Philip
gave the city to the Olynthians as a gift in order to deceive them.[62]

Pausanias and the scholiast on Demosthenes (VI, 20), however, present a different picture, but not difficult to explain.
Pausanias, for example, says that the Potidaeans were expelled
from their city twice, by the Athenians (in 429 B.C.) and then
by Philip, but that Cassander later restored them to their homes.[63]
Pausanias, by combining the two events in one sentence for
brevity, did not expand his statement to make the proper distinction between them. The fate of the inhabitants after each of
these episodes was different; but Pausanias eliminated this detail
and applied to 356 B.C. an event which only occurred in 429 B.C.
The statement of the scholiast on Demosthenes[64] that Philip destroyed the city by fire after he enslaved the inhabitants may not
be taken too seriously. He apparently followed the account given
by Diodorus and differs only in his insertion of the word   ἄψας
(set on fire) after the word ἐξανδραποδισάμενος (reduced to slavery). This insertion is probably an attempt on the part of the
scholiast to improve on Diodorus.[65]

The preceding discussion shows insufficient grounds for the
assumptions of Beloch,[66] Schaefer,[67] West,[68] and others that the
city was completely destroyed. Partial destruction may be regarded
as probable, but many of the inhabitants must have continued
to live in the town, though as slaves or subjects. Until 348 B.C.,
Potidaea was subject to the Olynthians. Following the capture and
destruction of Olynthus, it fell into the hands of Philip and the
Macedonians.[69] Potidaea then lapsed into obscurity; nothing has
been found that can safely be assigned to the period 356-316 B.C.
Future excavations of the site may throw some light on this dark
period of its history.

THE BRONZE COINAGE OF POTIDAEA

Until 1928 only a few bronze coins from Potidaea were known. The four archaeological campaigns at Olynthus under the direction of D. M. Robinson since then have brought to light a great number of such coins. These coins have been published in the following series of the *Excavations at Olynthus:* Part III, *The Coins Found at Olynthus in 1928,* pp. 101-105, nos. 814-818, 820-825, 827-833, 835-860;[70] Part VI, *The Coins Found at Olynthus in 1931,* pp. 89-92, nos. 777-825 and pl. XIX;[71] Part IX, *The Chalcidic Mint and the Coins Found in 1928-1934,* pp. 226, 305-309, 390-391 (with inventory numbers and findspots), and pl. XXX, no. 31 (= inv. no. 320); Part XIV, *Terracottas, Lamps, and Coins Found in 1934 and 1938,* pp. 418, 456 (with inventory numbers and findspots), and pl. 172, no. 8 (= inv. no. 226).

The total number of published Potidaean bronze coins from Olynthus is 179. Of these, 44 were found in 1928, 49 in 1931, 74 in 1934, and 12 in 1938. Three coins found at Mecyberna in 1934 and included in *Olynthus,* IX, pp. 253 and 396, may be added here, thus making a total of 182 excavation coins from these two sites.[72]

The types of the coins are:

1. *Obv.* Head of Athena, to right or to left, wearing Corinthian helmet; occasionally a border of dots.
   Rev. Trident with legend ΠOT, EIΔ to the right and left. The letters are in many cases defaced, but it seems that there were no more than ΠOTEIΔA. *See* pl. XXIII, a-i, and Robinson and Clement, *Olynthus,* IX, p. 226.[73] This Athena/Trident type is represented by 175 specimens from Olynthus and 3 from Mecyberna.
2. *Obv.* Head of Athena, right, wearing Corinthian helmet.
   Rev. Winged Pegasus walking right; legend ΠOT[EIΔ] around Pegasus, starting from below. *See* pl. XXIII, j-l. This type is represented by only four specimens from Olynthus.[74]

A third type representing a female head to right on the obverse and a butting bull on the reverse was previously assigned to Potidaea,[75] but is now generally attributed to Bottiaea.[76] The basis for the first assignment was the reading of the legend on the obverse of one of the specimens as ΠOTEI instead of BOTTI.[77] The legend is slightly worn, but BOTTI can be made out clearly.

In the discussion of the silver coinage of Potidaea in Chapter V, the time just before the revolt from Athens in 432 B.C. was taken as a *terminus post quem non*. It is also probable that at this time, following the alliance of Potidaea with Corinth and the rest of the Peloponnesians, the city started issues of bronze coinage. There can be no absolute certainty about this date. The answer depends upon whether conditions at Potidaea between 432-429 B.C. could be regarded as favorable for the issuing of coins and whether any extant coins could be assigned to this period with some degree of certainty.

Soon after the revolt Potidaea was blockaded by Athens. Within the city there were about 2000 Corinthian and Peloponnesian troops, a number of which were mercenaries from various cities of Peloponnesus. Some means of exchange among the citizens themselves would be necessary, and if Potidaea had to contribute a share to the pay of the mercenary troops in the city, the need for exchange would be even greater. With the city in such straitened circumstances, certainly no new issues of silver coinage could be expected. Therefore it would not be advisable to wholly disregard bronze coinage in this period only because, due to the bad state of preservation of the coins extant and the lack of definite archaeological evidence, no specific examples may be cited.

In 429 B.C., when the Potidaeans surrendered to the Athenians, they were allowed to take a fixed sum of money with them from the city. As they wandered through Chalcidice seeking shelter wherever it could be found, it is reasonable to expect a number of them to have settled at Olynthus. Such a settlement would account to some extent for the relatively high number of legible Potidaean coins from the Olynthus excavations. Commercial relations between the two cities in the fourth century and the annexation of Potidaea and her territories by Olynthus following the capture by Philip II in 356 B.C. must not be discounted as contributing factors to the presence of these coins at the excavations, however. Potidaean issues from these excavations exceed the number present from any other major city of the Chalcidic peninsula. Potidaea is represented by 179 coins, Acanthus by 88, Amphipolis by 155, Aphytis by 49, Mende by 37, Scione by 114, and Torone by 60.

Considering these facts and the strong Corinthian influence on the types, it is reasonable to assign at least the first of the Potidaean bronze issues to the period of the revolt from Athens in

432 B.C. and the subsequent siege. During this period, the alliance with Corinth and the presence of Corinthian citizens within Potidaea must have strengthened the relations between the two cities. The types of Athena, wearing a Corinthian helmet, with Pegasus or Trident on the reverse are strictly Corinthian.

It is possible, then, to assume that the Potidaeans started their bronze issues during this period and that, when they returned to their city after the battle of Aegospotami, they resumed the issues either with the same coin types or perhaps the Athena/Trident type for the first time. Intimate relations with Corinth may be assumed following the repatriation of the Potidaeans. The trident on the reverse might have its antecedent in the silver coinage issues with Poseidon and the trident or in the contemporary Corinthian Pegasus/Trident type. The Corinthian diobols with Pegasus on both the obverse and reverse are dated between ca. 430 B.C. and ca. 338 B.C., while the Corinthian bronze coins with Pegasus on the obverse and Trident on the reverse are usually dated ca. 400 B.C. to ca. 300 B.C.[78] There may also be some significance in the fact that no Potidaean coins of the Athena/Pegasus type were found in Hoard II of the Olynthus bronze coins, dated by Robinson and Clement on the basis of style in the first half of the fourth century, while five examples of the Athena/Trident type were contained in the Hoard.[79] The presence of the latter type, if not purely accidental, along with the rarity of the Athena/Pegasus type, may point to some chronological sequence of the Potidaean issues. It could be assumed that the Athena/Pegasus type represents an earlier period, starting with 432 B.C.

Stylistically, the ultimate conclusions to be drawn would place the bronze coins of Potidaea in the first half of the fourth century. This would agree with Head,[80] Gaebler,[81] and Robinson and Clement.[82] Babelon, however, had dated the extant bronze coins of Potidaea, in view of the paucity of specimens at the time of his work and the Corinthian influence on the types, in the years 432-429 B.C. and stated that Potidaea issued no coins in the fourth century.[83] While it is possible that Potidaea may have started coining bronze issues as early as 432-429 B.C., this period cannot be accepted as marking the end of the issues in view of the activity of Potidaea during the first half of the fourth century and advanced knowledge gained about the style of the coins from the Olynthus excavations. Potidaea ceased coining money when the city was captured by Philip II in 356 B.C.

THE FINAL PHASE AND THE FOUNDING OF CASSANDREIA

The importance of the location of Potidaea was once again realized and in 316/5 B.C. Cassander of Macedon founded a new city on approximately the same site. He named it Cassandreia, after himself.[84] The new city included Potidaea and many inhabitants of the neighboring region, especially the Olynthians who had survived the destruction of their city by Philip in 348 B.C., settled there.[85] The presence of citizens of neighboring towns in Potidaea-Cassandreia suggests the possibility of solving Chalcidic questions through further excavations on the site. The synoecism seems to have been extensive, as our sources and the prominence of the new city indicate, and the new inhabitants must have brought with them all the possessions they could. Building material for the new homes also must have been supplied from the ruins of nearby cities.[86] Cassandreia soon became one of the wealthiest and most powerful cities of Macedonia[87] and played a prominent role during Hellenistic, Roman, and Byzantine times, until destroyed by the Huns in the sixth century of our era.[88]

NOTES

CHAPTER I

LOCATION AND TOPOGRAPHY OF POTIDAEA; PRESENT REMAINS

1. The usual term for Poseidon in the Corinthian (Doric) alphabet is Ποτειδάϝων or Ποτειδάν, hence Potidaea, a city founded in his honor. The name of the city appears in ancient literature and inscriptions either as Ποτίδαια (generally, in Herod., VIII, 126, etc.; Xen., *Hell.*, V, ii, 15; Isocrates, XV, 108; and others), or as Ποτείδαια (consistently on inscriptions such as *I.G.*, I², 201, 397, and 949; and generally in Thuc., I, 56, etc., though in some editions the former spelling is given; Dem., VI, 20, etc., but here also the former spelling may appear). On coins, as much as Ποτειδα appears.

The citizens of Potidaea are designated as Ποτειδεᾶται or Ποτιδαιᾶται. Both are found in editions of Thucydides (I, 58, 62, and elsewhere); Ποτειδεᾶται is found on inscriptions such as the Tribute Lists (see n. 27, chap. IV), *I.G.*, 205, while Ποτιδαιάτης for Athenodoros is on the inscription from Philippi (see n. 85, p. 125). The adjective is given as Ποτειδεατικὸς in Thuc., I, 118.

2. Cf. also Strabo, VII, fr. 27: ἐπὶ τῷ ἰσθμῷ κεῖται; and Scylax Caryandeus (*Periplus*, 66); Παλλήνη ἄκρα . . . Ποτίδαια ἐν τῷ μέσῳ τὸν ἰσθμὸν ἐμφράττουσα. . . . Numerous other statements could be added to these from Herodotus, Thucydides, and others. Isocrates, however, mentions Potidaea and Torone as cities τῶν ἐπὶ Θρᾳκης. Stephanus Byzantius speaks of it as being πόλις Θρᾳκης and that the same place was later called Cassandreia, but he calls the latter a city of Macedonia πρὸς τῇ Θρᾳκῃ, ἡ ποτέ Ποτίδαια. Of course, these statements are not disturbing; they only show how undefined the boundaries of Macedonia and Thrace were and how loosely the latter term was used.

3. Cf. Arvanites, Ἡ Μακεδονία Εἰκονογραφημένη, p. 136; Struck, *Makedonische Fahrten,* I, *Chalkidike,* p. 43.

4. Strabo, VII, 330, 25.

5. Struck, *op. cit.,* p. 43: und such die hohe Nordmaur ist nur zum geringsten Teile antik; bloss kleinere, aus Quadern gefügte Partien der Substruktion gehören der klassischen Zeit an. Struck also includes a description of the wall.

6. Procopius, *De Aedificiis,* IV, 3. The Huns had captured Cassandreia by storm in 539 A.D. *Ibid., De Bello Persico,* II, 4.

7. Struck, *op cit.,* p. 43; Kolocotronis, *La Macédoine et l'Hellénisme* (Paris, 1919), pp. 348-50.

8. Struck, *op cit.,* p. 43.

9. *Ibid.*

10. Foundations of large cut stones without mortar were located about 250 m. from the E. end of the canal and were traced westward, in two parallel lines, for about 300 m. The location of these wall foundations is included in the canal.

Masonry using large cut stones without mortar can still be seen parallel to the wall foundations on the N. side of the canal. (Pl. XI, fig. 2). See Map 2.

11. Thuc., I, 63.

12. *Ibid.*, II, 58.

13. Diod., XII, 46. Some information as to how the walls were guarded is obtainable from the attempt of Brasidas in 422 B.C. to surprise Potidaea, as related in Thuc., IV, 135.

14. *Ibid.*, I, 56. See also I, 64.

15. *Ibid.*, IV, 129. For the sites of Mende and Scione cf. Meritt, *A.J.A.*, XXVII, 1923, pp. 447-60.

16. Demitsas, Ἡ Μακεδονία, no. 770 (27). Duchesne et Bayet, *Mémoire sur une Mission au Mont Athos* (Paris, 1876), p. 73, no. 114.

17. Duchesne et Bayet, *op. cit.*, no. 113; Demitsas, *op. cit.*, no. 763 (20); Michel, *R.I.G.*, no. 321; Ditt., *Syll.³*, 332; and others.

18. Duchesne et Bayet, *op. cit.*, no. 115; Demitsas, *op cit.*, no. 766 (23); *S.E.G.*, II, 414. The monument is republished, with measurements and a photograph, by D. M. Robinson in the *T.A.P.A.*, LXIX, 1938, pp. 66f. and pl. XVI, 20. In addition to this monument, a Roman portrait bust dated about the middle of the third century A.D. was found near the site of Potidaea. It is mentioned briefly in *ibid.*, p. 67, n. 49.

19. *Rev. Phil.*, XLII, 1918, pp. 60-62. For a correction of Foucart's error and a discussion of the name Hero Heropythos cf. Tod, *J.H.S.*, XLII, 1922, pp. 181-83. For an account of funeral banquet scenes on grave stelae cf. Gardner, *J.H.S.*, V, 1884, pp. 105-42.

20. Duchesne et Bayet, *op. cit.*, no. 116; Demitsas, *op cit.*, no. 767 (24).

21. Forest fires have caused much destruction on the peninsula. In August, 1936, a great fire destroyed much of the forest of Stavroniketa, the largest and most beautiful in Pallene.

22. For the Corinthian division of the Potidaean and Chalcidic coins see chap. V. The Polyxenas inscription from Olynthus has been published in *T.A.P.A.*, LXII, 1931, pp. 40ff. Robinson thinks that Polyxenas may have been a Potidaean resident of Olynthus. The inscription is dated at the end of the sixth century B.C. Cf. also Gude, *A History of Olynthus, Prosopographia*, v. Πολυξένας. The Neumous inscription from Olynthus is published in *T.A.P.A.*, LXIX, 1938, pp. 43f., pl. I, fig. 1, and is dated at the end of the sixth century or beginning of the fifth century B.C. Robinson believes that the same stonecutter was responsible for both the Polyxenas and the Neumous inscriptions. A reference to the Polyxenas inscription may be found also in W. A. McDonald's *The Political Meeting Places of the Greeks* (Baltimore, 1943), pp. 235f. For the Corinthian influence on the Olynthus mosaics cf. Robinson, *Excavations at Olynthus*, V, p. 5 and n. 12; also *A.J.A.*, XXXVI, 1932, pp. 16-24; XXXVIII, 1934, pp. 500-10; Hinks, *Cat. of the Gr., Etr., and Rom. Paintings and Mosaics in the Br. Mus.* (1933), p. xiv; Von Lorentz, *Röm. Mitt.*, LII, 1937, pp. 168ff. For the close relationship between Potidaean and Olynthian bronze objects, see pp. 11-13, and notes.

23. A brief summary of the excavations is given in *J.H.S.*, XLIX, 1929, p. 234; in *Year's Work in Classical Studies*, 1928-1929, p. 109; and in *Jahrbuch*, XLIII, 1928, p. 602.

24. Cf. Ch. Macaronas in *Makedonika*, II, 1941-1952 (Thessalonica, 1953), p. 623 and notes 6 and 8; *J.H.S.*, LXIV, 1944, p. 93 and LXXII, 1952, p. 40; *B.C.H.*, LXVIII-LXIX, 1944-1945, p. 431 and LXXI-LXXII, 1947-1948, p. 438.

25. In 1938 there were seven inscriptions from Potidaea in the Thessalonica Museum: a small Ionic capital, a corner triglyph, a marble statuette of Heracles, and several fragmentary scruptural pieces. These belong to the Cassandreian period.

In addition to the traces of the ancient wall, to a mudbrick wall with mortar parallel to it and located about 275 m. from the E. end of the canal (Pl. XI, 1), and to a large pithos (Pl. XII, 1) exposed during construction, some masonry of large cut stones with mortar was also found (indicated on the canal plan). These stones were pillaged from an ancient temple. The location of the masonry is slightly north of the line of the wall and about 525 m. from the E. end of the canal. Near here were found a number of sarcophagi of which marble fragments could be seen on the N.E. end of the canal. Many of these fragments are inscribed and some had been brought to the schoolhouse. During my stay at Nea Potidaea in 1938 I was able to locate near the N.E. tower about ten more inscribed fragments of which squeezes have been taken.

On the S.E. side of the canal other architectural fragments are visible of which a triglyph and several poros blocks with dove-tail and H-type clamps are of importance. I happened to locate a foot of a marble statue here (Pl. XII, 2). The toes are broken off but part of the base below the foot is preserved. The greatest dimensions are: Thickness of foot, 10 cm.; of base, 5 cm.; length of foot, 19 cm.; width, 10 cm.

The sculptural and inscribed pieces in Nea Potidaea belong to the Cassandreian period. Photographs and squeezes of the inscriptions of these and the specimens in the Thessalonica Museum have been taken.

D. M. Robinson in his article "Inscriptions from Macedonia, 1938," *T.A.P.A.*, LXIX, 1938, pp. 43-76, discusses a number of inscriptions from Hagios Mamas, some of which may have originally been connected with Potidaea-Cassandreia, and six from Nea Potidaea belonging to the Cassandreian period of the site. For the latter see *op. cit.*, pp. 64-68 and plates XII, 16; XIII, 16a, 17; XIV, 18; XV, 19; XVI, 20; XVII, 22.

26. Macaronas, *op. cit.*, p. 623. For the agonistic inscription, see Robinson, *T.A.P.A.*, LXIX, 1938, p. 64 and pl. XII, 16.

27. These terracottas were described in my original manuscript in 1939 and have appeared since in Robinson's *Excavations at Olynthus*, XIV, 1952, pp. 5f.

28. For parallels to the Amphipolis terracottas cf. Mary Ross' dissertation, "Terracotta Figurines of Macedonia and Thrace" (Johns Hopkins, 1939).

29. *Excavations at Olynthus*, II, p. 120, fig. 284; also, XIV, pp. 118-25 and plate 42, for the similarity of the figurine to the Attis type found at Olynthus and for references to the geographical distribution of the Cybele and Attis cult. The Olynthus type is dated in the late fifth or early fourth century B.C.

30. For the figure of Pegasus on the Potidaean bronze coins and the Corinthian influence on the type cf. chap. VII. For an account of Pegasus cf. West, "Pegasus in Classical Literature and Art" (Diss., Johns Hopkins, 1937).

31. *Br. M. Q.*, VI, 1932, p. 82.

32. *Br. M. Q.*, VIII, 1934, p. 108.

33. Another bronze pendant of the same Olynthus type is compared with a similar one from Potidaea in the British Museum (*loc. cit.*), dated as early as the eighth century B.C. Cf. Robinson, *op. cit.*, p. 124, pl. XXV, 420, and n. 213. For a comparison of Potidaean bronze rings (*Br. M. Q.*, VIII, 1934, p. 108, pl. XXXVe) with one from Olynthus and some from various places, see Robinson, *op. cit.*, p. 510, n. 104, and pl. CLXVI, 2585; in addition, cf. pp. 520-27, especially p. 521, n. 135, and pl. CLXVIII, 2624, for other miscellaneous bronze and iron objects of uncertain use from Olynthus which are similar to some in the British Museum from Potidaea (*op. cit.*, VI, 1932, pp. 82f., pl. XXXVIII) and other places in Thrace and Macedonia.

CHAPTER II

FROM THE FOUNDING OF POTIDAEA TO THE PERSIAN WARS

1. Herod., VII, 123.

2. *Ibid.*, IX, 28.

3. *Makedonische Fahrten*, I. *Chalkidike*, p. 45: H. Kiepert, *Lehrbuch der alten Geographie*, p. 317.

4. Cf. Glotz, *Histoire Grecque*, I (*Histoire Ancienne*, part II), pp. 162, 181f. For early Corinthian trade in the west, cf. also Blakeway, *B.S.A.*, XXXIII, 1932-3, pp. 170-208; *J.R.S.*, XXV, 1935, pp. 129-49. A detailed examination of the evidence for the history and archaeology of Corinth in the archaic period is presented by Will in *Korinthiaka* (Paris, 1955); see especially pp. 295-362, for the period of the Bacchiads.

5. Strabo, VI, 2, 4; Timaeus, fr. 53 (Müller, *F.H.G.*, I, p. 203). The Corinthians found Euboean settlers on these sites, Eretrians in Corcyra and Chalcidians in Syracuse, all of whom they dispossessed. Cf. Bury, *Hist. of Greece*, I, p. 104; Holm, *Hist. of Greece*, p. 287. The coinage of Corcyra was influenced more by Euboea than by Corinth.

6. *The History and Antiquities of the Doric Race* (tr. by H. Tufnell and G. Lewis), I, p. 130.

7. *Ancient Corinth*, p. 155. Cf. also Grote, *History of Greece*, III, p. 402.

8. Herod., III, 49.

9. O'Neill, *op. cit.*, p. 148.

10. Corcyra remained independent during Cypselus' reign according to Appian, *Bell. Civ.*, II, 39; cf. *C.A.H.*, III, p. 551. The battle between Corinth and Corcyra is described by Thuc., I, 13, as the first sea-fight in history.

11. Cf. O'Neill, *op. cit.*, p. 18. The Bacchiads were noted in antiquity for their oppression, and Strabo, VIII, 378, uses the word tyrants to describe them.

12. Strabo, VIII, 7, 6; X, 2, 8; I, 3, 18. Cf. Grote, *op. cit.*, III, p. 402 and Glotz, *op. cit.*, p. 322. To these colonies the three illegitimate sons of Cypselus were sent as governors, Gorgus in Ambracia, Pylades at Leucas, and Echiades at Anactorium. According to Aristotle (*Pol.*, 1315b 23), Cypselus was a popular ruler.

For general accounts of Corinthian colonization, see O'Neill, *op. cit.*, ch. VI; Raue, *Untersuchungen z. Geschichte d. Korinthischen Bundes* (Diss.), Marburg, 1937. For a recent account of the colonial policy of the Cypselids, cf. Will, *op. cit.*, pp. 517ff.

For the relations of Corinth and Argos in the seventh century B.C., cf. the article of A. Andrewes, "The Corinthian Actaeon and Pheidon of Argos," in the *Cl. Q.*, XLIII, 1949, pp. 70-78.

13. Cf. Bury, *op. cit.*, p. 162; Robinson, *A Short History of Greece*, p. 57.

14. Cf. O'Neill, *op. cit.*, p. 125.

15. For the cause and character of Greek colonization in general, see Gwynn, "The Character of Greek Colonization," *J.H.S.*, XXXVIII, 1918, pp. 88-123; Glotz, *op. cit.*, I, pp. 153-60; also, Trever, *Cl. Phil.*, XX, 1925, p. 132.

In 626 or 625 B.C., Corcyra colonized Epidamnus and invited Corinth to send an oecist. Phalius was sent. Cf. Thuc., I, 24 and 26. For a brief and balanced account of the rule of the Bacchiads and Cypselids at Corinth see Andrewes, *The Greek Tyrants*, pp. 43-53; a more detailed account is to be found in Will, *op. cit.*, chapters IV (for the Bacchiads) and V-VI (for the Cypselids).

16. For an account of the Lelantine War and the reasons for dating it toward the end of the seventh century, see O'Neill, *op. cit.*, pp. 162ff., and Appendix II. Will (*op. cit.*, p. 431) dates the war in the first half of the sixth century. There is a good deal of doubt about the chronology of the war, the contestants, and the part that Corinth played in it, but it does seem that Periander's activity in Euboea

and especially in the Lelantine plain was not limited to a single event. For Periander's intervention in Euboea see also Andrewes, *op. cit.*, p. 51.

Eretria lost the war, and the Lelantine plains were taken by Chalcis (Herod., V, 77; VI, 100). But Chalcis was weakened shortly afterwards by civil strife (Aristotle, *Pol.*, VIII, 10, 3). The decline of the Euboean cities must have offered an excellent opportunity for Corinth to gain a foothold in Chalcidice. Cf. Glotz, *op. cit.*, pp. 313f. Will (*op. cit.*, p. 402, n. 5 and p. 546) maintains that it is not clear whether Periander fought on the side of Chalcis or Eretria, but admits (*loc. cit.* and p. 431) that his intervention in the Lelantine War could have been the occasion for him to assure the interests of his city by "new directions," that is, by founding Potidaea.

17. Cf. Hasebroek, *Trade and Politics in Ancient Greece*, p. 108.

18. Cf. Cary, *The Geographical Background of Greek and Roman History*, pp. 51, 290; Andrewes, *op cit.*, pp. 50f., remarks that the founding of Potidaea "may be connected with the overland route from the Adriatic, for though Potidaea is not at the point where this road reaches the Aegean, it is in a strong position not far away."

19. Periander died ca. 586/5 B.C. Psammetichus' insignificant rule lasted from 585 to 583. Cf. *C.A.H.*, III, p. 559; Gwynn, *op. cit.*, pp. 116f.; Andrewes, *op. cit.*, p. 52.

According to Aristotle (*Pol.*, 1315b), the reign of the Cypselids at Corinth lasted for 73 years and 6 months. Cypselus ruled for 30 years, Periander for 40½, and Psammetichus for 3. Apollodorus of Athens (Jacoby, *F.G.H.*, II, B, 244), as quoted by Diogenes Laertius, states that Periander began his reign about the thirty-eighth Olympiad (628/7-625), ruled for 40 years and died at the age of 80, before the forty-ninth Olympiad (584/3-581) and forty-one years before the death of Croesus (546/5). On the strength of this essentially sound tradition and of the views of most modern scholars, we have adopted the period between 657 to 584/3 for the rule of the three Cypselids at Corinth. However, serious doubts have been cast on this traditional chronology. Beloch (*Gr. Gesch.*, I¹, pp. 343-71; I², pp. 274-318), places the beginning of the rule of the Cypselids about 623 B.C. O'Neill, (*op. cit.*, p. 116) finds Beloch's hypothesis "untrustworthy," and Prentice (*op. cit.*, p. 81, n. 11) unconvincing. Cf. also, Ure, *The Origin of Tyranny*, ch. VII; Glover, *Herodotus*, pp. 80f.; Wells, *Studies in Herodotus*, pp. 41-43, 70-73.

More recently, Will in his *Korinthiaka* (ch. V, pp. 363ff.) re-examines the evidence on the chronology of the Cypselids and presents interesting arguments for a later date, ranging from about 620 to 550 B.C., but he admits (p. 440) that his conclusion is "susceptible de reservoir des corrections." Kent in his review of the *Korinthiaka* (*Amer. Hist. Rev.*, LXI, 1956, p. 397) concludes that the author "seems to have solved the vexed problem of the chronology of the Cypselid tyranny," while Benson in his review (*A.J.A.*, LXII, 1959, p. 306), referring to Will's contribution on the subject, remarks that it has only a possible, not a probable, validity and that "it remains a tidy but unconfirmed hypothesis."

In Hammond's recent publication, *A History of Greece to 322 B.C.* (Oxford, 1959), the traditional dates for the rule of the Cypselids are retained (pp. 146ff.): Cypselus began his rule ca. 657, Periander ca. 627, and Psammetichus in 586.

20. Müller, *F.H.G.*, III, p. 393, fr. 60.

21. Cf. O'Neill, *op. cit.*, p. 125 and n. 39, ascribing the view to Holm, *op. cit.*, p. 308, and Meyer, *Ges. d. Alt.*, II, p. 624. *Webster's Geographical Dictionary* (1949) gives 609 B.C. as the date for the founding of Potidaea; Hammond, in his article on Potidaea in the *Oxford Classical Dictionary* (1949), places the event about 600 B.C., and also adopts this date in his book, *A History of Greece to 322 B.C.*, p. 116.

22. Roscher, III, p. 1339, v. *Pallene*. Cf. Hegesippus in Stephanus Byz., v. *Pallene*; Eustathius *ad Dionysium Periplus*, 327; Parthenius, 6, in *Erotici Scriptores Graeci*,

I (Biblio. Teubn.). Pallene also was the name of one of the daughters of Alcyoneus who fell from the Canastraeum promontory of the peninsula and was changed into a bird by Aphrodite (Roscher, *op. cit.*).

23. Herod., VII, 123. A reference to Phlegra can be found also in Aeschylus, *Eum.*, 295, which Verrall (*ad. loc.*), Macan (*Herod.*, VII, 123), and others interpret as referring to the peninsula of Pallene. This is contrary to the view of Paley (*ad loc.*) who feels that Aeschylus meant the volcanic district of Campania which, according to the Latin version (Ovid, X, 151), was the scene of the battle between Jupiter and the giants. Verrall further remarks that Aeschylus had in view "particularly its principal city, Potidaea."

24. Stephanus Byz., v. *Pallene*.

25. Müller, *Geographi Graeci Minores*, I, Anonymi (Vulgo Scymni Chii) *Orbis Descriptio*, p. 634.

26. Cf. Grote, *op. cit.*, III, p. 440.

27. Pindar, *Nem.*, I, 100; *Isthm.*, IV, 47; Aristoph., *Birds*, 824f., a jest; Lycophron, 1408; Apollodorus, I, 6, 1; Strabo, *Epit.*, VII, p. 330; Stephanus Byz., v. *Pallene*.

28. Strabo, *loc. cit.* Cf. also *Epist. Socrat.* (in *Epistolographi Graeci*, ed. Hercher, p. 630f.); Stephanus Byz., *loc. cit.*, gives the accounts of Hegessipus and Theagenes. The former refers to the battle as having been fought between the gods and the giants; the latter speaks of Heracles as defeating the giants, and the story becoming connected with the gods only because of the thunder and lightning which occurred during the battle.

29. Dionysius of Halicarnassus, I, 49, 124.

30. Thuc., IV, 120. Cf. *C.A.H.*, III, p. 651, where this is interpreted as suggesting late Minoan antecedents.

31. Herod., VII, 123; [Scymnus of Chios], V, 627. Cf. Grote, *op. cit.*, III, p. 440 and n. 2; Struck, *op. cit.*, pp. 35, 44.

32. Cf. Holm, *op. cit.*, I, p. 273.

33. For a description of Chalcidice cf. Griseback's *Reisen*, II, pp. 6-16; Leake's *Travels*, III, p. 152; also article in *R-E.*, v. *Chalkidike*.

34. Cf. West, *Hist. Chal. League*, p. 5; Casson, *Macedonia, Thrace and Illyria*, p. 94.

35. Cf. Hasebroek, *op. cit.*, p. 43.

36. *Deipnosophistae*, XI, 784 c (ed. Meinike).

37. Cf. Struck, *op. cit.*, pp. 39, 43; Casson, *op. cit.*, p. 30.

38. Diod., XII, 46 (ed. Dindorf).

39. Thuc., I, 63.

40. *Ibid.*, IV, 129.

41. Keramopoullos, Ἀρχ. Ἐφ., 1927-1928, pp. 57f., believes that the bronzes with Corinthian influence found in the archaic graves of the Necropolis of Trebenishte came from Potidaea.

42. Holm, *op. cit.*, p. 272.

43. Thuc., I, 25.

44. *B.C.H.*, IX, 1885, p. 276; Hermann, *A Manual of the Political Antiquities of Greece* (translation), § 87, p. 168. Hermann observes that changes from aristocracy or oligarchy to democracy manifested themselves earlier in the colonies than in the colonizing states. To what extent this could apply to Potidaea is difficult to say.

45. Holm, *op. cit.*, p. 272.

46. Bury, *op. cit.*, p. 159.

47. Hermann, *op. cit.*, § 86, pp. 165f. Corcyra was finally subjugated by Periander toward the end of his reign, but regained her independence after his death. Cf. Grote, *op. cit.*, III, p. 404.

48. Thuc., I, 38: cf. Grote, *op. cit.*, V, p. 323.

49. Bury, *op. cit.*, I, p. 159; O'Neill, *op. cit.*, pp. 158f.

50. Hasebroek, *op. cit.*, pp. 54, 110.

51. Thuc., I, 38.

52. Thuc., I, 56.

53. The presence of the Corinthian epidemiourgi at Potidaea is interpreted by Hermann (*op. cit.*, p. 81) as a policy on the part of Corinth to dominate Potidaea by interfering in her internal administration. Cf. Kahrstedt, *Griechisches Staatsrecht*, I, p. 361. The fact that Potidaea, though an ally of Athens, following the Persian wars, continued to receive the epidemiourgi from Corinth and the fact that, in times of war and with no indication of alliance, the Corinthian colonies are grouped constantly on the side of Corinth lends considerable support to this view. Cf. Will, *op. cit.*, p. 523 and notes 5 and 9; p. 524 and n. 1.

54. O'Neill, *op. cit.*, p. 158.

55. Cf. Müller, *The Hist. and Antiq. of the Doric Race*, II, p. 138; Hermann, *op. cit.*, p. 81, 1.

56. For the references to the epidemiourgi at Delphi see Daux, *Delphes au II*ᵉ *et au I*ᵉʳ *Siècle*, p. 430; also, Pomtow, "Die delphischen Schiedsrichter Texte und die Epidamiurgen," *Klio*, XVIII, 1923, pp. 259-95.

57. Cf. Daux, *loc. cit.*, and n. 1.

58. Müller, *op. cit.*, p. 146.

59. Hesychius, *Lex.*, v. *damiourgos*.

60. Cf. Müller, *op. cit.*, p. 145; *B.C.H.*, IX, 1885, p. 290.

61. Schömann, *Antiquities of Greece*, p. 143.

62. Cf. *B.C.H.*, IX, 1885, p. 293: The demiourgi had political significance, not sacerdotal.

63. They appear in the sixth and fifth century inscriptions from Olympia. Cf. Roehl, *Inscr. Gr. Ant.*, 111, 112, 113, 122.

64. Thuc., V, 47; *R.I.G.*, no. 195.

65. *C.I.G.*, 1567 (Achaea), 2653-2654 (Cnidus), *J.H.S.*, IV, 1883, pp. 136f. (Camirus).

66. *Rev. Arch.*, XIV, p. 337; *J.H.S.*, IV, 1883, p. 137 and n. 1. Cf. also Latychew in *B.C.H.*, IX, 1885, p. 291.

67. *B.C.H.*, VII, 1883, pp. 489, 491.

68. Cf. Gaillemer in Daremberg and Saglio, v. *demiourgoi*. For references to demiourgi in other cities, cf., among others, *ibid.*, *loc. cit.*; *B.C.H.*, IX, 1885, pp. 290ff.; Müller, *op. cit.*, pp. 145f.; Glotz, *The Greek City*, pp. 89f.

69. Gaillemer, *loc. cit.*

70. O'Neill, *op. cit.*, p. 206.

71. Schömann, *op. cit.*, p. 143.

72. *Nem.*, VI, 40; *Isthm.*, V, 5.

73. Herod., VIII, 129.

74. Himerius, *Or.*, 3, 10. Cf. Farnell, *Cults of the Greek States*, IV, p. 14, and n. 4d. The image of the god does not appear on Corinthian coins; there are sixth century B.C. terracotta plaques, however, from Corinth which show Poseidon on horseback holding a trident in his right hand and the reins in his left. Cf. Farnell, pl. 1, fig. a.

For the worship of Poseidon at Corinth and for an account of the theories of the origin of the cult, see also O'Neill, *op cit.*, pp. 107-13. For a general account of the cult, cf. F. Schachermeyer, *Poseidon und die Entstehung des griechischen Götterglaubens* (Bern, 1950).

75. Farnell, *op. cit.*, IV, p. 14.

76. *Ibid.*, and n. 4d; Lavedan, v. *Poseidon*, p. 779.

77. For the legends of Poseidon-horse and horse sacrifice see Farnell, *op. cit.*, IV, p. 15 and pp. 20ff.

78. "Sur la Signification de Types monétaires des Anciens," *B.C.H.*, XVIII, 1894, p. 119. A coin of Rhaucus with a bust of a horse and a star is also mentioned by Svoronos (*loc. cit.*). Cf. Babelon, *Traité*, I, p. 1149 and n. 3.

79. The torso of the statuette of Poseidon is dated in the time of the Antonines in *Jahrbuch*, XLIII, 1928, p. 603.

80. The height of the figure is 1.13 m. In 1938 the relief was in the office of the mayor of the modern town. For a brief mention of the monument and an account of a Latin inscription on the back of it, cf. D. M. Robinson, "Inscriptions from Macedonia, 1938," *T.A.P.A.*, LXIX, 1938, p. 16 and pl. XV, 19.

81. A restoration of the inscription is given in *I.G.*, IV, 673. Cf. also *C.I.G.*, 1165.

82. Pindar, *Nem.*, IV, 44, with the scolion. Cf. Smith, *Dict. of Gr. and Rom. Biogr. and Myth.*, v. *Alcyoneus*.

83. Pindar, *Isthm.*, VI, 45; Ephorus in Müller's *F.H.G.*, I, 255, 70; Diod., IV, 15; Theagenes in Stephanus Byz., 497, 17. Cf. *R-E.*, Suppl. III, p. 955.

84. Thuc., II, 70.

85. Herod., VIII, 129.

86. Paus., X, 11, 5.

87. *Loc. cit.*

88. In the case of the treasury of the Cnidians, Pausanias (X, 11, 5) states that he does not know whether it was built in commemoration of a victory or as a display of their wealth. This statement is very interesting and may be taken as an indication of Pausanias' inquiring into the reason for the erection of the treasuries. Pausanias shows no doubt as to the reason for the erection of the Potidaean treasury.

89. Herod., VIII, 129.

90. Paus., X, 13, 5. After the expulsion of the tyrants the name of Corinth was substituted on the dedicatory inscription for that of Cypselus. Herod., I, 14; Frazer, *Paus.*, V, pp. 295ff.

91. Paus., X, 11, 5.

92. The inscribed block containing the name of the Syracusans was found in 1895. Cf. Frazer, *Paus.*, V, p. 282.

93. Cf. Dinsmoor in *B.C.H.*, XXXVI, 1912, p. 459.

94. For the numbers given see pl. VIII of Dinsmoor's article in *B.C.H.*, XXXVI, 1912, pp. 439-493; and pl. L in De La Coste-Messelière, *Au Musée de Delphes*. Dinsmoor (*loc. cit.*, p. 458 and n. 1) is right in rejecting no. XII as unsuitable for a Doric building because of the thickness of its wall (1.30 m.). Such a thickness implies an Ionic superstructure. This building has been suggested as possibly a Syracusan or a Potidaean treasury by Robinson in *A.J.P.*, XXXI, 1910, p. 220.

95. Dinsmoor, *loc. cit.*, pp. 461f.

96. *Ibid.*

97. For the identifications of V see Dinsmoor, *loc. cit.*, p. 462. De La Coste-Messelière, pl. L, gives it as Megarian or Syracusan; Keramopoullos, *Guide*, 1935, p. 34 and plan, identifies it as Siphnian.

98. *Ibid.*, p. 36 and plan. De La Coste-Messelière, *op. cit.*, pp. 469ff., and 474; *R-E.*, Suppl. IV, col. 1260, and no. 32 in plan.

99. Cf. Dinsmoor, *loc. cit.*, p. 262; also De La Coste-Messelière, *op. cit.*, p. 469.

100. Dinsmoor, *loc. cit.*, pp. 460f. For treasury XIII and its final attribution to Cyrene, see Jean Bousquet, *Le Trésor de Cyrene, Fouilles de Delphes*, II, *topographie et architecture*, (Paris, 1952), and Dinsmoor's review in *A.J.A.*, LXI, 1957, p. 403.

101. Cf. Dinsmoor, *loc. cit.*, p. 460; Pomtow in *B.P.W.*, XXIX, 1909, p. 190. Both date them in the first half of the fifth century B.C. De La Coste-Messelière, *op. cit.*, p. 472, gives 510-480 B.C.; *R-E.*, Suppl. IV, col. 1275, dates VIII a little earlier than 510; Keramopoullos, *Guide*, 1935, p. 36, dates both before 548 B.C.

102. Dinsmoor (p. 460) rejected VIII and IX on the ground that neither one fitted the dates for the Syracusan treasury. This has been disproved by later excavations.

103. Cf. De La Coste-Messelière, *op. cit.*, p. 471.

104. The order of the treasuries has been reversed, but not on sufficient evidence. Potidaean IX, Syracusan VIII; Homolle in *C.R.*, 1894, p. 584; Pomtow, *Delphi*, II, p. 20; in *B.P.W.*, XXIX, 1909, p. 190; XXXI, 1911, p. 1647; Frazer, *Paus.*, V, p. 282, following Homolle.

105. For Potidaean VIII, Syracusan IX, see Keramopoullos, *loc. cit.*

106. De La Coste-Messelière, *op. cit.*, p. 59, n. 2.

107. *Ibid.*, p. 76. For the comparison between these two buildings see *ibid.*, p. 59.

108. P. Perdrizet in *R.E.A.*, I, 1899, pp. 208-10; Ditt., Syll.³, 15.

109. Delphi Museum inv. nos. 2254, 3080. Lolling, *Berlin. Sitzungsber.*, 1888, p. 581.

110. Ditt., *loc. cit.* For a facsimile see Roehl, *Imagines*, 3rd ed., p. 44, 6; also, Perdrizet, *op. cit.*, p. 209.

111. The maximum dimensions of the two fragments are: h. $= 0.26$ m., w. $= 0.42$ m., th. $= 0.20$ m. (*R-E.*, Suppl. IV, col. 1276). The height of the letters of the dedication is 0.02 m., and the height of the letters of the signature, 0.0035 m. (Perdrizet, *op. cit.*, p. 209).

112. The reading *Therepes* suggested at first by Lolling, *loc. cit.*, cannot stand. *Theygenes* has been read by Baunack, *Philologus*, XLVIII, 1889, p. 385, and has been accepted by Perdrizet, *op. cit.*, p. 210, and others.

113. Cf. Wilhelm, *Beiträge zur Griechischen Inschriften-kunde* (Vienna, 1909), p. 6.

114. Nikitsky (*Revue Russe de Philologie*, 1894, p. 109), when the first fragment was found, made a facsimile of it and suggested that the third line was not the artist's signature but the end of the dedication. The discovery of the second fragment made it clear that the line in question was taken by the artist's name. Cf. Perdrizet, *op. cit.*, p. 208.

115. Cf. *R-E.*, Suppl. III, col. 346.

116. Cf. Perdrizet, *op. cit.*, p. 209.

117. *Ibid.*, p. 209, and *I.G.A.*, 165, 206.

118. Perdrizet, *op. cit.*, p. 210; *I.G.A.*, 373.

119. Baunack, *Philologus*, XLVIII, 1889, p. 386; *R-E.*, Suppl. III, col. 346; Suppl. IV, col. 1276.

CHAPTER III

POTIDAEA DURING THE PERSIAN WARS

1. Herod., VII, 122ff.

2. *Ibid.*, 123.

3. Torone, Galepsus, Sermyle, Mecyberna, and Olynthus.

4. Herod., VII, 185. This number is considered too great for 480 B.C. by Munro in *C.A.H.*, IV, p. 273.

5. Herod., VII, 126; 128.

6. Grundy, *The Great Persian Wars*, p. 429.

7. Herod., VIII, 127.

8. *Ibid.*

9. Herod., VIII, 128.

10. *Ibid.*; cf. Aeneas Tacticus, XXXI, 25-27.

11. It is to this period that Svoronos ("L'Hellénisme Primitif de la Macédoine, Prouvé par la Numismatique," *Journ. Int. Arch. Num.*, XIX, 1918-19, pp. 207-211) assigns the issue of a number of electrum coins, of Persian fabric but in the types of Olynthus at that time, to Artabazus for the expenses of the long siege of Potidaea during which (p. 209) "Les statères d'or auraient joué le même rôle *stratégique* que les dariques 'archers' qui seuls plus tard chassèrent d'Asie, l'armée d'Agesilas." Svoronos further believes (p. 210) that the Potidaeans and their Pallenean allies issued electrum staters at this time on the Euboic standard. From the "uncertain

coins of Asia Minor" he assigns a coin with the head of a bull on the reverse and a swastika in relief on the reverse to Potidaea. The swastika, of course, is found on the reverse of the coins of Corinth as well as on those of her colonies, Corcyra and Syracuse. To Mende he assigns a coin with the head of an ass on the obverse and an incuse square on the reverse (Pl. XIX, 28 for Potidaea, 26 for Mende).

12. Polyaenus, *Strategemata*, VII, 33, 1 (ed. Melber). This method of communication is often employed by the ancients. Cf. Herod., V, 35; Caesar, *Bell. Gall.*, V, 48.

13. Herod., VIII, 128.

14. *Ibid.*, 129.

15. *Ibid.*

16. *Ibid.*

17. *Ibid.*

18. *Ibid.*

19. Earthquakes were also ascribed to him. According to Herodotus (VII, 129) the Thessalians believed that Poseidon made the passage through which the river Peneios flows. Myres in his book *Herodotus, Father of History* (Oxford, 1953), p. 46, describes the incident as an earthquake.

20. Herod., IX, 28. The other Corinthian colonies mentioned by Herodotus as having participated in this battle are Ambracia with 500 men, Leucas and Anactorium with 800. Myres, *op. cit.*, p. 287, places the Potidaean and Corinthian hoplites in the II regional brigade.

21. Herod., IX, 31.

22. *Ibid.*, 81.

23. *Ibid.*

24. Diod., XI, 33, 1.

25. For the inscription on the Delphic monument see Ditt., *Syll.*³, 31; Tod, *Greek Historical Inscriptions*, 19. For the history of the monument see *I.G.A.*, 70. The name of Potidaea appears on the fifth coil of the bronze triple-bodied serpent. For the inscription on the monument at Olympia see Paus., V, 23.

26. Munro in *C.A.H.*, IV, p. 329; E. Meyer, III, 235 n.

27. Pausanias (V, 23) mentions 27 names as appearing on the Olympian monument; Herodotus gives 25 names as having taken part at Plataea; and on the Delphic monument 31 names are recorded.

28. Macan, *Herodotus, The Seventh, Eighth, and Ninth Books*, IX, 28.

29. Bauer, *Wienen Studien*, 1887, pp. 223f.

30. Herodotus relates (IX, 81) that the cost of the monument was paid out of the spoils won at Plataea. Thucydides (I, 132) definitely implies that the names of the states which helped to overthrow the barbarian were inscribed on the tripod. The heading of the inscription which took the place of the original arrogant epigram of Pausanias also contradicts Bauer's view. Cf. also Frazer's *Pausanias*, V, p. 306.

Larsen ("Federation for Peace in Ancient Greece," *Cl. Phil.*, XXXIX, 1944, p. 151 and n. 14) regards the inscription on the serpent-column as giving "something in the nature of an official list at the time of the battle" and includes Potidaea among the participants.

A more comprehensive account of the entire question is presented by Merritt, Wade-Gery and McGregor in their monumental work, *The Athenian Tribute Lists* (henceforth cited as *A.T.L.* or authors of *A.T.L.*), III, ch. I, "The Serpent Column and the Covenant of Plataia," pp. 95ff.; the differences between the Delphi and Olympia monuments are explained (p. 95) as perhaps due to the inexact copying by Pausanias, while the Delphic list is regarded as a probable master-copy.

31. Cf. Thuc., I, 132; [Demosthenes] in *Near.*, 97. Also Herod., VIII, 82, for the inclusion of the Tenians on the Delphic inscription because of their participation at the battle of Salamis.

32. Cf. the lists given in Frazer's *Pausanias*, V, p. 305. Rawlinson, *History of*

Herodotus, IV, p. 469, considers the restoration of Mantineans after Hermionians as probable. He suggests the Paleans among his conjectural restorations to fill one of the apparent lacunas in the lists. Cf. also Tod, *op. cit.,* p. 24.

33. Meyer, III, 235 n.

34. How and Wells, *A Commentary on Herodotus,* IX, 28, 3.

35. *Op. cit.,* p. 472.

36. *Ibid.,* p. 473.

37. Along with the Mykanes, Kynthioi, Siphnioi.

38. *Ibid.,* p. 469.

39. Herod., VIII, 82.

40. Cf. *Ibid.,* VIII, 126-28, and our previous account of the revolt in Pallene and Olynthus.

41. Frazer, *Pausanias,* V, 304.

42. Hicks-Hill, *A Manual of Greek Historical Inscriptions,* p. 24.

43. Paus., I, 23.

44. Arist., *Rhet.* II, 22. See also commentary of Anonymous on the passage (ed. H. Rabe, p. 131, 30).

CHAPTER IV

FROM THE END OF THE PERSIAN WARS TO THE REVOLT FROM ATHENS

1. Thuc., I, 92; Plut., *Arist.,* 23; Diod., XI, 44, places the number of Peloponnesian ships at 50.

2. Thuc., I, 95. Cf. also Plut., *Arist.,* 23; 24; 25; Diod., XI, 46.

3. Thuc., *loc. cit.*

4. Herod., VI, 72; Diod., XI, 48.

5. Arist., *Ath. Pol.,* XXIII, 5. The first assessment of Aristides was imposed in the third year after the battle of Salamis and is dated in the archonship of Timosthenes (478/7); therefore the Confederacy must have been organized as early as the end of 478 B.C. Cf. Bury, *op. cit.,* I, p. 353; E. Cavaignac, *Etudes sur l'Histoire Financière d'Athènes au Ve Siècle,* p. 37; *C.A.H.,* V, p. 40. For more extensive discussions on the founding and early history of the Delian Confederacy, see L. I. Highby, *Klio,* Beiheft XXXVI, 1936, pp. 39-57; Larsen, "The Constitution and Original Purpose of the Delian League," *Harvard Studies in Cl. Phil.,* LI, 1940, pp. 176-212; Gomme, *A Historical Commentary on Thucydides* (henceforth cited as *Commentary*), I, especially pp. 272-95. For a more recent account, see *A.T.L.,* III, chapters III and V.

6. Thuc., I, 96; III, 10; VI, 76; Diod., XI, 37ff.; Plut., *Arist.,* 5.

7. Herod., VI, 42; Plut., *Arist.,* 24.

8. Thuc., I, 96.

9. *Ibid.* Cf. also Diod., XII, 40; Plut., *Arist.,* 24.

10. Thuc., I, 99. Cf. *A.T.L.,* III, pp. 237f.

11. Plut., *Arist.,* 25; *Per.,* 12; Diod., XII, 37. Cf. Cavaignac, *op. cit.,* pp. 48, 61ff.; Glotz, *Histoire Grecque,* II, p. 155; *A.T.L.,* III, p. 262, where it is stated that there is nothing improbable in the proposal coming from the Samians at this time.

12. Herod., VII, 106.

13. *Ibid.;* Thuc., I, 98; Plut., *Cimon,* 7; 9; 14. The Greek cities on the coast of Thrace and Hellespont were reduced by Cimon in 476/5 B.C.

14. Walker, *C.A.H.,* V, pp. 43f.

15. *Am. Hist. Rev.,* XXXV, 1929-1930, p. 273.

16. *A.T.L.,* III, p. 223.

17. Cf., among others, Grote, *op. cit.,* V, p. 121.

18. See n. 13, above.

19. Thuc., V, 18, 5. This passage of Thucydides has been interpreted by some (Grote, *op. cit.,* V, p. 122) as implying that the cities mentioned were listed in the

first assessment of Aristides. Walker in *C.A.H.*, V, p. 44 and n. 1, regards this inference as fallacious and argues that the phrase *the tribute of Aristides' time* "would be employed for the assessment of new accessions to the League," so long as Aristides was acting as assessor. The phrase admits both interpretations, that the cities in question were listed in the first assessment of Aristides (478/7) and therefore were original members of the Confederacy, or that they were assessed during the period of years when Aristides was acting as assessor. This is also recognized by the authors of *A.T.L.*, III, p. 221, who further emphasize that if the phrase "is interpreted strictly then cities which paid Aristeides' tribute were original members of the Confederacy."

Francotte, *Les Finances des Cités Gr.*, pp. 101f., does not accept the idea that the Chalcidic cities were first assessed by Aristides, but admits that they entered the league at an early date. Concerning the cities assessed by Aristides, cf. Agricola, *De Aristidis Censu* (Diss.), Berlin, 1900. For a general discussion of the topic cf. also Beloch, *Rhein. Mus.*, 1888, p. 75; Busolt, *Griech. Gesch.*, III, 1, p. 228; West, *Hist. Chalc. League*, p. 11 and n. 18b.

20. For the tribute lists see *S.E.G.*, V; *A.T.L.*, I, pp. 127ff.; II, pp. 7ff.; Hill, *Sources for Greek History* (new ed. by Meiggs and Andrewes, Oxford, 1951), pp. 404-23.

21. Herod., VIII, 1.

22. Pp. 93f. and n. 66 where reference is given to West's article in the *Am. Hist. Rev.*, XXXV, 1930, p. 274. West includes (pp. 273f.) Potidaea among the cities that contributed ships and thinks that the change from this form of contribution in the case of Potidaea took place in 444 B.C., when her name appears for the first time on the tribute lists.

23. *A.T.L.*, III, pp. 58, 238, and 249ff.; for the list of fourteen allies, which, in the judgment of the authors of *A.T.L.*, may still have been furnishing ships in 454 B.C., see pp. 267f. and n. 11. This list includes Potidaea and the states which West (*op. cit.*, pp. 273f.) had regarded as among the charter members of the Confederacy.

24. The persistence of Potidaea and other charter members of the Confederacy who had supplied ships from the beginning is ascribed by West (*op. cit.*, especially p. 275, n. 26) to a feeling of equality and prestige they enjoyed because of their contribution in the battles against Persia. Cf. also *A.T.L.*, III, p. 249, with reference to West's remarks.

25. Thuc., I, 97-99. The affair of Naxos offers an early example. After Athens conquered this island and confiscated its fleet, a tribute was imposed on the inhabitants (*ibid.*, I, 98).

26. Wade-Gery in his article on "The Question of Tribute in 449/8 B.C." (*Hesperia*, XIV, 1945, pp. 212-23) maintains that it was Cimon's plan for an efficient force that gradually led to increased transfers from ships to money, and the number of names in the quota list of 450/49 "suggests a considerable transfer . . . at the great Panathenaea of 450, while Kimon still lived and the Persian war looked likely to last" (pp. 219f. and n. 17); he further presents (p. 226) a convincing case for no tribute being paid in the year following the Peace of Callias (450/49) and that when the tribute was reimposed "during 449/8, to be paid in 448/7 and thenceforward" (p. 226), a new basis was established since the doctrine that the tribute was for "the war against the barbarian" could no longer be maintained. This basis for a new policy Wade-Gery finds (p. 222) in Pericles' Congress Decree reported by Plutarch, *Per.*, 17, and in the fact that Spartan unwillingness to participate in the Congress for a permanent understanding gave Athens the opportunity to think of the tribute as a "Defense Fund" for any eventuality of war (p. 224 and n. 30).

According to the authors of *A.T.L.* (III, p. 250), the transfer from ships to money by all remaining naval allies except Samos, Chios and Lesbos "began about 454 and was completed by the end of Period II (perhaps, except for Potidaia, at the

Panathenaia of 450)" and is described as part of the reorganization of the Empire following the removal of the treasury from Delos to Athens, with Cimon encouraging the allies to accept this new policy.

For additional treatment of the question of tribute for 449/8, see references in Wade-Gery, *op. cit.*, p. 212. For the Peace of Callias, cf., in particular, Wade-Gery's article in *Harvard Studies in Cl. Phil.*, Suppl. I, 1940, pp. 121-56; Cary, *Cl. Q.*, XXXIX, 1945, pp. 87-91; *A.T.L.*, III, ch. VIII, "The Peace of Kallias," pp. 274-300, where the peace is dated in the spring of 449, soon after the Dionysiac festival (pp. 274 and 281).

27. Following is the tribute of Potidaea that is preserved or can safely be restored on the tribute quota lists. The references are to *A.T.L.*, I, pp. 127ff., by list number, year, column, and line followed by the amount of tribute paid (converted from Attic to Arabic numerals).

No.	Year	Column	Line	Tribute Paid
9	446/5	III	7	[6]
10	445/4	II	4	6
11	444/3	III	14	6
12	443/2	III	31	6
13	442/1	III	30	[6]
14	441/0	I	42	6
15	440/39	II	50	6
19	436/5	V	20	[6]
20	435/4	VI	5	6
21	434/3	V	21	[15]
22	433/2	II	70	15

28. *Ibid.*, pp. 142f. Skapsaioi, Sermaioi, Neopolitai, and Spartolioi for 439/8; Ikioi, Stolioi, Skablaioi, Asseritai, Argilioi, and Mendaioi for 438/7; Hill, *op. cit.*, pp. 410-14.

29. *A.T.L.*, I, p. 144.

30. *Ibid.*, III, pp. 64f. Recently this view has been adopted by Gomme, *op. cit.*, III, p. 608, where the increase is described as "doubtless part of the pressure brought to bear on her [Potidaea] at this time and helps to explain her secession in 432." Gomme, however, in vol. I, p. 211, n. 5, regarded the increase as probable for 434/3 and thought it "more likely that Thucydides would have mentioned so big an increase if it had immediately preceded the revolt."

31. See also Gomme, *op. cit.*, I, p. 211, n. 5. Cf. preceding note for the variation of Gomme's view.

32. *A.T.L.*, III, pp. 64-65.

33. Cf. *A.T.L.*, *loc. cit.*; p. 321 and n. 89; Gomme, *op. cit.*, III, p. 608.

34. Changes in tribute within assessment periods are less likely, though not uncommon. Cf. also *A.T.L.*, III, p. 65 and n. 1.

35. The Athenians, conscious of their new strength in this area, proceeded to raise old tribute quotas and to impose new assessments. Cf. *A.T.L.*, III, p. 319. For Brea's location between Therma and Aeneia and its founding ca. 438 B.C., cf. Woodhead, "The Site of Brea: Thucydides I, 61. 4," *Cl. Q.*, N.S., II, 1952, pp. 57-62. This location for Brea seems to be more preferable than somewhere in Bisaltia, and its founding can better explain the changes in tribute in this area about this time than the founding of Amphipolis. With Brea in Bisaltia, the authors of *A.T.L.* (III, pp. 64f. and 321 with n. 89) are more inclined to attribute these changes to the founding of Amphipolis.

36. *A.T.L.*, III, p. 319.

37. The following list has been prepared from *A.T.L.*, I, pp. 127ff. After the name of each city and under list number and the years indicated, the amount of tribute

is given in number of talents followed by the column and line in which it appears on the quota lists.

Years:	10, 445/4			12, 443/2			22, 433/2		
City	Talents Paid	Col.	Line	Talents Paid	Col.	Line	Talents Paid	Col.	Line
Acanthus	3	II	6	3	III	19	[3]	II	67
Dium	Not recorded. (In 446/5: 1	II	12)	1	II	35	[1]	II	58
Torone	Not recorded. (In 446/5: 6	II	28)	6	III	18	Not recorded. (In 432/1: 6	II	51)
Sermylia	5	II	25	5	III	28	Not recorded. (In 434/3: 4½	V	9)
Olynthus	Not recorded. (In 450/49: 2	III	30)	[2]	III	14	(Name of city restored) 2	II	45
Potidaea	6	II	4	6	III	31	15	II	70
Aphytis	1	II	23	1	III	12	Not recorded. (In 432/1: 3	II	38)
Neapolis	[½]	II	29	½	III	4	½	II	47-8
Scione	6	II	21	6	III	22	Not recorded. (In 435/4: 15	VI	6)
Mende	Not recorded. (In 444/3: 5	III	5)	9	III	20	Not recorded. (In 434/3: 8	V	6)

38. The comparisons are made from *A.T.I.*, *loc. cit.* See also Hill, *op. cit.*, pp. 410-14.

39. For the Corinthian constitution cf. O'Neill, *op. cit.*, pp. 143ff. The authors of *A.T.L.* (III, pp. 149f.) emphasize that the evidence scarcely justifies the general belief, as maintained by Walker (*C.A.H.*, V, pp. 471f.), that Athens insisted upon democratic constitutions and cite the presence of the annual Corinthian magistrates to Potidaea as an example; they describe the Potidaean constitution as being "in all probability oligarchic." Cf. also Gomme, *op. cit.*, I, pp. 380f.

40. Thuc., I, 56-58.

41. For Athenian personnel in the Empire, see especially *A.T.L.*, III, pp. 142-45, and Gomme, *op. cit.*, I, pp. 380-83, II, p. 34. Both references agree that no Athenian board of magistrates was permanently appointed in every city. The authors of *A.T.L.* further indicate that a city with inspectors might be autonomous depending on its behavior, though the one with a garrison was not.

42. Walker, *C.A.H.*, V, p. 94 and n. 1; Gomme, *op. cit.*, I, pp. 239-44 and 383.

43. For Corinthian-Athenian relations during this period, cf. especially O'Neill, *op. cit.*, pp. 189-94. Cf. also Grundy, *Thucydides and the History of His Age* (2nd ed., 1948), I, pp. 183f. and 233.

44. Thuc., I, 103; Diod., XI, 79. For the relations between Athens and Megara during this period, see Highbarger, *The History and Civilization of Ancient Megara*, (Baltimore, 1927), pp. 155ff.

45. Thuc., I, 108.

46. O'Neill, *op. cit.*, pp. 192f.

47. Thuc., I, 112.

48. *Ibid.*, 103.

49. For the identification of Phlegra with Pallene, see p. 17, above.

50. *A.T.L.*, III, p. 321 and n. 88.

51. Grundy, *op. cit.*, pp. 191-97.

52. Diod., XII, 10, 3.

53. At least the Corinthians so report it; cf. Thuc., I, 41.

54. Grundy, *op. cit.*, p. 198. Cf. also O'Neill, *op. cit.*, p. 196, who follows Grundy in his account of the Corinthian-Athenian relations during this period.

55. Thuc., I, 24ff.

CHAPTER V

THE COINAGE OF POTIDAEA TO 432 B.C.

1. Seltman, *Greek Coins*, p. 67; cf. also p. 290 and pl. VII, 4-5, where a Potidaean tetradrachm is dated ca. 530 B.C. and a drachm ca. 520 B.C. The same views and references appear in the 2nd edition, London, 1955.

2. Babelon, "Trouvaille de Tarente," in *Rev. Num.*, Serie 4, XVI, 1912, pp. 1-40.

3. *Ibid.*, p. 39.

4. Cf. Seltman, *op. cit.*, p. 67 and pl. VII, 5.

5. Seltman (*loc. cit.*) and Gardner (*History of Ancient Coinage*, p. 197), contrary to the view of Head, Babelon and others, contend that Potidaea and the other cities of Chalcidice, although they follow the Attic standard in their issues of tetradrachms, in their lower units follow the Corinthian division in drachms and their fractions. This seems to be right. So what has been termed a tetrobol or a diobol in referring to the coins of these cities is really a Corinthian drachm or a hemidrachm. Only a coin attributed to Acanthus has a weight equivalent to the Attic drachm (Head, *H.N.^{2}*, 205, wt. 4 grms.), but the attribution is considered as doubtful by Gardner (p. 198).

The Corinthian stater was 8.58 grms. and was divided into three drachms of 2.25-2.91 grms.; these were subdivided into hemidrachms of 1.16-1.49, obols of 0.32-0.48 and hemiobols of 0.20-0.25. The Attic tetradrachm weighed about 17.43 grms. and had the following divisions: drachm $= 4.36$, triob. $= 2.18$, diob. $= 1.45$, trihem. $= 1.09$, obol $= 0.72$, and hemiob. $= 0.36$ grms.

6. The dangers of dating coins solely on the basis of style have often been pointed out. Cf. D. M. Robinson, *A Hoard of Silver Coins from Carystus* (*Num. Notes and Monographs*, no. 124), p. 42, n. 85.

7. Herod., VIII, 129.

8. Seltman, *op. cit.*, p. 290, dates a drachm illustrated on his pl. VII, 5, ca. 520 B.C.

9. Babelon, *loc. cit.*, p. 39. The Hoard was found in 1911.

10. For the primitive concept of Poseidon still evident in the sixth century cf. Dr. Thalia Phillis Howe's article, "Zeus Herkeios," *A.J.A.*, LIX, 1955, p. 289 and n. 21, where the following comment appears: "Poseidon's innate primitivism is best exemplified on the coins of Potidaea where he sat naked on horseback holding the trident and the reins."

11. These three coins were found at Olynthus during the excavations in 1931. There is no reason to consider them as modern forgeries as Regling (*Deutsche Literaturzeitung*, XXXIV, 1933, p. 1613) and Gaebler (*Sitzungsber. d. preuss. Akad. d. Wiss. phil.-hist. Klasse*, 1935, p. 841) do. Regling's argument has been refuted by Robinson in *A.J.A.*, XXXIX, 1935, p. 247, and n. 2. The genuineness of these coins has been upheld by Schwabacher, *A.J.A.*, XLII, 1938, pp. 70-76; by Newell, *A.J.A.*, XL, 1936, p. 397. Cf. also, Robinson and Clement, *Excavations at Olynthus*,

IX, p. 307 and n. 255. It is significant that Gaebler has not included the three Potidaean tetradrachms among the forgeries which he lists in his *Antiken Münzen Nord-Gr.*, III², pp. 207ff.

12. Babelon, *Traité*, I, p. 1149, no. 1638, incorrectly says that the trident is held in the left hand and the reins in the right. The hand drawn back cannot be the left, as comparison with other examples shows.

13. As stated previously, the star beneath the horse is meant to give a planetary character to the horse. The star appears on both tetradrachms and drachms, with the number of rays varying from five to eight.

14. Because of the general use of applying the terms tetrobol, diobol, etc., to the divisions of the Potidaean tetradrachm, though they were not meant as such (cf. above, n. 5), we insert these terms in parentheses along with the correct denominations in order to avoid any confusion.

15. Gardner, "Coinage of the Athenian Empire," in *J.H.S.*, XXXIII, 1913, p. 151; Babelon, *Rev. Num.*, XVII, 1913, p. 468; Gomme, *Commentary*, I, p. 384.

16. Gardner, *loc. cit.*, p. 150.

17. Nesselhauf, *Unters. zur Gesch. der Del.-Att. Symmachie* (1933), pp. 34f. The *symmachia* changed into an *arche* at the time of the peace with Persia (450/49 B.C.). On Athenian imperialism, see Meiggs, "The Growth of Athenian Imperialism," *J.H.S.*, LXIII, 1943, pp. 21-34.

18. A fragment was found at Smyrna, another in Siphnos, and two at Syme. For these fragments cf. Tod, 67. In 1928 Robinson found a fifth fragment in Aphytis, a city near Potidaea, and published it in the *A.J.P.*, LVI, 1935, pp. 149-54. The Aphytis fragment gives several lines preceding the beginning of the other fragments. For a full bibliography on these fragments see Segre's article, *Clara Rhodos*, IX, 1938, p. 151 and notes on that page. A reprint of the Coan fragment may be found in *A.T.L.*, I, 1939, p. 579.

Similar references to the above and a brief summary of Athenian policy to institute unification of coinage, weights and measures throughout the Empire may be found in Gomme, *op. cit.*, pp. 383f. and 206. For the decree cf. also *I.G.*, I², p. 295; *S.E.G.*, X, 25: Robinson and Clement, *Excavations at Olynthus*, IX, pp. xxviii, 273f.; Seltman, *Greek Coins*, pp. 111f.; Tod, *J.H.S.*, LIX, 1939, pp. 251f.; LXV, 1945, p. 87; Dinsmoor, *Hesperia*, Suppl. V, 1941, pp. 152f.; E.S.G. Robinson, *Hesperia*, Suppl. VIII, 1949, pp. 324-40. For additional bibliography see Tod, I², 1946, pp. 263f., and especially *A.T.L.*, II, pp. 61-68, where the complete decree is restored. A composite text of the decree is to be found also in Hill, *Sources of Greek History* (Oxford, 1951), pp. 295f.

19. *A.T.L.*, II, pp. 61-68.

20. Segre, *loc. cit.*, p. 171; *A.T.L.*, II, p. 61. D.M. Robinson refers to this decree and to the fragment he found at Aphytis in his monograph, *A Hoard of Silver Coins from Carystus*, p. 32 and n. 66, and still dates it between 438-423 B.C.

21. Cf. Segre, *loc. cit.*, p. 173.

22. Gold and electrum were not included in the monetary decrees and their issues were not suspended by Athens. Cf. Segre, *loc. cit.*, p. 171.

23. Cf. Segre, *loc. cit.*, p. 172.

24. *Hist. Num.²*, p. 212; *B. M. Cat.*, Macedonia, pp. 161, 21. Cf. also Robinson, *Excavations at Olynthus*, III, p. 26, no. 65; Gaebler, *op. cit.*, III², p. 104, no. 4.

25. Casson, *Macedonia, Thrace and Illyria*, p. 104.

26. Babelon, *Traité*, I, p. 1151, no. 1640.

27. Naville VI, pl. 15, 442, offers a good illustration.

28. Casson, *op. cit.*, p. 104, n. 9 and fig. 24.

29. *B. M. Cat.*, pl. XXV, 1-9.

30. Cf. Robinson, *Excavations at Olynthus*, III, p. 26.

31. The possibility of a city named Pallene near the isthmus before the coming of the Corinthians might easily account for the influence on the type of the Potidaean coins. For a pre-Corinthian occupation of the isthmus see ch. II, pp. 16-18.

32. Seltman, *op. cit.*, p. 67 and pl. IV, 15. Cf. Robinson, *Excavations at Olynthus*, VI, p. 35, where the head on coin number 134 is spoken of as resembling that of Aphrodite on Corinthian drachms.

33. Cf. Lavedan, *Dictionaire Illustré de la Mythologie et des Antiquités Gr. et Rom.*, p. 778.

CHAPTER VI

DURING THE PELOPONNESIAN WAR

1. Thuc., I, 54. A valuable contribution to our knowledge of the Peloponnesian War and of many phases of 5th century Grecian affairs has recently been made with the publication of Gomme's intensive study, *A Historical Commentary on Thucydides*, I (Oxford, 1945), II and III (Oxford, 1956). The fourth and final volume is most anxiously awaited.

2. Thuc., I, 40.

3. *Ibid.*, I, 56.

4. *Ibid.*, I, 38.

5. *Ibid.*, I, 44.

6. *Ibid.*

7. Thuc., I, 49; 50; 51. The Athenians at first sent ten ships under the command of Lacedaemonius, Diotimus and Proteas, with orders not to engage unless Corinth sailed against Corcyraean territory. Later, twenty more ships under Glaucon and Andocides were sent.

8. Leucas sent ten ships, Ambracia twenty seven, and Anactorium one against Corcyra. Cf. Thuc., I, 46. Previously, Leucas had sent ten ships and Ambracia eight with the Corinthian expedition against the Corcyraeans who were attacking Epidamnus. Cf. Thuc., I, 27.

9. Thuc., I, 56; Diod., XII, 34, 2.

10. Thuc., I, 56. The phrase *meta tauta euthys* in this passage does not necessarily eliminate the possibility of the delivery of the Athenian ultimatum as late as March, 432. Potidaea paid her tribute at this time as usual which may indicate that events had not yet reached the critical stage. We cannot be certain; the best that can be said is that the ultimatum was sent sometime during the winter of 433 or early spring of 432. For the use of *euthys* in Thucydides, cf. Gomme, *Commentary*, I, p. 199, where our phrase is regarded as "a possible expression, even though some months elapse."

11. Thuc., I, 56; 57. The rivalry between Perdiccas and Philip is suggested by Thucydides (II, 100, 3) and in the extant record of a treaty between Philip and Athens (*I.G.*, I², 53) which Schweigert ("Epigraphical Notes," *Hesperia*, VIII, 1939, pp. 170f.) dates in the year 433/2 B.C. For Philip's territory from the valley of the Axius river and to the east, cf. Gomme, *op. cit.*, I, pp. 202f., 212 and II, p. 248; in *A.T.L.*, III, Philip is mentioned as ruling in northern Macedonia (p. 317), and the year 434 B.C. is suggested as a probable date for his alliance with Athens (p. 319).

Derdas is described by the Scholiast on Thucydides as the son of Arrhidaeus and nephew of Perdiccas and Philip.

12. The number of generals is given as ten in the Ms. of Thucydides (I, 57, 6), but this cannot be correct. Four is the number adopted in place of ten in many texts. Two, however, with Archestratus as the third, is a more likely number and has been adopted by Wade-Gery (see review of Meritt's *Athenian Financial Documents of the Fifth Century* in *J.H.S.*, LIII, 1933, p. 135), following the suggestion of Woodward for *I.G.*, I², 296, where the first payments to the generals campaigning in the North are recorded; this is also considered as the more probable reading by Gomme, *op. cit.*, I, p. 209.

13. Thuc., I, 57. It is interesting to note that there is no implication in Thucydides of any Athenian garrison being stationed at Potidaea or in neighboring cities. Garrisons in the Athenian Empire may not be assumed except in strategic places or those subject to some existing threat, local or outside. See also Gomme, *op. cit.*, II, p. 34.

14. Thuc., I, 58.

15. *Ibid.*

16. August 8th-September 12th. The chronology adopted here and in the following pages for the period of 432-429 B.C. is that accepted by Robinson and Clement, *Excavations at Olynthus*, IX, pp. 142-47. The chronological problem of this period depends on the account of Thucydides and on the interpretation of *I.G.*, I², 296. Cf. Busolt, *Gr. Gesch.*, III, pp. 799ff.; Beloch, *Gr. Gesch.*, II², 2, pp. 219ff.; West, *Cl. Phil.*, X, 1915, pp. 34-53; *C.A.H.*, V, pp. 475f. In addition, the investigations of Kolbe, *Thukydides im Lichte der Urkunden*, pp. 15ff.; Merrit, *Ath. Financial Documents*, pp. 63-83; Wade-Gery, *J.H.S.*, LIII, 1933, pp. 135f.; Gomme, "*I.G.* i.² 296 and the Dates of Τὰ Ποτειδεατικά," *Cl. Rev.*, LV, 1941, pp. 59-67; *Commentary*, I, pp. 199ff., 209ff., 396, and especially 222-24 and 420-25.

Gomme in re-evaluating the evidence disagrees with the commonly accepted chronology and arrives (*Commentary*, pp. 424f.) at the following chronological sequence in reference to the "Potideatica" of Thucydides, I, 56-65:

Athenian demands on Potidaea, and Potidaea's delegations to Athens and Sparta, Jan. 433-32; sailing of Archestratus' expedition and the Potidaean revolt, mid-Apr.; sailing of Callias' expedition, ca. May 20; arrival of Aristeus at Potidaea, end of May; battle of Potidaea and beginning of the siege, mid-June; Phormio's expedition, Sept. or October 432-31; Theban attack on Plataea, beginning of March; Peloponnesian invasion of Attica, ca. May 20.

Gomme's arguments for these conclusions are very ingenious and stimulating, but not entirely convincing. Basically, they involve a number of chronological probabilities and necessitate a change in the manuscript reading. The manuscript change suggested is Thucydides, II, 2, 1, where it is stated that the Theban attack on Plataea took place in the sixth month after the battle of Potidaea. This attack is placed early in March shortly before the 8th, the date of the third new moon of 431 (p. 422), and it is claimed that the battle of Potidaea must have taken place after Sept. 12 of 432, since an earlier date in September would place it in the seventh month before March 7 (p. 422, n. 2). But the date for the Theban attack on Plataea cannot be established so precisely. In any case, Gomme is led to the conclusion that there is a numerical corruption in the manuscript reading (pp. 422f.), that is, *in the sixth month* should read *in the tenth month;* and the battle of Potidaea was therefore fought not later than the middle of June of 432. However, in view of the manuscript tradition and the lack of more definite evidence especially from epigraphical sources, it seems preferable to retain the generally accepted date.

More recently, Hammond (*A History of Greece to 322 B.C.*, Appendix 5, p. 660), commenting on the date of the Theban attack on Plataea, presents a convincing argument for a date late in March of 431 and places the date of the battle at Potidaea late in September of 432.

17. Thuc., I, 58. Corinth in 421 B.C. refused to give up her Chalcidic allies who had revolted with Potidaea at this time. Cf. *ibid.*, V, 30.

18. *Ibid.*, I, 58; Diod., XII, 34. For the extent of the original revolt see West, *Hist. Chalc. League*, pp. 17f. and n. 15; *A.T.L.*, III, p. 322; Gomme, *Commentary*, I, pp. 210ff.

19. Cf. Thuc., I, 56; Aristodemus, 18 in Jacoby, *F.G.H.*, 104 and in Hill, *Sources for Greek History*, p. 23.

20. Thuc., I, 59. Thucydides informs us (I, 57) that both Philip and Derdas rebelled against Perdiccas, and that the Athenians made an alliance with them.

The use of the perfect *esbeblekoton* in the passage (I, 59, 2) implies that some action by Philip and Derdas' brothers against Perdiccas was already in progress by the time of the arrival of Archestratus in Macedonian waters. Cf. C. D. Morris, *Thucydides, Book I* (Boston, 1888), note *ad loc.*; Gomme, *op. cit.*, I, p. 212.

21. Thuc., I, 60.

22. The problem has been fully discussed by Pelekides in *Epeteris Philosophikes Scholes*, VI, Thessalonica, 1950, pp. 1-36, and we are in general agreement with his arguments. As stated in Thuc., I, 60, Aristeus' forces arrived in the Thraceward region forty days after the revolt of Potidaea. Pelekides reasonably takes this indication of time to mean the duration of the entire task of the expedition—recruiting, preparation, and journey—rather than only the last part of it, which would have made the movement by land more probable. The statement of Thucydides, he remarks (p. 34), merely gives the date of the event, that is, the arrival of the army of Aristeus. Although ships are not indicated, this cannot be taken to mean that the Corinthians went to Potidaea by land. Thucydides' silence on this point, Pelekides explains (p. 36), is easily understood in view of Corinth's position as a sea-power, whereas it would not have been the case had the Corinthian expedition reached Potidaea by land.

Gomme (*op. cit.*, I, p. 213), however, feels that Aristeus arrived "almost certainly" by land after eluding the Athenian Archestratus at Pydna. He dismisses (p. 215) Classen's view that the last part of the journey was made by sea in order to avoid the Athenians at Pydna, since, had this been the case, "Thucydides' silence would be even stranger." But it could be maintained that, whether by sea or by land, there is no evidence for any Athenian attempt to intercept the movements of Aristeus.

23. According to Thucydides (I, 46), ninety Corinthian ships had taken part in the battle of Sybota.

24. Thuc., I, 65.

25. Diod., XII, 46.

26. Thuc., I, 61, 1-2. Diod., XII, 34. For the date in September/October, cf. Robinson and Clement, *op. cit.*, p. 145.

27. Thuc., I, 61, 3.

28. The text of Thucydides (I, 61, 3-4), is the object of a wide controversy concerning the movement of Callias from Pydna to the Chalcidic coast. For attempts to clarify the meaning, cf., among others, Gomme, *op. cit.*, I, pp. 215-18; "Notes on Thucydides," *Cl. Rev.*, N.S., I, 1951, pp. 137f.; Meritt, Wade-Gery, and McGregor, *A.T.L.*, especially vol. III, pp. 314-23; Pelekides, *loc. cit.*, pp. 36-47, with a good summary of the various arguments on pp. 38-43; Woodhead, "The Site of Brea: Thucydides I. 61. 4," *Cl. Q.*, N.S., II, 1952, pp. 57-62; Edson, "Strepsa (Thucydides, I. 61. 4)," *Cl. Phil.*, L, 1955, pp. 169-90.

29. For the arguments in favor of the interpretation given here, see my article, "Thucydides and the Expedition of Callias against Potidaea, 432 B.C.," *A.J.P.*, LXXXIII, 1962, pp. 265-87.

30. Woodhead, *loc. cit.*, has presented quite a convincing case for such a location for Brea.

31. Edson (*op. cit.*, pp. 171-73, 184, and notes) prefers a location for Strepsa near Therma and on or near the northern or northeastern shore of the Thermaic Gulf. This is in general agreement with the view adopted by the authors of *A.T.L.* (I, pp. 550ff. and map, where Strepsa is tentatively placed northwest of Therma; III, p. 220, n. 122 and pp. 314ff. with notes 62 and 64). For a location to the south of Therma, see Gomme, *Commentary*, I, p. 218; Pelekides, *loc. cit.*, p. 43 and map on p. 45; see also my article cited in n. 29, above.

32. Pausanias, mentioned here for the first time, is generally assumed to be one of Derdas' brothers, but is otherwise unidentifiable. The Scholiast on Thuc., I, 61,

4, comments that according to some Pausanias was the son of Derdas; according to others, his brother. Gomme (op. cit., I, p. 218) regards both of these suggestions as "probably only guesses" and is inclined to identify him as another member of the Macedonian royal house.

33. Thuc., I, 61, 5. The location of Gigonus is not exactly known except that it was to the northwest of, and not too far from, Potidaea. The city is mentioned by Herodotus (VII, 123) and by the Scholiast on Thucydides (ad loc.). Cf. West, Hist. Chalc. League, p. 34, n. 12; A.T.L., I, pp. 478, 539-41; Gomme, op. cit., p. 217; Edson, op. cit., p. 184 and n. 160.

34. Thuc., I, 62. Perhaps the forced alliance concluded at Pydna between Perdiccas and the Athenian generals was not meant to be kept by either party. With the Athenians out of his territory and with Philip and Pausanias, his enemies, now in the service of Athens, Perdiccas saw no reason to refrain from actively supporting his former allies in Chalcidice.

35. Thucydides (I, 63) gives the distance as being 60 stades from Potidaea. Strabo, VII, fr. 28, speaks of the distance between the two cities as being 70 stades.

36. Thuc., I, 62.

37. Ibid., I, 63, 1. Thucydides does not state whether Aristeus was on the left or the right wing. That he decided to force his way to Potidaea through the Athenian line, instead of attempting to reach Olynthus through hostile Macedonian cavalry, may suggest that he commanded the left wing on the western side of the isthmus. The phrase para ten chelen dia tes thalasses provides some evidence for the existence of a harbor here, if by chele we understand a claw-like projection of the end of the wall. Cf. also Gomme, op. cit., I, p. 219. That Potidaea must have had a western harbor is implied in Thuc., IV, 129.

38. Thuc., I, 63, 2.

39. Ibid., I, 63, 3; Diod., XII, 34, 4, speaks of the number of Potidaeans and allies killed as being more than 300.

Socrates is mentioned by Plato, Charmides, 153 A-C, as having taken part in this battle, and in the Symposium, 220 D-E, as having saved Alcibiades, wounded. In the Apology, 28 E, Socrates is represented as having fought in the battles of Potidaea, Amphipolis, and Delium. Cf. also, Epistolae Socraticae in Epistolographi Graeci (ed. Hercher), p. 612, and Diogenes Laertius, Socrates, II, 5, n. 7. Athenaeus, Deipnosophistae (ed. Meineke), 215d, e, 216b, c, e, refutes the testimony of Plato, but we cannot trust him. Cf. Clinton, Fasti Hellenici under the year 429 B.C.

40. Kaibel, Epigrammata Graeca ex Lapidibus Conlecta, no. 21; I.G., I², 945; Tod, Gr. Hist. Inscr., 59. It is an epitaph inscribed on a marble stele and was found on the site of the Athenian Academy; it is now in the British Museum (C.E. Newton, Ancient Greek Inscriptions in the Br. Mus., part I, 37). It is generally thought that originally there was a relief, now lost, above the epitaph, representing three soldiers (I.G., I², 945 notes; Tod, p. 128). This has been disproved by Professor Meritt who thinks the idea arose from a wrong association by Boeckh of two different drawings which appeared on the same page in Fauvel's notes. The top of the monument is smooth and no object was placed upon it. See reference to Professor Meritt's letter in J. H. Oliver's article, "The Monument with the Marathon Epigrams," Hesperia, V, 1936, p. 134. Below the epitaph in another piece, now lost, the names of Callias and the 150 Athenians who fell in the engagement must have been inscribed. The epitaph is in elegiac meter and has twelve lines. According to Tod (p. 128), it is composed of three epigrams of four lines each, representing those selected after a competition. For the latest restoration of the epitaph see Tod, op. cit., no. 59.

Farnell (Greek Hero Cults, p. 398) considers the inscription to be the first monument containing any eschatological idea, and refers to the first two lines of the second epigram. At the same time, he doubts whether it "has any religious eschatological value"; he would rather interpret it as expressing "the quasi-physical perception that the soul escaped like a breath into the upper air." A fuller discussion of the eschatological significance of the Potidaean epigrams and their association with religious conceptions common in Orphism and Pythagorianism may be found in R. Mondolfo's excellent treatise on *L'Infinito nel Pensiero dei Greci* (Florence, 1934), p. 218, note 3; p. 219 and note 2; p. 318 and notes 1, 2, and 3; p. 322, and notes 1, 2, and 3.

For the forms of public epitaphs in the fifth century and for a similarity of feeling between the Potidaean epigrams and those on the battle of Marathon see F. Jacoby's article, "Some Athenian Epigrams from the Persian Wars," *Hesperia*, XIV, 1945, no. 3, pp. 167-74 and notes 37, 60, and 67.

A similarity between the order of ideas in the entire inscription and the Funeral Speech of Pericles, as given in Thucydides, II, 35ff., has been pointed out by Powell in a paper referred to in *Cl. Rev.*, XXI, 1907, pp. 61f. It is not likely, however, that our inscription is a memorial of the subsequent siege of Potidaea, as Gomme in his *Commentary*, I, p. 220, is inclined to suggest.

41. Thuc., I, 64.

42. *Ibid.* For the presence of Phormio at Potidaea, cf. Diod., XII, 37, 1; Isocr., XVI, 29; Polyaen., III, 4, 1. For the date of his expedition, cf. Robinson and Clement, *op. cit.*, p. 146; *C.A.H.*, V, p. 475.

43. Thuc., I, 65.

44. *Ibid.* It was about this time, after the blockade of Potidaea was completed, that the original number of seventy ships was reduced to thirty. Thuc., III, 17. Cf. West, *Hist. Chal. League*, p. 36 and note 19.

45. Thuc., I, 65. The Sermylians evidently had remained loyal to Athens and had shown no interest in the revolt.

46. *Ibid.*, I, 66; 67.

47. *Ibid.*, I, 67.

48. *Ibid.*, I, 67-71, especially 71; cf. also I, 58. In their speech before the Spartan Assembly the Corinthians refer to Potidaea (*ibid.*, I, 68, 4) as the most strategic place for operations in the Thraceward region.

49. *Ibid.*, I, 72-78.

50. *Ibid.*, I, 79-88.

51. *Ibid.*, I, 87; 119.

52. *Ibid.*, I, 119; 125; II, 2.

53. *Ibid.*, I, 126, first Spartan embassy; I, 139, second and third embassies. The second embassy specifically demanded that the Athenians raise the siege of Potidaea, revoke the decree against Megara, and give liberty to Aegina.

54. *Ibid.*, II, 23; 25; 26.

55. *Ibid.*, II, 29.

56. *Ibid.* Whether Therma belonged to Perdiccas when Archestratus captured it (Thuc., I, 61, 2) is a disputed point. The authors of *A.T.L.* (I, p. 546 and note 3; III, note 123 on pp. 220f.; p. 322 with note 91) equate Therma (Therme) with the Serme of the tribute lists. Edson (*Cl. Phil.*, XLII, 1947, pp. 100-104) and Gomme (*op. cit.*, I, p. 91) object to this equation and understand Thucydides' phrase (II, 29, 6), "Therma to be restored," to imply that originally the city belonged to Perdiccas and was not one of the tributary allies of Athens.

57. Thuc., II, 29; 95; Aristoph., *Acharn.*, 141ff. Cf. also, Robinson and Clement, *op. cit.*, p. 146 and note 120.

58. Thuc., II, 29; 95.

59. *Ibid.*, II, 58.

60. *Ibid.*, II, 31. It is stated parenthetically that the number of Athenian troops at Potidaea at this time was 3000.

61. *Ibid.*, II, 58. Cf. West, *Hist. Chal. League*, p. 37 and note 28.

62. Thuc., II, 58, 1. In a previous passage (II, 56, 1-2), Thucydides mentions that the expedition of Pericles around Peloponnesus included 100 ships with 4000 hoplites on board, 300 cavalry in horse transports, and 50 Chian and Lesbian vessels. The passage cited here would suggest that this entire force under Pericles was now placed under the command of his colleagues, Hagnon and Cleopompus; but later, in the same paragraph (58, 3), only 4000 hoplites and an unspecified number of ships are mentioned under Hagnon. This seems to be more likely.

63. Thuc., II, 58; Diod., XII, 46.

64. Thuc., *loc. cit.;* Diod., *loc. cit.* According to Diodorus more than 1000 talents had been spent by this time in the siege, and because of the size of the sum and the ill feeling of the Athenians toward the Potidaeans (they were the first to revolt), Hagnon was afraid to raise the siege.

65. Thuc., II, 67, 1; Herod., VII, 137, 2-3.

66. Thuc., *loc. cit.*

67. *Ibid.*

68. Thuc., II, 67, 2-4.

69. *Ibid.,* II, 70.

70. *Ibid.;* Diod., XII, 46. Isocrates (XV, 113), in referring to the capture of Potidaea by Timotheus (364/3 B.C.) financed by the general himself, mentions that the 432-429 siege cost Athens 2,400 talents. According to Diodorus (XII, 46) more than 1,000 talents had already been spent by the time Hagnon and Cleopompus were besieging the town. In another passage (XII, 40) the same author says that 4,000 talents had been spent for the building of Propylaea and the siege of Potidaea. The passage of Thucydides cited above places the expenses of the siege at 2,000 talents. In another passage (III, 17), Thucydides mentions that each soldier received two drachmas a day, one for himself and one for his servant. There is also an inscription (*I.G.,* I², 296 and 309a) which records the money spent by the Athenians during the year 432/1. For this inscription cf. *S.E.G.,* X, 223; Hill, *Sources for Greek History,* pp. 312f.; Meritt, *Ath. Fin. Doc.,* pp. 68-83; Kolbe, *Thukydides im Lichte der Urkunden,* pp. 1-49; Robinson and Clement, *Excav. at Olynthus,* IX, pp. 143f.

Modern calculations based on the above data have not given us any more definite answer as to the expenses of the siege. Cf. Cavaignac, *Le Trésor d' Athènes de 480 à 404,* pp. 108, 121; Francotte, *Les Finances des Cités Gr.,* p. 169; Ferguson, *The Treasuries of Athena,* pp. 160, 167; Andreades, *A History of Gr. Public Fin.,* I, pp. 221f.; *A.T.L.,* I, p. 597; II, pp. 96, 106; III, pp. 123f., 323, 340; Gomme, *op. cit.,* II, pp. 20f., 144f.

71. Thuc., II, 70; Diod., XII, 46.

72. Thuc., II, 70. This is an indication of the strong determination of the Athenians to capture Potidaea and explains their persistent efforts to realize that aim. Strict orders must have been given to the generals to continue the siege. Cf. Diodorus, XII, 46, where Hagnon is afraid to raise the siege because of the large sum already spent and the ill feeling of the Athenians toward the Potidaeans.

Though there is no definite evidence that the generals received bribes from the Potidaeans or of an actual accusation to that effect, an echo of this may be found in Aristophanes, *Knights,* 438-9, where the comedian charges Cleon with receiving ten talents from Potidaea. There is no mention in the sources that Cleon was connected with the generals when Potidaea capitulated. On the contrary, one would expect a man like Cleon to seize such an opportunity to degrade the generals by accusing them of bribery (cf. Roger, *The Comedies of Aristophanes,* note *ad loc.*). The *Knights* was produced in 424 B.C., five years after the fall of Potidaea, and Aristophanes, in his zeal to ridicule Cleon, did not bother to verify his facts. In verse 834 of the same play Cleon is charged with having received bribes from Mytilene in 428/7. This charge is more appropriate, since a decree, revoked soon afterwards, was passed upon the motion of Cleon to put to death the instigators of the revolt in that island.

For bribery being a common charge against all demagogues, see Aristoph., *Wasps*, 671.

73. Thuc., II, 79. Though not mentioned by name, Xenophon's two colleagues probably are with him in the operations against Spartolus. Diodorus, XII, 47, refers to Xenophon and Phanomachus, but omits Hestiodorus. Cf. Gomme, *op. cit.*, II, pp. 203f.

74. Thuc., II, 70, 4.

75. Diod., XII, 46.

76. *I.G.*, I, 340; *I.G.*, I² 397; Ditt., *Syll.³*, 74; Michel, *R.I.G.*, 1035; Hicks, 45; Hicks and Hill, 59; Lolling, *Catal.*, 98; Pittakis, *Eph.*, 1082; Rangabé 370; Ussing, *Inscr. Gr. Ined.*, 68; Tod, *Gr. Hist. Inscr.*, 60; etc. The inscription is not stoichedon as has generally been said. Cf. Austin, *The Stoichedon Style*, p. 64, n.

77. Cf., among others, *A.T.L.*, III, p. 285, where apoikoi and epoikoi are regarded as the same, "differing only in meaning as do our words 'emigrant' and 'immigrant'."

78. Ehrenberg, *Cl. Phil.*, XLVII, 1952, pp. 145ff., especially in reference to the epoikoi at Aegina; Walker, *C.A.H.*, V, pp. 96f., speaks of colonies with apoikoi or epoikoi (Potidaea included) as cleruchies. The fact that the ancient writers also confused these terms simply indicates how loosely the terms came to be used after their official or technical meaning lost its original significance. For instance, Demosthenes (VI, 20 and elsewhere) refers to the cleruchs of 362/1 B.C. at Potidaea as apoikoi, while Plutarch (*Per.*, 34, 2) speaks of the epoikoi at Aegina (431 B.C.) as cleruchs.

79. Tod, *op cit.*, 44, commentary on lines 26, 28; II, 146, commentary, where the epoikoi are described as being sent "to supplement the city's depleted population." Ehrenberg, *op. cit.*, p. 144, elaborating on Tod's statement, speaks of the settlers as additional colonists. For still another explanation, cf. Gomme's remark (*Commentary*, II, p. 87) in reference to the epoikoi at Aegina, that the term is "perhaps here used . . . particularly to mean 'settlers who must keep watch'."

80. For the inscription, see also *A.T.L.*, II, D21, and below, n. 95.

81. The question of Athenian colonies and cleruchies has been discussed extensively by a number of eminent scholars. More recently the studies of Ehrenberg (*Aspects of the Ancient World*, ch. IX, pp. 116-43; "Thucydides and Athenian Colonization," *Cl. Phil.*, XLVII, 1952, pp. 143-49); and of the authors of *A.T.L.* (especially, vol. III, pp. 284-97) have greatly added to the clarification of certain points, but a good deal is still open to debate and further elucidation.

82. The term cleruchy is a recognized form, while apoecy has been adopted by Ehrenberg (*Aspects, loc. cit.*); epoecy may justifiably be introduced, for part of the difficulty in discussing the types of settlements is to be found in the general practice of using the same terms in describing different things. It should be added, however, that the form *epoikia* (epoecy) does not appear in Greek, but instead *apoikia* was used also for settlements with epoikoi; but this must not obscure the specific status of a settlement with epoikoi, as the Locrian inscription (Tod, I², 24) illustrates.

Ehrenberg (*op. cit.*, p. 34) distinguishes four types of Athenian colonies: the apoecy as a normal colony and as a dependent one within the Empire, the cleruchy as a municipal community and as a garrison. This is reasonable enough, but had Ehrenberg recognized the status of an epoecy as an intermediate form with features of both apoecy and a cleruchy, he would have seen the distinctions among the various types more accurately, and would not have classified the epoikoi at Potidaea simply as additional colonists (*Cl. Phil.*, XLVII, 1952, p. 144), those of Aegina as cleruchs (pp. 146, 148), and later (p. 148), in reference to Thucydides, VII, 57, would not have described the settlements of both Aegina and Hestiaea as "non-tributary" *apoikiai* or "independent cleruchies."

83. Cf. *A.T.L.*, III, p. 285. In some cases, a municipal organization in a cleruchy can be assumed, but this implied no change in the Athenian status of its members. Cf. Ehrenberg, *Aspects*, p. 134, where this type of cleruchy is described as nearer to the apoecy.

84. The Athenian settlers at Aegina are twice described by Thucydides (II, 27, 1; VIII, 69, 3) as epoikoi. In references to Potidaea, the word epoikoi appears once in Thucydides (II, 70, 4) and twice on Attic inscriptions (see above, pp. 75 and 78 with note 95). Other tributary allies who suffered a similar fate, particularly Hestiaea in Euboea (Thuc., I, 114, 3) and Scione in Pallene (*idem*, V, 32, 1), may have received epoikoi type of settlers and not apoikoi or klerouchoi, as is generally thought. The question regarding the type of Athenian settlement at Hestiaea is especially critical in view of the apparently conflicting epigraphical and literary evidence. The epigraphical record suggests that the Hestiaeans enjoyed municipal organization, but retained features of Athenian citizenship (*I.G.*, I², 40-42). Thucydides (VII, 57, 2), however, describes the Hestiaeans as apoikoi and groups them with the Aeginitans whom he has already mentioned as epoikoi.

Gomme (*Commentary*, I, pp. 345ff.), emphasizing the epigraphical record, regards Hestiaea as a cleruchy, while the authors of *A.T.L.* (III, pp. 288ff.), with emphasis on Thucydides (VII, 57, 2), consider it a colony (apoecy). Ehrenberg (*Cl. Phil.*, XLVII, 1952, pp. 145ff.), attempting to reconcile the epigraphical record with the evidence of Thucydides, recognizes (p. 146) that Hestiaea has features of both an independent apoecy and a cleruchy, but finally concludes (p. 148) that "the odds are strongly in favor of a cleruchy." Cf. also the conclusion of Chambers to the effect "that, in the present state of the evidence, it is better to regard it as a cleruchy" (*Studies in the Veracity of Thucydides*, Diss., 1954, as reported in *Harvard Studies in Cl. Phil.*, LXII, 1957, p. 142).

Reconciliation of the evidence and of the views resulting from it seems impossible unless the epoikoi type of settlement is recognized as an intermediate stage often associated, as we have seen, with an independent type of colony (apoikia) which, at the same time, displays the characteristics of a cleruchy. The position of Hestiaea in the text of Thucydides (VII, 57, 2) is parallel to that of Aegina which had received epoikoi type of settlers; the term apoikoi is used, apparently in its general sense, for the settlers of both places. This is not inconsistent with the special status of the term epoikoi. If the form apoikia could be used for epoikoi type of settlers also (as the Locrian inscription mentioned in note 82, above, illustrates), why not the term apoikoi for epoikoi? The Athenians knew the exact status of their settlers at both Aegina and Hestiaea. For an apoikia with epoikoi type of settlers, see also the Athenian decree of 325/4 B.C. in connection with the establishment of a colony in the Adriatic (*I.G.*, II², 1629; Tod, *op. cit.*, II, no. 200).

85. This feature of the epoecy is to be found also in what Ehrenberg (*Aspects*, p. 133) calls independent or municipal cleruchy. Though Ehrenberg does not recognize the epoecy as a distinct type of settlement, yet he realizes the need of accepting "several intermediary forms between the pure cleruchy and the pure apoecy.'

For Athenian revenue from the epoikoi at Aegina and Potidaea, cf. *A.T.L.*, III, pp. 342ff.

86. Arist., *Oecon.*, II, 2, 5.

87. For the introduction, general characteristics and nature of the eisphora, see Andreades, *History of Gr. Public Finance*, I (tr. by Brown), pp. 326-34; Oliver, *T.A.P.A.*, LXVI, 1935, pp. 196-98; Cary, *J.H.S.*, XLV, 1925, pp. 243-50; Busolt-Swoboda, *Griechische Staatskunde*, II (Munich, 1926), pp. 1223-27; W. Schwan in *Rhein. Mus.*, LXXXII, 1933, pp. 247-84; *A.T.L.*, III, pp. 337 note 49, 343 note 84,

and 345; Gomme, *Commentary*, II, pp. 32-33, 278-79; Meritt, "Indirect Tradition in Thucydides," *Hesperia*, XXIII, 1954, pp. 223-25.

According to Thucydides (III, 19, 1), the eisphora was levied at Athens for the first time in 428 B.C. By the time of the production of the *Knights* of Aristophanes (424 B.C.), the eisphora is regarded as a common thing (lines 774-78, 921). Meritt is probably right in believing that the need of the eisphora was removed with the high assessment of 425 B.C. (*op. cit.*, p. 223).

88. Cf. D. M. Robinson, "Inscriptions from Macedonia, 1938," *T.A.P.A.*, LXIX, 1938, pp. 58f. It is worth noting that Hagios Mamas still belongs to the district of Nea Potidaea.

Another Attic inscription on a bronze dicast's ticket, found during the 1938 excavations at Olynthus, mentions the deme of Phlya. But this is dated by Robinson in the first half of the fourth century and may be connected with a member of the Athenian cleruchy at Potidaea (362/1 B.C.) or with an Athenian visitor at Olynthus.

89. Thuc., II, 79. Xenophon was one of the generals when Potidaea capitulated (II, 70).

90. *Ibid.*, II, 79.

91. *Ibid.*, II, 80; 81.

92. Ditt., *Syll.*[3], 75; *I.G.*, I[2], 57; Hicks and Hill, 60; Michel, 74; Kahrstedt, *Klio*, XXXIII, 1940, p. 9; Tod, *J.H.S.*, LXV, 1945, pp. 65, 67 and *Gr. Hist. Inscr.*, I[2] no. 61; Meritt, *A.J.P.*, LXIX, 1948, p. 70, and for a more recent restoration and additional bibliography, cf. *A.T.L.*, II, 1949, pp. 48f. and photograph on pl. I.

93. A. B. West gives effective arguments for dating this decree in the spring of 429 B.C., after the capture of Potidaea (*A.J.A.*, XXIX, 1925, pp. 440ff.). Cf. Tod, *op. cit.*, 61; Meritt, *Ath. Fin. Docum.*, pp. 22f.

The authors of *A.T.L.* (III, p. 136 and note 11), in reply to West's arguments, take the clause referring to the Athenian soldiers in Potidaea "to mean the army besieging Poteidaia," which would date the decree before the capture of the city in the winter of 430/29; otherwise, they maintain, it would be difficult to understand the phrase "if the Athenian colony were in existence." But the phrase may easily be understood once we reflect that some time must have elapsed between Potidaea's capitulation and the arrival of the Athenian epoikoi; besides, with Potidaea as the base of Athenian operations in Chalcidice, the phrase, "the soldiers in Potidaea," could be justified even after the establishment of the Athenian settlers there.

94. Lines 29-32 provide that henceforth the people of Methone are to pay only the amount due to the goddess, the *aparche*, that is, a sixtieth of the total amount.

95. The inscription is stoichedon with 50 letters to the line. Lines 8-13 and 9-22 refer to the Athenian epoikoi at Potidaea; *A.T.L.*, II, p. 75.

96. For the decree cf. also *S.E.G.*, X, 1949, 67; J. and L. Robert, *R.E.G.*, LVII, 1944, pp. 191f.; Meritt, *Hesperia*, XIII, 1944, pp. 211-29; and, for additional references, *A.T.L.*, II, p. 75.

97. *I.G.*, I[2], 949, l. 40.

98. Simonides as commander was sent with Athenian forces and allied troops and captured the city of Eion, a colony of Mende. Cf. Thuc., IV, 7.

99. Thuc., IV, 78-81; cf. West, *Hist. Chal. League*, p. 46, note. 11.

100. Thuc., IV, 88.

101. *Ibid.*, IV, 106; IV, 109. This happened in the winter of 424/3 B.C.

102. *Ibid.*, IV, 110-16.

103. *Ibid.*, IV, 116.

104. *Ibid.*, IV, 117-19. Cf. West, *op. cit.*, p. 56.

105. Thuc., IV, 120.

106. *Ibid.*, IV, 122, 6.

107. *Ibid.*, IV, 120-21.

108. *Ibid.*, IV, 121.

109. *Ibid.*, IV, 123.

110. Aristonymus for the Athenians and Athenaeus for the Lacedaemonians were sent to announce the news of the armistice. All cities in Thrace had accepted except Scione. Thuc., IV, 122.

111. *Ibid.*, IV, 123.

112. *Ibid.*

113. *Ibid.*, IV, 129. Their forces were composed of 50 ships, of which 10 were Chian, 1000 hoplites, 600 archers and, in addition, 1000 Thracian mercenaries and some targeteers from their allies in that region. Professor Meritt assumes that Nicias was already at Potidaea when he was ordered to proceed against Mende and Scione. (*Ath. Fin. Docum.*, p. 134.)

114. Thuc., IV, 129. Poseidonium has been assumed by some to be a temple of Poseidon; cf. E. F. Poppo's edition of Thucydides, note *ad loc.*, and also Crawley, *Thucydides Peloponnesian War*. But for the Poseidium promontory, cf. Leake, *Travels in Northern Greece*, III, p. 157. Possibly the word refers to the promontory with a temple of Poseidon on it.

115. Thuc., IV, 130.

116. *Ibid.*, IV, 133. For the location of both Mende and Scione see Meritt's article, "Scione, Mende, and Torone," *A.J.A.*, XXVII, 1923, pp. 447ff.

117. Thuc., IV, 124; 129.

118. *Ibid.*, IV, 135.

119. *Hist. of Gr.*, IV, p. 228.

120. This we must understand by the word *diakenon* in Thucydides, *loc. cit.*

121. Another practice of guarding the walls seems to have been for the officer in charge of the sentinels to go on rounds with a bell. Cf. Aristoph., *Av.*, 842.

122. In the list of Athenian forces at Syracuse, Thucydides (VII, 57) includes the epoikoi of Aegina, but not those of Potidaea.

CHAPTER VII

FROM THE END OF THE PELOPONNESIAN WAR TO THE FOUNDING OF CASSANDREIA

1. Xen., *Hell.*, II, ii, 2; Plut., *Lys.*, 13.

2. Xen., *Hell.*, II, ii, 5-7.

3. *Ibid.*

4. Xen., *Hell.*, II, ii, 9. See also Plut., *Lys.*, 14, for the repatriation of the Aeginetans, Melians, and Scionaeans by Lysander after he expelled the Athenians from these places.

5. Xen., *Hell.*, III, v, 12-13; Diod., XIV, 13; Plut., *Lys.*, 13, 5. Cornelius Nepos (*Liber de Excellentibus Ducibus Exterarum Gentium*, VI, *Lysander*, 1 and 2) presents similar information.

6. *Op. cit.*, pp. 95f. and n. 46 where reference is given to Ed. Meyer's *Theopomp's Hellenika* (Halle, 1909), pp. 266ff.

7. Xen., *Hell.*, III, iv, 2. According to Xenophon, one of Lysander's motives in joining the expedition of King Agesilaus against Persia in 396 B.C. was to use the King's influence in re-establishing the decarchies. Cf. also *ibid.*, III, iv, 7-10, where Lysander's motive is finally exposed. For a re-evaluation of Lysander's part in the history of this period, cf. Smith's article, "Lysander and the Spartan Empire," *Cl. Phil.*, XLIII, 1948, pp. 145-56. Smith maintains that the year 403 B.C. does not represent "a grand political defeat for Lysander" and that the ephors' decree at the time regarding the decarchies applied primarily, if not exclusively, to cities in Asia Minor.

8. Dem., XVIII, 96.

9. Cf. *C.A.H.*, VI (1953), p. 44.

10. Cf. Isaeus, V, 46; Diod., XIV, 82; Jebb, *Attic Orators*, II, pp. 350f.; West, *op. cit.*, p. 98.

11. Ditt., *Syll.*³, 135; Tod, *Gr. Hist. Inscr.*, II, 111; Geyer, *Makedonien bis zur Thronbesteigung Philipps II*, pp. 112ff.; West, *op. cit.*, pp. 99-102; Gude, *op cit.*, pp. 24f., 101; Robinson and Clement, *op cit.*, pp. 154f. The text of the treaty is recorded on the upper part of a marble stele reported to have been found near Olynthus and given in 1844 along with a base from a grave at Potidaea to the Austrian government by its consul at Thessalonica. Cf. especially Robinson and Clement, p. 155, note 154 and Tod, p. 30. The treaty is generally dated near the beginning of the reign of Amyntas which is placed by some in the year 389 B.C. (Gude, p. 24) and by others about 393 B.C. (Tod, pp. 32f.).

12. Ditt., *op. cit.*, 11. 19-24.

13. Cf. West, *op. cit.*, p. 98; Kahrstedt, "Chalcidic Studies," *A.J.P.*, LVII, 1936, p. 438.

14. Xen., *Hell.*, V, ii, 12; 15; cf. V, ii, 24.

15. *Ibid.*, V, ii, 12.

16. *Ibid.*, V, ii, 15.

17. *Ibid.*, V, ii, 24. Cf. West, *op. cit.*, p. 98; Kahrstedt, *op. cit.*, p. 438; Robinson and Clement, *Excavations at Olynthus*, IX, p. 306; Hampl, "Olynth und der Chalkidische Staat," *Hermes*, LXX, 1935, p. 182.

For an account of the theories concerning the date of the formation of the Chalcidic League, see Gude, *A History of Olynthus*, pp. 18-23. Gude argues for the year 382 B.C. A more recent account, with a complete examination of the evidence both literary and numismatic, is given by Robinson and Clement, *op. cit.*, pp. 117-29. Here the arguments of Gude are strongly refuted and the formation of the league is connected with the alliance of the Potidaeans, the Bottiaeans, and the Chalcidians and their revolt against Athens in 432 B.C. Cf. also, *ibid.*, p. 142.

18. Xen., *Hell.*, V, ii, 23.

19. *Ibid.*, V, ii, 24. Diod., XV, 19; Isocr., IV, 126. The forces of Eudamidas are placed at 3000 by Diodorus (XV, 20). Cf. West, *op. cit.*, p. 105; Underhill, *Chronological Summary*, p. XCI. For the chronology of this war cf. also Meyer, *G.d.A.*, V, 894 A.

20. Xen., *Hell.*, V, ii, 24. There is no reason to believe with West (*op. cit.*, p. 105) that the submission of Potidaea to Eudamidas was brought about by an anti-Chalcidian party within the town which was strong enough to open the city's gates to him. Such a view, though not impossible, is not borne out by any evidence. We are inclined to believe that the alliance of the city with the Chalcidians may have been effected mainly because of fear of future attack upon the town. Eudamidas' presence is Potidaea's opportunity to break the alliance.

21. Xen., *Hell.*, V, ii, 40.

22. *Ibid.*, V, ii, 39. We might expect that Teleutias, upon his arrival at Potidaea, was joined by Eudamidas and his forces. This may at least be suggested by the word *syntaxamenos*, used in Xenophon's account. Although this word does usually mean to marshal soldiers for battle, we still might conclude that the soldiers of Eudamidas were included. Diodorus (XV, 21) definitely states that Teleutias received the soldiers of Eudamidas also.

23. For the account of this battle cf. Xen., *Hell.*, V, iii, 3-6; also Diod., XV, 21, who gives the number of Lacedaemonians killed as more than 1200.

24. Besides the Spartan and allied troops, volunteers from Thessaly, Amyntas, and Derdas joined him.

25. Diod., XV, 22. The soldiers who had escaped to Potidaea and the surrounding area reunited with the new forces.

26. Xen., *Hell.*, V, iii, 19; Diod., XV, 23.

27. Xen., *op. cit.*, V, iii, 26; Diod., *loc. cit.*

28. West, *op cit.*, p. 228; Kahrstedt, *op. cit.*, p. 443; M. Cary in *C.A.H.*, VI, p. 105. The passages usually quoted are Dem., II, 14; Isocr., XV, 113; Dein., I, 14; Polyaen., III, 10, 15. Epigraphical evidence for the campaigns, *I.G.*, II², 110; Ditt.³, 174. For Timotheus' campaigns in the North cf. also Papastavru, *Amphipolis* (*Klio*, Beiheft, XXXVII, 1936), pp. 27ff.

29. Cf. literary references on note above.

30. Cf. Gude, *A History of Olynthus*, pp. 31f. and note 32.

31. "Chalcidic Studies," *A.J.P.*, LVII, 1936, p. 443.

32. Isocr., XV, 113. Cf. also with 108, where there is no indication of any alliance.

33. Dein., I, 14.

34. Dem., II, 14. Cf. also Diodorus' account, XV, 81.

35. Isocr., XV, 108, 113; Dein., I, 14; Diod., XV, 81; Polyaen., III, 10, 15. Some of the other cities recovered by Timotheus were Methone, Torone and Pydna.

36. Diod., XV, 81.

37. Aesch., II, 30; Arist., *Rhet.*, II, 3, 13. For the chronology see West, *op. cit.*, p. 113 and note 31; Gude, *op. cit.*, p. 32 and note 33.

38. Dem., VI, 20, Schol.; VII, 10; Diod., XVI, 8; Hegesippus, *De Hal.*, 10. On Athenian cleruchies, cf. M. Wagner, *Zur Geschichte der attischen Kleruchien* (Diss.), Tübingen, 1914; Meyer, *Forschungen zur alten Geschichte*, II, pp. 182f.; *ibid.*, *G.d.A.*, IV, pp. 19f.; A. Boeckh, *Staatshaushaltung d. Athener³*, I, pp. 499ff.; *ibid.*, II, pp. 100ff.; P. Foucart, *Mém. acad. inscr.*, Sér. I, vol. IX, 1878. See also above, pp. 75f. and notes.

39. Ditt.³, 180; *I.G.*, II², 114; Michel, *R.I.G.*, 1453; Tod, II, 146. Perhaps, the three fragments of Pentelic marble (*I.G.*, II, 2, 960) found in the Acropolis and containing names of cleruchs may refer to the cleruchy sent to Potidaea at this time instead of to the one sent to Samos a few years before (365 B.C.). For the first fragment see also Roberts and Gardner, *An Introduction to Greek Epigraphy*, Part II, *The Inscriptions of Attica* (Cambridge, 1905), p. 413.

40. According to M. Cary in *C.A.H.*, VI, p. 106, the establishment of Athenian cleruchies at Samos (365 B.C.) and at Potidaea (361 B.C.) was contrary to the spirit of the Second Athenian Confederacy, but not contrary to the letter, since both places were not formally enrolled members. Tod, *Gr. Hist. Inscr.*, II, 146, commentary, agrees with Cary on this point.

41. Cf. Cloché, *La Politique Étrangère d' Athènes, de 404 à 338 avant J.-C.*, p. 130.

42. Dem., II, 7.

43. For the decree see *I.G.*, II², 118.

44. Diod., XVI, 8, 4 refers to them as "the Athenian garrison"; also, Ioannis Sardianus, *Commentarium in Aphonii Progymnasmata* (*Rhetores Graeci*, XV, ed. H. Rabe, Biblio. Teubner), ix. He follows Diodorus.

45. *Excavations at Olynthus*, X, pp. 500f., notes 59-61, and pl. CLXIV. In commenting on the dicast's ticket, Robinson remarks that he knows "only two other such tablets or tesserae found outside of Attica" (p. 500) and that this is the "only Athenian one so far outside of Attica, which gives an Athenian deme name" (p. 501). Cf. also his remarks in *T.A.P.A.*, LXIX, 1938, pp. 56f.

No other name can be connected with Potidaea's history during this period except that of Callicrates who was appointed thearodocus, a host at Potidaea to theoroi from Epidaurus, sometime after 365 B.C. Theoroi were sent by Epidaurus to different cities during the reign of Perdiccas III, 365-359 B.C., to collect money for the building and decoration of the Asclepieum. Cf. *I.G.*, IV², I, 94, 1b, line 12.

46. Dem., I, 9, 12; XX, 63; Diod., XXI, 8. For a detailed account of the activity of Philip during this period, cf. Cloché, "Philippe II, roi de Macédoine, de 359 à 351 avant J.-C.," *Etudes Classiques*, XVIII, 1951, pp. 403-09.

47. We now have an epigraphical record of this alliance. An inscription bearing a record of this treaty was found near Olynthus during the 1934 campaign. D. M. Robinson has published the treaty in the *T.A.P.A.*, LXV, 1934, pp. 103-22, with full commentary, and dated it in the year 357 B.C., just before the capture of Potidaea. For literary sources for the alliance, cf. Dem., II, 6f.; VI, 20; XXIII, 108; Diod., XVI, 8; Liban. on Dem., I; Scala, *Staatsverträge*, no. 185. Cf. also Segre, "Il Trattato tra Filippo e i Calcidesi," in *Riv. di Filol.*, XIII, 1935, pp. 497-502.

48. Cf. West, *op. cit.*, p. 119.

49. Diod., XVI, 8, 3.

50. Dem., VII, 10. It is not certain whether the statement of Demosthenes refers to a special alliance of the Athenians at Potidaea with Philip or a separate clause in the existing treaty between him and Athens. Again, it is not easy to explain the reference of the word *oikousin* in the passage. Does it point to the inhabitants of Potidaea in general or only to the Athenian cleruchs? The former seems to be more likely, and thus the passage of Demosthenes may be interpreted to mean that an alliance was sworn by Philip and the inhabitants of Potidaea in general. Naturally, then, the Athenian cleruchs were regarded as allies.

51. Dem., II, 7; Livy, XLIV, 11; Plut., *Alex*, 3. Soon after Philip had captured Potidaea three messages were reported to him, the victory of Parmenio over the Illyrians, the victory of his racehorse at the Olympic games, and the birth of Alexander. Cf. Robinson, *op. cit.*, p. 106; Cloché, *La Polit. Étrang. d'Athènes de 404 à 338 avant J.-C.*, p. 155; West, *op. cit.*, p. 119.

52. Dem., IV, 35; IV, 4f.; I, 9. Cf. also, Cloché, *loc. cit.; idem, Démosthènes*, p. 15: The Athenian fleet engaged with the revolt of the islands off Asia Minor arrived too late to save Potidaea, as it also did in the case of Pydna. Cf. also, West, *loc. cit.*

53. Dem., XX, 61.

54. *Ibid.*, IX, 26. For modern authorities who have treated the subject cf. Perdrizet in *B.C.H.*, XXI, 1897, pp. 117f.; Beloch, *Gr. Gesch.*, 2nd ed., III, p. 230; Schaefer, *Demosthenes und seine Zeit*, II², pp. 24-25; Gude, *op. cit.*, p. 76; West, *op. cit.*, p. 131, note 37; Hampl, "Olynth und der Chalkidische Staat," *Hermes*, LXX, 1935, pp. 176-96; Robinson and Clement, *Excavations at Olynthus*, IX, pp. 306f., and note 254.

55. Dem., VI, 20; VII, 9, 10, 13; VIII, 62, 65.

56. *Ibid.*, IX, 26.

57. *Ibid.*, XX, 61; Cf. XXIII, 107 and 116. The speech is dated in 352 B.C.; in 107, it is stated that Philip could have kept Potidaea if he had wanted to, but instead gave her to the Olynthians as a present.

58. Jacoby, *F. Gr. Hist.*, II, B, fr. 57, p. 657.

59. Diod., XVI, 8, 5.

60. *Ibid.*, XIX, 52, 2.

61. Lib., VIII, pp. 607ff. (ed. R. Foerster, Leipzig, 1915).

62. Suidas, v. *Karanos*.

63. Paus., V, 23.

64. On Dem., VI, 20 (ed. Sauppius, Scholion, p. 70b).

65. Robinson and Clement hold the same interpretation on this point in *Olynthus*, IX, p. 307, n. 254.

66. *Gr. Gesch.*, III², 1, p. 230 and n. 3.

67. *Demosthenes und seine Zeit*, II², pp. 24-25 and n. on page 25.

68. *Hist. Chal. League*, p. 131, n. 37. Potidaea, having been captured by Philip, was "handed over to the Chalcidians after it had been destroyed. . ."

69. Pydna and Potidaea paid allegiance to Philip after the capture of Olynthus. Cf. Jaeger, *Demosthenes*, p. 118. In the article on Potidaea in the *Oxford Classical Dictionary* (Oxford, 1949), Hammond states that after Potidaea fell into the hands

of Philip in 356 B.C., "It was perhaps destroyed in the Olynthian War (348)." This is not supported by the evidence at our disposal.

Of some interest here is the epigram of Adaeus (VII) concerning a hero named Philopragmon. According to Paton, *Greek Anthology (Loeb Class. Libr.)*, II, no. 694, the epigram is not sepulchral and reads as follows: "If thou passest by the shrine of the hero (his name is Philopragmon) that is at the cross-roads outside Potidaea, tell him on what task thou journeyest, and he at once will help thee to find a means of accomplishing it." The reference to Potidaea places the epigram before the founding of Cassandreia in 316 B.C.

For Adaeus, a Macedonian poet of the time of Alexander the Great, cf. *Anthologia Graeca*, ed. Jacobs, XIII, p. 832; Pape, *Worterbuch der griechischen Eigennemen*, v. *Adaeos*.

70. Nos. 819, 826, and 834, with female head to right on the obverse and butting bull to left on the reverse, originally assigned to Potidaea, have been excluded from *Olynthus*, IX, *The Chalcidic Mint and the Coins Found in 1928-1934*, p. 279 and n. 113, and were assigned by Robinson and Clement to Bottiaea where they properly belong.

71. Again, the two coins, nos. 775 and 776, originally assigned to Potidaea, have been excluded from the resumé of Potidaean coins in *Olynthus*, IX, p. 307, n. 260, and p. 279 and n. 114, and are assigned to Bottiaea.

72. For additional references to Potidaean bronze coins see Head, *Hist. Num.²*, p. 212; Babelon, *Traité*, 2, IV, p. 595, nos. 958, 960, and pl. CCCXIV, 5; Imhoof-Blumer, *Mon. Gr.*, p. 91, no. 112; Wroth, *Num. Chron.*, II, 1902, p. 316.

73. Pl. XXIII, a-i. Athena (to left)/Trident: a-d = *Olynthus*, III, pl. XX, 818, 830, 832, 833, respectively; e = *Olynthus*, VI, pl. XIX, 816; Athena (to right)/Trident: f-g = *Olynthus*, III, pl. XX, 837 and pl. XXI, 842, respectively; h = *Olynthus*, VI, pl. XIX, 780; i = *Olynthus*, XIV, p. 418, inv. no. 255 = pl. *61*, 7 in my article, "The Coinage of Potidaea," *Robinson Studies*, vol. II. I am grateful to Dr. Robinson for providing me with a photograph of Potidaean coins from Olynthus from which the plate in my article was prepared.

For other examples of the Athena/Trident type, with the head of Athena to left or to right, see especially *Olynthus*, III, pls. XX and XXI; VI, pl. XIX; IX, pl. XXX, 31. See also Babelon, *op. cit.*, pl. CCCXIV, 5.

74. Pl. XXIII, j-l. Athena/Pegasus: j = *Olynthus*, III, pl. XX, 814; k = *Olynthus*, VI, pl. XIX, 777; l = *Olynthus*, XIV, pl. *172*, 8 = pl. *61*, 8 in my article mentioned in preceding note. For the fourth Athena/Pegasus coin, with the Pegasus not as well preserved, see pl. *61*, 9 in my article and *Olynthus*, XIV, p. 418, inv. no. 18.

For other references and illustrations see Gaebler, *Ant. Mün. Nord-Griech.*, III², p. 155, no. 11, pl. XX, 29 (= Babelon, *loc. cit.*, no. 598) and no. 12, pl. II, 4 (= Wroth, *op. cit.*, p. 315, 2, pl. XV, 2); Head, *op. cit.*, p. 212.

75. Head, *op. cit.*, p. 212; Babelon, *op. cit.*, p. 595, no. 958; Imhoof-Blumer, *op. cit.*, p. 91, no. 112; Wroth, *op. cit.*, p. 316.

76. Gaebler, *op. cit.*, p. 51, no. 4, pl. XX, 28. Cf. also notes 70 and 71, above.

77. Cf. preceding note. The legend is found below the exergue line.

78. Robinson and Clement, *Olynthus*, IX, p. 351 and notes 612-15. In the Olynthus excavations, one Corinthian diobol of the Pegasus/Pegasus type, dated in the fourth century, was found in 1931 (*Olynthus*, VI, pl. VIII, 124) and three bronze coins with Pegasus/Trident, dated ca. 400-ca. 300 B.C., were found, one in 1931 (*op. cit.*, p. 81 and pl. XVII, 722) and two in 1934 (*Olynthus*, IX, p. 351).

79. *Olynthus*, IX, p. 191.

80. *Op. cit.*, p. 212.

81. *Op. cit.*, p. 103.

82. *Op. cit.*, p. 308; cf. also Robinson, *Olynthus*, III, p. 101; VI, p. 89; XIV, p. 418.

83. *Op. cit.*, pp. 595-96.

84. Diod., XIX, 52, 2-3; Strabo, VII, 330, frs. 25, 27; Paus., V, 23; Livy, XLIV, 11; Pliny, *N.H.*, IV 10 (17). *Webster's Geographical Dictionary* (1949) erroneously gives ca. 301 B.C. for the founding of Cassandreia.

85. Diod., XIX, 52, 2; Paus., V, 23, 3.

We may add here two persons who lived in other cities, but whose names reflect a Potidaean origin. Menekrates Poteidaiou Megareus, described as a didascalus in the Delphic Soteria of 268-65 B.C., seems to be the son of a Potidaean who had been granted citizenship by Megara. Cf. E. Capps, "Studies in Greek Agonistic Inscriptions," *T.A.P.A.*, XXXI, 1900, p. 118; Ditt., *Syll.³*, 424, A, col. I, 71. An inscription from Philippi containing an ephebic list mentions *Athenodoros Gorgiou Potidaiates* as a gymnasiarch. The date of the inscription is not certain. It has been published by Mertzides in his book on Philippi (pp. 122-4) and is dated, on the basis of writing, in the Macedonian period. Collart (*Phipippes*, p. 178, no. 2) reproduces the inscription, but with a question as to its genuineness, and dates it just before the capture of Potidaea by Philip in 356 B.C. chiefly because Athenodoros is mentioned as being Potidaean. This does not necessarily follow since the ethnic *Potidaeates* might have been kept by Potidaeans residing in other cities even after the fall of their own city.

86. The results of the excavations at Olynthus indicate that the abandonment of the northern area and the end of the post—348 B.C. coins found there coincide with the settlement of Cassandreia. Cf. Robinson and Graham, *Olynthus*, VIII, pp. 12f. and Robinson and Clement, *Olynthus*, IX, pp. 372 and 374, where, in addition, it is stated that a similar situation may be assumed for the neighboring Mecyberna, though numismatic evidence indicates that the town captured by Philip in 348 B.C. was not destroyed but continued to exist "until the founding of Cassandrea and then indeed was depopulated in favor of its new large neighbor" (p. 374). For the abandonment of Mecyberna by 316 B.C. see also Robinson, *Olynthus*, XIV, p. 43.

87. Diod., XIX, 52, 3. Cf. also Athenaeus, *Deipnosophistae*, XI, 784c.

88. Cf. Diod., XXXIII, 17 (Cassandreia under the dominion of the Tyrant Apollodorus, 279 B.C.); Livy, XXVIII, 8 (principal naval arsenal under Philip, the son of Demetrius); *ibid.*, XLIV, 11, 12 (a Roman fleet, in conjunction with Eumenes of Pergamum failed to capture the city, 169 B.C.); *ibid.*, XLIII, 23, and Pliny, *N.H.*, IV, 10 (Roman colonization of the city during the time of Augustus); Procopius, *De Aedificiis*, IV, 3, and *De Bello Persico*, II, 4 (the Huns captured the city by storm in 539 A.D. and left scarcely any traces of it; rebuilt by Justinian soon afterwards).

ABBREVIATIONS

◻

Am. Hist. Rev.	—*American Historical Review*
A.J.A.	—*American Journal of Archaeology*
A.J.P.	—*American Journal of Philology*
Arch. Anz.	—*Archaeologischer Anzeiger* (Appendix to *Jahrbuch*)
'Αρχ. 'Εφ.	—'Αρχαιολογικὴ 'Εφημερίς (Athens)
A.T.L.	—*Athenian Tribute Lists*
B.P.W.	—*Berliner Philologische Wochenschrift*
B.M.Cat.	—*British Museum Catalogue*
Br. M.Q.	—*British Museum Quarterly*
B.C.H.	—*Bulletin de Correspondance Hellénique*
B.S.A.	—*Annual of the British School at Athens*
Cahn *Cat.*	—Cahn, *Auktions Katalog* 68, Munich, 1930
C.A.H.	—*Cambridge Ancient History*
C.I.G.	—*Corpus Inscriptionum Graecarum*, Berlin, 1828-77
Cl. Phil.	—*Classical Philology*
Cl. Q.	—*Classical Quarterly*
Cl. Rev.	—*Classical Review*
C.R.A.I.	—*Comptes Rendus de l'Académie des Inscriptions et Belles-Lettres*
Daremberg-Saglio	—*Dictionnaire des Antiquités Grecques et Romaines*
Hirsch *Cat.*, XIII, XIV	—*Monnaies Grecques et Romaines, Ars Classica*, Geneva, 1928, 1929
I.G.	—*Inscriptiones Graecae*
I.G.A.	—*Inscriptiones Graecae Antiquissimae*
Jahrbuch	—*Jahrbuch des Deutschen Archäologischen Instituts*
Jameson Collection	—*Collection R. Jameson, Monnaies Grecques Antiques*, I, Paris, 1913
J.H.S.	—*The Journal of Hellenic Studies*
Journ. Int. Arch. Num.	—*Journal International d'Archéologie Numismatique*
McClean Collection	—*Catalogue of the McClean Collection of Greek Coins*, Cambridge (England), 1923
Naville I, IV, V, VI	—*Monnaies Grecques Antiques*, Naville et Cie, Geneva, 1920, 1922, 1923, 1923
_____ X	—*Monnaies Grecques et Romaines*, Naville et Cie, Geneva, 1925
Num. Chron.	—*Numismatic Chronicle*
R-E.	—*Real-Encyclopädie der classischen Altertumswissenschaft*
Rein. Mus.	—*Reinisches Museum für Philologie*
Rev. Arch.	—*Revue Archéologique*
R.E.A.	—*Revue des Etudes Anciennes*
R.E.G.	—*Revue des Etudes Grecques*
R.I.G.	—*Recueil d'Inscriptions Grecques*
Rev. Num.	—*Revue Numismatique*
Rom. Mitt.	—*Mitteilungen des Deutschen Archäologischen Instituts, Romische Abteilung*
S.E.G.	—*Supplementum Epigraphicum Graecum*
Weber Collection	—*The Weber Collection*, vol. II, *Greek Coins, Macedon, Thrace*, etc., London, 1924
Zeit. f. Num.	—*Zeitschrift für Numismatik*

BIBLIOGRAPHY

□

I. Ancient Sources

Aeneas Tacticus *(Loeb Class. Library)*.
Aeschylus, *Eumenides*.
Adaeus, *(Anthologia Graeca)*.
Aristodemus, 18 (Jacoby, *F. Gr. H.*, 104).
Aristophanes, *Knights, Birds*.
Aristotle, *Oeconomica, Rhetoric, Athenaion Politeia, Politica*.
Athenaeus, *Deipnosophistae*.
Deinarchus, *Orations*.
Demosthenes, *Orations*.
Diodorus Siculus, *Bibliothecae Historicae quae Supersunt*.
Diogenes Laertius, *Socrates*.
Dionysius of Halicarnassus, *Antiquitatum Romanarum*.
Epistolae Socraticae (Epistolographi Graeci, ed. Hercher).
Herodotus, *History*.
Hesychius, *Lexicon*.
Isocrates, *Orations*.
Libanius, VII.
Livy, XLIV.
Nepos, *Liber de Excellentibus Ducibus Exterarum Gentium*, VI,
    Lysander.
Nicolas of Damascus, fr. 60 (Müller, *F.H.G.*, III, 393).
Parthenius, 6 *(Erotici Scriptores Graeci*, I, Biblio. Teubn.).
Pausanias, *Description of Greece*.
Pindar, *Nemeans, Isthmians*.
Plato, *Apology, Charmides, Symposium*.
Pliny, *Natural History*.
Plutarch, *Lives: Alexander, Aristides, Cimon, Lysander, Pericles*.
Polyaenus, *Strategemata*, IV.
Procopius, *De Aedificiis*, IV, *De Bello Persico*, II.
Scylax Caryandeus, *Periplus* (*Geogr. Gr. Min.*, ed. Müller).
Scymnus of Chios, *Orbis Descriptio* (*Geogr. Gr. Min.*, ed. Müller).
Stephanus Byzantius.

Strabo, *Geographica.*

Suidas, *Lexicon.*

Thucydides, *History* (ed. H. Stuart Jones, Oxford, 1942).

Xenophon, *Hellenica.*

II. Modern Works

Abbott, G.F., *Thucydides, A Study in Historical Reality,* London, 1925.

Alexander, John A., "The Coinage of Potidaea," *Studies Presented to David Moore Robinson,* ed. by G.E. Mylonas and D. Raymond, vol. II, St. Louis, 1953, pp. 201-17 and pl. 61.

——————, "Thucydides and the Expedition of Callias Against Potidaea, 432 B.C.," *A.J.P.,* LXXXIII, 1962, pp. 265-87.

Andreades, A.M., *A History of Greek Public Finance,* vol. I. Revised and enlarged edition. Tr. by C.N. Brown, Cambridge (Mass.), 1933.

Andrewes, Anthony, *The Greek Tyrants,* London, 1956.

Austin, R.P., *The Stoichedon Style in Greek Inscriptions,* London, 1938.

Babelon, E., "La Politique Monétaire d'Athènes au Vᵉ Siècle avant Notre Ère," *Rev. Num.,* XVII, 1913, pp. 457-85.

——————, *Traité des Monnaies Grecques et Romaines,* Paris, 1901, etc.

——————, "Trouvaille de Tarente," *Rev. Num.,* Serie 4, XVI, 1912, pp. 1-40.

Babelon, J., *Catalogue de la Collection de Luynes. Monnaies Grecques: II Grèce Continentale et Iles,* Paris, 1925.

Beloch, K.J., *Griechische Geschichte,* Strassburg, Berlin, and Leipzig, 1912-1927.

Bonner, R.J., *Aspects of Athenian Democracy,* Berkeley, Cal., 1933.

Bury, J.B., *A History of Greece to the Death of Alexander the Great,* 2 vols., London, 1902.

Busolt, G., *Griechische Geschichte,* Vol. III, Gotha, 1897.

——————, *Griechische Staatskunde* (Zweite Hälfte, bearbeitet von Dr. Heinrich Swoboda. *Handbuch der Altertumswissenschaft,* vol. IV), Munich, 1926.

Cahn, A.E., *Auktions Katalog* 68, Munich, Nov., 1930.

The Cambridge Ancient History, ed. by J.B. Bury, *et al.,* New York and Cambridge (England), 1923, etc.

Cary, M., "Athens and Histiaea," *J.H.S.,* XLV, 1925, pp. 243-50.

——————, *The Geographical Background of Greek and Roman History,* Oxford, 1949.

Casson, S., *Macedonia, Thrace and Illyria,* Oxford, 1926.

Cavaignac. E., *Études sur l'Histoire financière d'Athènes au Vᵉ siècle. Le Trésor d'Athènes de 480 à 404,* Paris, 1908.

Clinton, H.F., *Fasti Hellenici. The Civil and Literary Chronology of Greece from the LVth to the CXXIVth Olympiad,* 3rd ed., Oxford, 1841.

Cloché, P., *Démosthènes et la Fin de la Démocratie Athénienne,* Paris, 1937.

——————, "Philippe II, roi de Macédoine, de 359 à 351 avant J.-C.," *Études Classiques,* XVIII, 1951, pp. 403-09.

——————, *La Politique Étrangère d'Athènes de 404 à 338 avant J.-C.,* Paris, 1934.

Collart, P., *Philippes, Ville de Macédoine, depuis ses origines jusqu'à la fin d'époque romaine,* Paris, 1937.

Cramer, J.A., *A Geographical and Historical Description of Greece,* vol. I, Oxford, 1828.

Daux, G., *Delphes au IIe et au Ier Siècle,* Paris, 1936.

De La Coste-Messelière, P., *Au Musée de Delphes. Researches sur quelques monuments archaiques et leur décor sculpté,* Paris, 1936.

Demitsas, M.G., ‘Η Μακεδονία, Athens, 1896.

De Romilly, Jacqueline, *Thucydide et l'Impérialisme Athénien. La Pensée de l'Historien et la Genèse de l'Oeuvre,* Paris, 1947.

Dinsmoor, W.B., "Studies of the Delphian Treasuries," *B.C.H.,* XXXVI, 1912, pp. 439-93.

Dittenberger, W., *Sylloge Inscriptionum Graecarum,* 3rd ed., Leipzig, 1915-1921.

Duchesne, L., and Bayet, M., *Mémoire sur une Mission au Mont Athos,* Paris, 1876.

Edson, Charles, "Notes on the Thracian Phoros," *Cl. Phil.,* XLII, 1947, pp. 88-105.

——————, "Strepsa (Thucydides, I, 61. 4)," *Cl. Phil.,* L, 1955, pp. 169-90.

Ehrenberg, Victor, *Aspects of the Ancient World, Essays and Reviews,* New York, 1946.

——————, "Thucydides and Athenian Colonization," *Cl. Phil.,* XLVII, 1952, pp. 143-49.

Farnell, L. R., *The Cults of the Greek States,* vol. IV, Oxford, 1907.

——————, *Greek Hero Cults and Ideas of Immortality,* Oxford, 1921.

Ferguson, W. S., *The Treasurers of Athena,* Cambridge (Mass.), 1932.

Finley, John H., Jr., *Thucydides,* Cambridge (Mass.), 1947.

——————, "The Unity of Thucydides' History," *Harvard Studies in Cl. Phil.,* Suppl., vol. I, 1940, pp. 255-98.

Forrer, L., *The Weber Collection,* vol. II, *Greek Coins, Macedon, Thrace,* etc., London, 1924.

Francotte, H., *Les Finances des Cités Greques,* Paris, 1909.

Frazer, J. G., *Pausanias's Description of Greece,* vols. III, V, London, 1898.

Gaebler, H., *Die Antiken Münzen Nord-Griechenlands*. Band III, *Makedonia und Paionia*, Berlin, 1935.

Gardner, P., "Coinage of the Athenian Empire," *J.H.S.*, XXXIII, 1913, pp. 147-88.

——————————, *The Earliest Coins of Greece Proper* (from the Proceedings of the British Academy, vol. V) , London, 1912.

——————————, *History of Ancient Coinage*, Oxford, 1918.

Geffcken, J., and Ziebarth, E., *Friedrich Lübkers Reallexikon des Klassischen Altertums*, Berlin, 1914.

Geyer, F., *Makedonien bis zur Thronbesteigung Philipps II*, *Historische Zeitschrift*, Beiheft XIX, Munich and Berlin, 1930.

Glotz, G., *The Greek City and Its Institutions*, New York, 1930.

——————————, *Histoire Grecque*, vols. I-III, Paris, 1925, 1931, 1936.

Glover, T. R., *Herodotus*, Berkeley, Cal., 1924.

Gomme, A. W., *A Historical Commentary on Thucydides*, vols. I-III, Oxford, 1945-1956.

——————————, "I.G., I², 296 and the Dates of Τὰ Ποτειδεατικά," *Cl. Rev.*, LV, 1941, pp. 59-67.

——————————, "Notes on Thucydides," *Cl. Rev.*, N.S., I, 1951, pp. 135-38.

Granier, Fr., *Die Makedonische Heereswersammlung, Ein Beitrag zum antiken Staatsrecht*, Munich, 1931.

Grose, S.W., *Catalogue of the McClean Collection of Greek Coins*, vol. II, Cambridge (England) , 1926.

Grote, G., *A History of Greece*, 12 vols., London, 1869.

Grundy, G.B., *The Great Persian War and its Preliminaries; A Study of the Evidence, Literary and Topographical*, London, 1901.

——————————, *Thucydides and the History of His Age*, London, 1911; vols. I (2nd ed.) and II, Oxford, 1948.

Gude, Mabel, *A History of Olynthus*, Baltimore, 1933.

Gwynn, A., "The Character of Greek Colonization," *J.H.S.*, XXXVIII, 1918, pp. 88-123.

Hammond, N.G.L., *A History of Greece to 322 B.C.*, Oxford, 1959.

Hampl, F., *Die Griechischen Staatsvertäge des 4. Jahrhunderts v. Christi Geb.*, Leipzig, 1938.

——————————, "Olynth und der Chalkidische Staat," *Hermes*, LXX, 1935, pp. 177-96.

Harrison, E., "Chalkidike," *Cl. Q.*, VI, 1912, pp. 93-103, 165-78.

Hasebroek, J., *Trade and Politics in Ancient Greece*, tr. from the German by L.M. Frazer and D.C. MacGregor, London, 1933.

Head, B.V., *British Museum Catalogue of Greek Coins, Macedonia, etc.* London, 1879.

——————————, *Historia Numorum*, 2nd ed., Oxford, 1911.

————————————, and Svoronos, J.H., Ἱστορία τῶν Νομισμάτων, Athens, 1898.

Henderson, B.W., *The Great War between Athens and Sparta, A Companion to the Military History of Thucydides*, London, 1927.

Hercher, R., *Epistolographi Graeci*, Paris, 1873.

Hermann, K.F., *A Manual of the Political Antiquities of Greece, Historically Considered* (tr. from the German), Oxford, 1836.

Hicks, E.L. and Hill, G.F., *A Manual of Greek Historical Inscriptions*, Oxford, 1901.

Highbarger, E.L., *The History and Civilization of Ancient Megara*, Baltimore, 1927.

Highby, L.I., *The Erythrae Decree. Contributions to the Early History of the Delian League and the Peloponnesian Confederacy, Klio*, Beiheft XXXVI, N. Folge, Heft 23, 1936.

Hill, G.F., *Sources for Greek History between the Persian and Peloponnesian Wars*, ed. by R. Meiggs and A. Andrewes, Oxford, 1951.

Hinks, R.P., *Catalogue of the Greek, Etruscan and Roman Paintings and Mosaics in the British Museum*, London, 1933.

Holm, A., *History of Greece*, 4 vols., London and New York, 1894-1898.

How, W.W., and Wells, J., *A Commentary on Herodotus*, Oxford, 1912.

Imhoof-Blumer, F., "Nymphen und Chariten auf griechischen Münzen," *Journ. Int. Arch. Num.*, XI, 1908, pp. 1-213.

Jacoby, F., *Die Fragmente der Griechischen Historiker*, Berlin, 1923.

————————————, "Some Epigrams from the Persian Wars," *Hesperia*, XIV, 1945, pp. 157-211.

Jaeger, W.W., *Demosthenes, The Origin and Growth of His Policy*, Berkeley, Cal., 1938.

Jameson, R., *Collection R. Jameson, Monnaies Grecques Antiques*, I, Paris, 1913.

Kahrstedt, U., "Chalcidic Studies," *A.J.P.*, LVII, 1936, pp. 416-44.

————————————, *Griechisches Staatsrecht*, I, *Sparta und Seine Symmachie*, Göttingen, 1922.

Kaibel, G., *Epigrammata Graeca ex Lapidibus Conlecta*, Berlin, 1878.

Keramopoullos, A.D., Ὁδηγὸς τῶν Δελφῶν, Athens, 1935.

Kiepert, H., *Lehrbuch der alten Geographie*, Berlin, 1878.

Kolbe, W., *Thukydides im Lichte der Urkunden*, Stuttgart, 1930.

Kolocotronis, V., *La Macédoine et l'Hellénisme. Étude Historique et Ethnologique*, Paris, 1919.

Laistner, M.L.W., *A History of the Greek World from 479 to 323 B.C.*, London, 1936; 2nd ed., 1947.

Larsen, J.A.O., "The Constitution and Original Purpose of the Delian League," *Harvard Studies in Cl. Phil.*, LI, 1940, pp. 176-213.

Lavedan, P., *Dictionnaire illustré de la Mythologie et des Antiquités Grecques et Romaines*, Paris, 1931.

Leake, G., *Travels in Northern Greece*, vol. III, London, 1835.

Macan, R.W., *Herodotus, the Seventh, Eighth, and Ninth Books*, vol. I, parts I-II, London, 1908.

Macaronas, Ch., " Χρονικά 'Αρχαιολογικά," *Makedonika*, vol. II, 1941-1952, Thessalonica, 1953, pp. 590-678.

Marshall, F.H., *The Second Athenian Confederacy*, Cambridge, 1905.

Meiggs, R., "The Growth of Athenian Imperialism," *J.H.S.*, LXIII, 1943, pp. 21-34.

Meritt, B.D., *Athenian Financial Documents of the Fifth Century*, Ann Arbor, 1932.

―――――, "Scione, Mende, and Torone," *A.J.A.*, XXVII, 1923, pp. 447-60.

―――――, "Indirect Tradition in Thucydides," *Hesperia*, XXIII, 1954, pp. 185-231.

―――――, Wade-Gery, H.T., and McGregor, M.F., *The Athenian Tribute Lists*, vol. I, Cambridge, Mass., 1939; vols. II-IV, Princeton, 1949-1953.

Mertzides, S., Οἱ Φίλιπποι, Constantinople, 1900.

Meyer, E., *Geschichte des Altertums*, Stuttgart, 1893.

Michel, C., *Recueil d'Inscriptions Grecques*, Paris-Brussels, 1900-1927.

Momigliano, A., *Filippo il Macedone, Saggio sulla Storia Greca del IV Secolo A.C.*, Florence, 1934.

Müller, K., *Fragmenta Historicorum Graecorum*, Paris, 1841-1873.

―――――, *Geographi Graeci Minores*, Paris, 1882.

―――――, *The History and Antiquities of the Doric Race*, tr. from the German by H. Tufnell and C.C. Lewis, two vols., Oxford, 1830.

Myres, John L., *Herodotus, Father of History*, Oxford, 1953.

Nesselhauf, H., *Untersuchungen zur Geschichte der Delisch-Attischen Symmachie, Klio*, Beiheft XXX, 1933.

O'Neill, J.G., *Ancient Corinth*, Part I, *From the Earliest Times to 404 B.C.*, Baltimore, 1930.

Oliver, J.H., "The Athenian Decree Concerning Miletus in 450/49 B.C.," *T.A.P.A.*, LXVI, 1935, pp. 177-98.

Oxford Classical Dictionary, ed. M. Cary, *et al.*, Oxford, 1949.

Paparregopoulos, K., Ἱστορία τοῦ Ἑλληνικοῦ Ἔθνους, 3rd ed., Athens, 1896.

Papastavru, J., *Amphipolis, Geschichte und Prosopographie, Klio*, Beiheft XXXVII, Leipzig, 1936.

Pelekides, S., " Γύρω ἀπὸ τὰ Ποτειδεατικά," *Epeteris Philosophikes Scholes*, Thessalonica, VI, 1950, reprint, pp. 1-47.

Raue, H.O., *Untersuchungen z. Geschichte d. Korinthischen Bundes*, Marburg, 1937.

Rawlinson, G., *History of Herodotus,* vol. IV, London, 1875.

Regling, K., *Die Griechischen Münzen der Sammlung Warren,* Berlin, 1906.

Robinson, D.M., *Excavations at Olynthus,* III, *The Coins Found at Olynthus in 1928;* V, *Mosaics, Vases, and Lamps of Olynthus Found in 1928 and 1931;* VI, *The Coins Found at Olynthus in 1931;* X, *Metal and Minor Miscellaneous Finds;* XII, *Domestic and Public Architecture;* XIV, *Terracottas, Lamps, and Coins Found in 1934 and 1938,* Baltimore, 1931-1952.

————————————, "Inscriptions from Macedonia, 1938," *T.A.P.A.,* LXIX, 1938, pp. 43-76, pls. I-XXVII.

————————————, "Inscriptions from Olynthus, 1934," *T.A.P.A.,* LXV, 1934, pp. 103-37.

————————————, "A New Fragment of the Athenian Decree on Coinage," *A.J.P.,* LVI, 1935, pp. 149-54.

————————————, "New Inscriptions from Olynthus and Environs," *T.A.P.A.,* LXII, 1931, pp. 40-56.

————————————, *A Short History of Greece,* New York, 1936.

————————————, and Clement, P., *Excavations at Olynthus,* IX, *The Chalcidic Mint and the Excavation Coins Found in 1928-1934,* Baltimore, 1938.

————————————, and Graham, J.W., *Excavations at Olynthus,* VIII, *The Hellenic House,* Baltimore, 1938.

Robinson, E.S.G., "The Athenian Currency Decree and the Coinage of the Allies," *Hesperia,* Suppl. VIII, 1949, pp. 324-40.

Roehl, H., *Imagines Inscriptionum Graecarum,* 2nd ed., Berlin, 1894; 3rd ed., Berlin, 1907.

————————————, *Inscriptiones Graecae Antiquisimae praeter Atticas in Attica Repertas,* Berlin, 1882.

Roscher, W.H., *Ausführliches Lexikon der Griechischen und Römischen Mythologie,* Leipzig, 1897-1909.

Schaefer, A., *Demosthenes und Seine Zeit,* II, Leipzig, 1886.

Schaefer, H., "Die attische Symmachie im 2. Jahrzehnt ihres Bestehens," *Hermes,* LXXI, 1936, pp. 129-50.

Schömann, G.F., *The Antiquities of Greece: The State,* tr. from the German by E.G. Hardy and J.S. Mann, London, 1880.

Schwan, W., "Die attische εἰσφορά," *Rhein. Mus.,* LXXXII, 1933, pp. 247-84.

Segre, M., "La Legge Ateniese Sull' Unificazione della Moneta," *Clara Rhodos,* IX, 1938, pp. 151-78.

Seltman, C.T., *Greek Coins,* London, 1933; 2nd ed., 1955. References are to the 1st ed., unless otherwise indicated.

Smith, W., *A Dictionary of Greek and Roman Biography and Mythology,* London, 1880.

——————————————, *A Dictionary of Greek and Roman Geography*, London, 1873.

Stanley, C., "Economic Equilibrium in the Mediterranean World 750-432 B.C.," *L'Acropole*, III, 1928, pp. 49-72.

Struck, A.H., *Makedonische Fahrten*, I, *Chalkidike*, Vienna and Leipzig, 1907.

Svoronos, J.N., "L'Hellénisme Primitif de la Macédoine, Prouvé par la Numismatique," *Journ. Int. Arch. Num.*, XIX, 1918-1919.

——————————————, "Sur la signification des Types monétaires des Anciens," *B.C.H.*, XVIII, 1894, pp. 101-28.

Tod, M.N., *A Selection of Greek Historical Inscriptions to the End of the Fifth Century B.C.*, Oxford, 1933; I², Oxford, 1946; II, *From 403 to 323 B.C.*, Oxford, 1948.

Underhill, G.E., *A Commentary on the Hellenica of Xenophon*, Oxford, 1900.

Ure, P.A., *The Origin of Tyranny*, Cambridge (England), 1922.

Wade-Gery, H.T., "The Question of Tribute in 449/48 B.C.," *Hesperia*, XIV, 1945, pp. 212-29.

Webster's Geographical Dictionary. A Dictionary of Names of Places with Geographical and Historical Information and Pronunciations, Springfield, Mass., 1949.

Wells, J., *Studies in Herodotus*, Oxford, 1923.

West, A.B., "The Chronology of the Years 432 and 431 B.C.," *Cl. Phil.*, X, 1915, pp. 34-53.

——————————————, "The Formation of the Chalcidic League," *Cl. Phil.*, IX, 1914, pp. 24-34.

——————————————, *The History of the Chalcidic League*, Madison, 1918.

——————————————, "The Tribute Lists and the non-Tributary Members of the Delian League," *Am. Hist. Rev.*, XXXV, 1929-1930, pp. 266-75.

Will, Edouard, *Korinthiaka: Recherches sur l'Histoire et la Civilization de Corinthe des Origines aux Guerres Médiques*, Paris, 1955.

Woodhead, A.G., "The Site of Brea: Thucydides I. 61. 4," *Cl. Q.*, N.S., II, 1952, pp. 57-62.

INDEX

ILLUSTRATIONS

PLATE I

FIG. 1. Nea Potidaea seen from the southeast. The Thessalonica-Cassandra road is at the left, the Thermaic Gulf in the background.

FIG. 2. Nea Potidaea seen from the pump-house. The second knoll south of the canal is at the right.

PLATE II

FIG. 1. View from Nea Potidaea southward. The Metochion Dochiariou is on the horizon to the left. The Pyrgos (tower) can be seen on the east side of the hill, right.

FIG. 2. View from the Pyrgos toward the canal.

PLATE III

Fig. 1. Nea Potidaea seen from the northwest. Remnants of the mediaeval wall are in the foreground, between the canal and the town.

Fig. 2. Houses on the west side of Nea Potidaea. A tower of the mediaeval wall is at the upper left.

PLATE IV

Fig. 1. Ruins of the temple of Poseidon, discovered by Professor Pelekides, seen from the southwest.

Fig. 2. Ruins of the Metochion Dochiariou seen from the east.

PLATE V

FIG. 1. The eastern part of Nea Potidaea. Remains of the wall along the edge of the canal.

FIG. 2. View from the northeast end of the canal. The third knoll south of the canal with the remains of the Metochion upon it may be seen.

PLATE VI

The eastern shore of the peninsula at Potidaea.

PLATE VII

The ferryboat and the district northwest of the canal.

PLATE VIII

FIG. 1. The western section of the mediaeval wall; probable location of a harbor is in the foreground.

FIG. 2. Detail of a tower of the mediaeval wall illustrated above.

PLATE IX

FIG. 1. Remains of the mediaeval wall westward from the modern Thessalonica-Cassandra road. A trench revealing remains of a more ancient wall is in the foreground.

FIG. 2. Another view of the mediaeval wall remains on either side of the road.

PLATE X

Fig. 1. The northeast end of the canal showing the east tower of the mediaeval wall.

Fig. 2. Remains located east of the tower seen in fig. 1.

PLATE XI

Fɪɢ. 1. A mudbrick wall with mortar located on the north side of the canal.

Fɪɢ. 2. Remains of a wall located near the area shown in fig. 1.

PLATE XII

Fig. 1. A pithos found near the northeast side of the canal.

Fig. 2. Ancient remains on the southeast side of the canal.

PLATE XIII

Fɪɢ. 1. Ancient remains located west of those of pl. XII, fig. 2.

Fɪɢ. 2. Ancient poros blocks located near those shown above.

PLATE XIV

Fig. 1. Ancient poros blocks with dove-tail clamps found near those shown on pl. XIII, fig. 2.

Fig. 2. Architectural poros block found near those above.

PLATE XV

Fig. 1. The capital of a Doric poros column located on the old Thessalonica-Cassandra road near the south side of the canal.

Fig. 2. The capital of another Doric poros column found with that in fig. 1.

PLATE XVI

FIG. 1. The capital of a Doric poros column located southeast of the modern town.

FIG. 2. Part of a Doric poros column found near the south side of the modern town.

FIG. 3. A typical sight at Nea Potidaea.

PLATE XVII

Fig. 1. An ancient block showing a T-shape clamp found near the capitals illustrated on pl. XV.

Fig. 2. An ancient block found near that of fig. 1.

PLATE XVIII

FIG. 1. The sacred precinct of Apollo at Delphi viewed from the northeast. The Athenian treasury is in the foreground; the remains of the Potidaean treasury are behind the Athenian.

FIG. 2. The remains of the Potidaean treasury seen from the east.

PLATE XIX

FIG. 1. The Potidaean treasury from the southeast showing reused material.

FIG. 2. The Potidaean and Syracusan treasuries seen from the southeast.

PLATE XX

Fig. 1. The Potidaean treasury seen from the northeast. The omphalos is at its southeast corner; the terrace of the Athenian treasury is at the left.

Fig. 2. The Sicyonian treasury seen from the west.

PLATE XXI

FIG. 1. Sculptured material dated in the Cassandreian period at Nea Potidaea.

FIG 2. Samples of pottery dated in the Cassandreian period at Nea Potidaea.

PLATE XXII

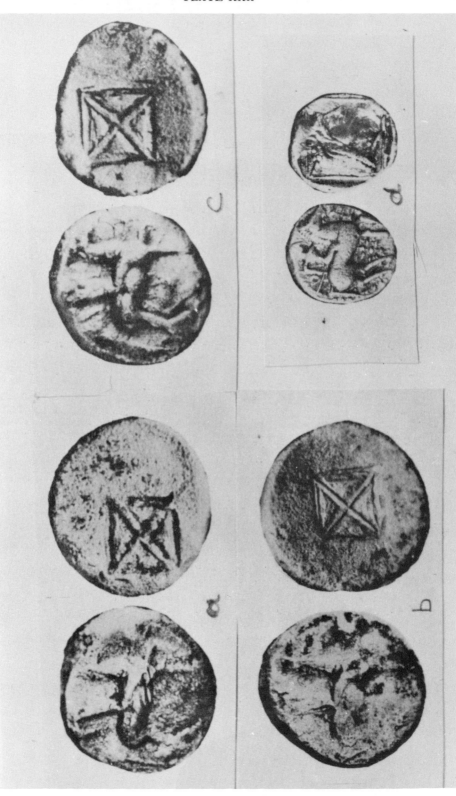

PLATE XXIII

Potidaean bronze coins from the Olynthus excavations. *Reproduced by permission of the Johns Hopkins Press.*

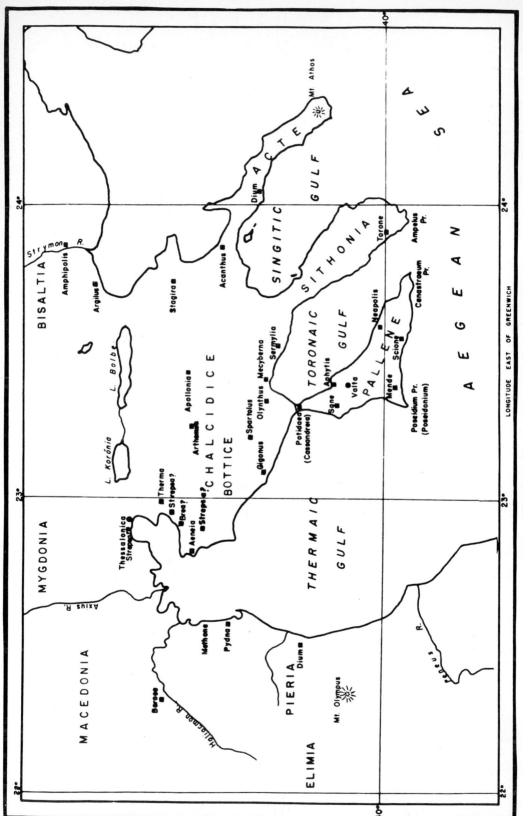

MAP 1: The Chalcidic peninsula and adjacent territory.

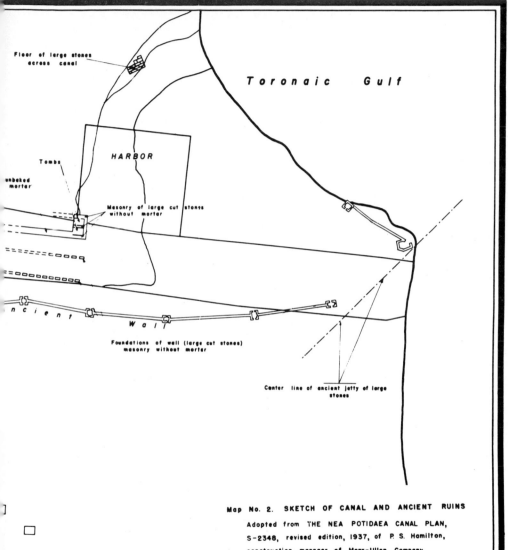

Floor of large stones
across canal

Tombs

unbaked
mortar

HARBOR

T o r o n a i c   G u l f

Masonry of large cut stones
without mortar

n c i e n t   W a l l

Foundations of wall (large cut stones)
masonry without mortar

Center line of ancient jetty of large
stones

Map No. 2.   SKETCH OF CANAL AND ANCIENT RUINS

Adopted from THE NEA POTIDAEA CANAL PLAN,
S-2348, revised edition, 1937, of P. S. Hamilton,
construction manager of Monx-Ullen Company.

METERS

FEET
SCALE

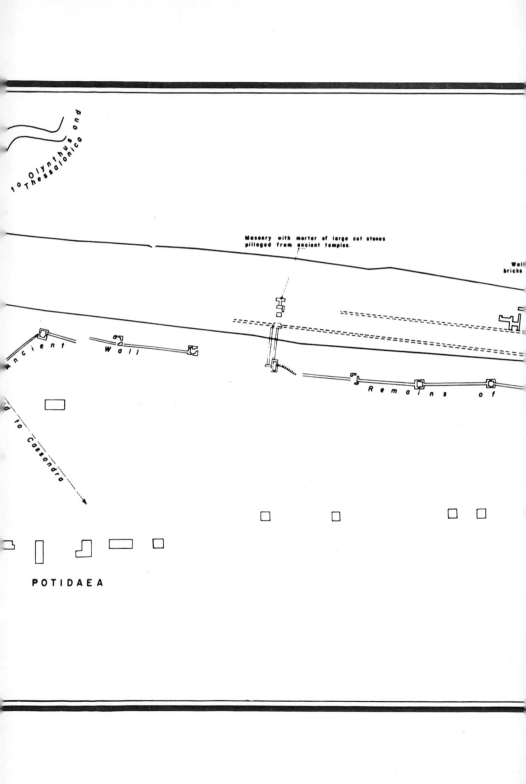

to Olynthus and
to Thessalonica

Masonry with mortar of large cut stones
pillaged from ancient temples.

Wall
bricks

ncient   Wall

Remains   of

to Cassandra

POTIDAEA

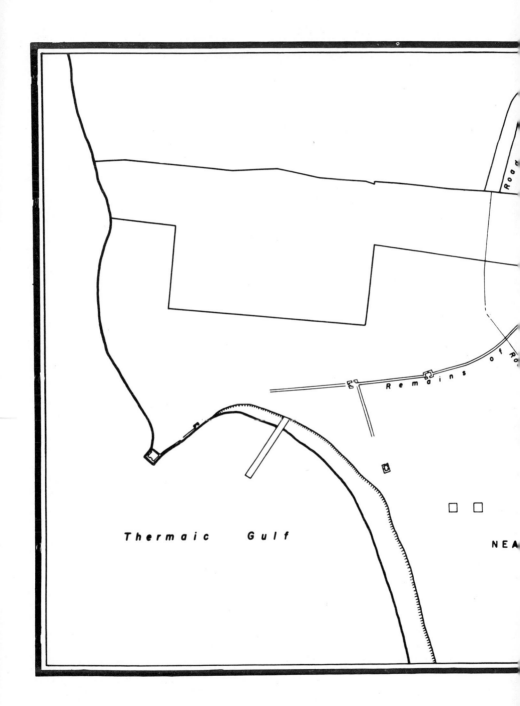

Road

Remains of Ro

Thermaic   Gulf

N E A

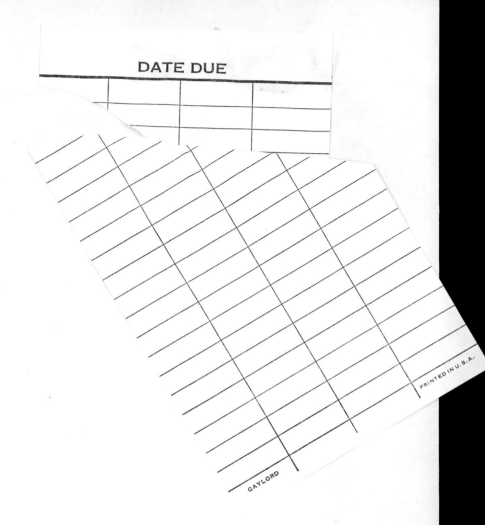

DATE DUE

GAYLORD

PRINTED IN U.S.A.